Stopped in Our Tracks
Third Series

My teaching, if that is the word you want to use, has no copyright. You are free to reproduce, distribute, interpret, misinterpret, distort, garble, and do what you like; even claim authorship, without my consent or the permission of anybody.

— U.G.

Stopped in Our Tracks

Third Series

By
K. Chandrasekhar

Translated from Telugu and edited by
J.S.R.L. Narayana Moorty

Foreword by
Mahesh Bhatt

Epilogue by
Sunita Pant Bansal

**MOTILAL BANARSIDASS
INTERNATIONAL
DELHI**

2025, Delhi

© Author
All Rights Reserved

ISBN : 978-81-939855-3-0 (Cloth)
ISBN : 978-81-969855-4-7 (Paper)

Also available at
MOTILAL BANARSIDASS INTERNATIONAL
H. O.: 41 U.A. Bungalow Road, (Back Lane)Jawahar Nagar, Delhi - 110007
4261 (Basement) Lane # 3, Ansari Road, Darya Ganj, New Delhi - 110002
12/1A, 2nd Floor, Bankim Chatterjee Street, Kolkata - 700073
Shop #. 6, 241, Luz Ginza Complex, Luz Corner, Mylapore, Chennai - 600004
Stockist : Motilal Books, Ashok Rajpath, Near Kali Mandir, Patna - 800004

No part of this book may be reproduced in any form or by any electronic or mechanical means including information storage and retrieval systems without permission in writing from the publishers, excepts by a reviewer who may quote brief passages in a review.

Printed in India
MOTILAL BANARSIDASS INTERNATIONAL

Foreword

Life is a movie. A lie that feels alive. You sit in the dark, watching people walk, birds fly, waves crash — everything moving, everything real. But nothing is moving. What you see is a trick. A sequence of still pictures played fast enough to fool the eye.

Between these pictures lies a sliver of darkness. Invisible, unnoticed, but present. In every hour of film, you spend minutes in darkness, caught between frames. Thirty whole minutes in the days of old projectors — half your time given to emptiness, to nothingness.

Life, too, is a sequence of frames. A smile. A tear. A moment of clarity. Between them lies the void. Silent. Empty. The place where life really lives. But we never see it. We move from frame to frame, forever blind to the gaps in between.

This is the heart of *Stopped in Our Tracks*: *Third Series* by K. Chandrasekhar — the enigma of a man who lived like a flame and refused to leave even smoke behind. UG Krishnamurti, the most subversive man to walk this earth, hated all traces of permanence. "I want to go unsung, unwept, unremembered," he said.

And he did.

When UG left on March 22, 2007, he gave me one task: make sure no one knows where his ashes rest. I obeyed. I made them vanish. No shrine, no symbol. Nothing to hold onto. Even I don't know where they are now.

But UG's fire doesn't vanish. It lingers. Chandrasekhar, UG's oldest companion, has gathered the fragments — photos, letters, tapes, clippings — sparks from a life that refused to be contained.

Can these fragments capture UG? No. They never could. They only remind us of his defiance, his rage, his refusal to be trapped. "You will never know what life is," he said. "Whatever you say, that's not it."

Perhaps the best way to understand what Chandrasekhar has done is to think of the old days in a cinema hall. When the projector frame jammed, the heat of the bulb would burn it. The screen would erupt in chaos — a volcano of molten celluloid. The sound would stop, and the illusion would shatter.

For a moment, the theatre would fall silent. The spell was broken. The story disappeared. The projectionist would fix the reel, and the film would start again. But something was lost. The magic couldn't return. The audience saw the lie.

This is what Chandrasekhar's book does. Like the stuck frame in a projector, he interrupts the illusion. He stops us in our tracks, forcing us to see the darkness between the frames. UG was always a story-buster. A man who tore down myths and burned the lies we live by.

But UG's fire was not just meant to destroy. It was meant to rebirth you — a new you, unrecognizable and untouched by the old. If you truly met UG, you would never be the modified continuity of who you were. You would be something entirely different. The fire he lit left no traces, no roots of the old self to grow back.

In *Stopped in Our Tracks: Third Series*, Chandrasekhar picks up the torch. He doesn't preserve UG. He doesn't even try. Instead, he reminds us of the fire that burned. He shows us the ashes, then leaves us in the void between the fragments — where the real mystery of life resides.

To be stopped is no small thing. To have your reel of illusions paused, your enchantment shattered — that is the gift of this book. UG's fire wasn't meant to comfort us. It was meant to destroy us, yes — but also to rebirth us, free of all that we once thought we were.

Stopped in our tracks, we stand before the void — silent, shattered, reborn, and alive.

Mahesh Bhatt
Mumbai, 2025

CONTENTS

Foreword   *v*

Editor's Note   *xiii*

Part - I : Palm Springs Diary 1998-99

Getting Ready for the Journey	3
Palm Springs	5
"Each day there is danger, yet you live to be a hundred years!"	11
Aruna and Venkat Arrive	31
Mystical Experiences	33
The Body will Take Care of Itself	35
"God is in the Vagina" – Sri Ramakrishna	35
Strange Business Transactions	37
The Guhas	38
"He is my Enemy No.1"	41
"You must all be reduced to the level of animals..."	43
Karma Cards	44
Kiran	46
Claire and Larry	47
Mahesh Leaves...	47
Lakshmi and Guha	48
Conflict between Moorty and UG	50
Aruna, a Hard-working Girl	53
Money due to Mahesh	54
Lisa's Stay in the House	55

"Came down quickly!"	56
Air Museum and War Heroes	57
Larry and Susan	58
Aruna's Departure	60
Paul Lynn and Family	61
Palm Springs on New Years' Eve	62
Lakshmi and Guha (continued)	64
Moorty Walks Out	67
Indian Canyon	70
Working at a Job	72
My Writing	74
Why Did Moorty Get Mad at UG?	81
Kinkos	82
Scotty's E-mail	84
99-Cent Market	85
At Paru's	86
Clinton's Son	90
The Future of America	94
Pleasure Seeking and the Continuity of the 'I'	96
Clean-Up Time	99
Moorty Phones	101
A Near-Miss	106
Punit and Family	106
Trip to Las Vegas	110
What's There to be Proud of?	118
'Public Enemy No. 1'	124
Fair in Palm Springs	125
Photos for My Book	126
UG's Kuja Stage	128

Lisa's Gift for Mario	130
Last Day in Palm Springs	132
Julie's Diary	134
En Route to Seaside	136
Seaside	140
With Aruna and Venkat	144
Livermore Temple	145
Chinatown in San Francisco	147
John Allen	148
Telugu Language and Telugu People	149
UG's Friends	151
Chalam's Sudha	158
Chalam's and Dhurjati's Writing Styles	159
Eddy's Prank	162
Tranquility of Mind	163
The Struggle	167
Return Trip	173
After Getting Back to the Nest	179
Pictorial Memories of Palm Springs, California	180-185

Part - II : Gstaad Diary 1999

Switzerland - July 1999	187
In Switzerland with UG	195
Paul Sempé	196
Gstaad - Ludi Haus	197
Chandrahas	200
Srinivas	205
John Piatras	215
Experiencing...	217
Swiss Independence Day	219
Lisa and Mario	220
Leboyer	222

Leboyer at Dinner	225
Francis	229
Krim	231
Hymn to Annapurna	244
Auto-writing – Rajyalakshmi's Story	245
UG Website	248
UG's Consoling People	249
Zurich – Hotel Hilton	254
About Krim Again	255
UG's Euphoria – Internet Links	261
UG and Julie	263
Gottfried and Bodil	269
Lisa and Mario - II	270
Sabyasachi Guha's Life	271
About Volker – My meeting with him	275
Guha's Life - II	277
UG's Initial Meetings with Others	277
Bharati's Predictions – My Guru Daśa	288
Julie's Punishment (Training)	293
Trip to Neuchatel and La Chaux-de-Fonds	295
Censorship	297
Francis – II	306
UG's Field of Attraction	310
Rukmini Arundale	315
"You are talking even when you're silent...."	316
Mr. Raju, the Astrologer	321
Raju with UG – UG's Past life	322
Mrs. Saraswati and Mr. Raju	326
Programming the Body	328
UG Talks About...	332
Pictorial Memories of Gstaad, Switzerland	343-349
Epilogue	351

Editor's Note

Chandrasekhar sent me the materials for this book at the same time that he sent the excerpts for his second book (*Stopped in our Tracks – Second Series*). Although they are continuous diaries of his travels abroad to visit UG in Palm Springs, California, USA and Gstaad, Switzerland in the years 1998 and 1999, they too are distinguished by the same kind of accounts of UG's encounters with people and self-reflections. In addition, they contain his impressions of the environs of the places he visits. The reader cannot but share his joys and sorrows as well as his frustrations in relating to UG.

Thanks to Julie Thayer for her proofreading corrections and comments.

Many thanks, once again, to Wendy Moorty for her unstinted help in editing the translation.

J.S.R.L. Narayana Moorty
Seaside, California
August 24, 2007

Part I

Palm Springs Diary

1998-99

December 16, 1998 Wednesday

Getting Ready for the Journey

I am thrilled to see that preparations are underway for such a major travel the day after tomorrow. I received the tickets yesterday. However, I started worrying about the trip as soon as I woke up. Why this torture of traveling again? If it seems like a torture to us, how much more so should it be to UG? Going to a strange place once every couple of months – although they are old faces, indeed, they all look new to him. The cold is becoming more severe here. It will only get worse each day. It must be much colder there in Palm Springs. God only knows why all this is happening. Apparently, UG told Suguna that we will be in Los Angeles on Saturday. Perhaps Mr. And Mrs. Malladi Krishnamurti will leave by then. Meanwhile, we are getting ready.

For a man who has no encumbrances, what a big family UG has! But none of this touches him. He remains as worry-free as someone watching images on a movie screen. My mind, entrenched in the notion that I am my body, writhes with every disturbance. For whom all this anxiety? Although I have been questioning myself like this and trying forcibly to wipe out the notion that I am the body and adopt the idea that I am the Universal Self, I am unable to see my own foolishness. To think that all this doesn't concern me – how do I even know "that I exist"? Thinking – it's not as easy as thinking. There is an ocean of difference between the 'I' notion and the thinking that "I am such and such, and I am my body." This belief is pretty deep-rooted. It's very tricky. It's easy to talk. Bhagavan asks, as though it's so easy, "Isn't it enough to think that 'I am not this'?" In the flood of thoughts arising wave after wave, how small is this little boat of belief! It will capsize in a moment if the ego raises its head. The struggle starts again. This has been going on for so many years. Still, my confidence in my own abilities does not end.

Even at this moment, what am I thinking about? – I'm thinking about what I should take with me. Any books? Among the books I have, which ones should I take? Any of the books that I have written? Must I ask Moorty and take those that he recommends? – My mind thinks along these lines. It doesn't remember that this time I am going there as a naked man and not to show myself off. What do I have to show off, in the first place? If UG is creating such an opportunity to be in his presence, it is due to his mercy. As a matter of fact, does he have mercy and compassion? Would a great soul who dispenses to each what he or she deserves think that he should show special compassion to a particular person? Is there any difference for him between a stone image in a temple, a photo image, or the bodily forms moving in his presence? If there is, does it only exist in my imagination? I don't understand any of this. The only solution is to sit at the feet of UG and give myself up. "I beseech UG for only one thing! I can't battle you. I can't please you with my power of poetical creations. Please forgive my helplessness. This is the way I am. Let me be. Give me the ability to lay down my weapons." Isn't that the true renunciation? Who cares about my superficial lectures?

* * *

December 17, Thursday

We leave tomorrow. Preparations are underway. Close friends are coming to say goodbye. Indiramma and Shyamalamma will stay here while we are gone.

The medicines to take along cost Rs. 1,000. We have bought clothes and gifts. I have spent Rs. 5,000. ... I just called UG. Apparently Aruna will not be coming to the airport. "It's more important for me to be with you. Aruna is important only after you," I told UG. "Aha, you're trying to trick me," says UG. "I'm telling you the truth," I replied.

Thoughts about the school are crowding in.

*   *   *

December 18, Friday: New Moon Day

We are leaving at 4 o'clock in the afternoon for Madras. The Jet Airways flight was postponed till 5:30 pm. Still there was no problem. The airport manager, Sastri, puts us in a nice VIP lounge. The effect of the new moon day has waned thanks to UG's influence.

Palm Springs

December 20, Sunday – Day 1

What shall I write? How should I start? I woke up at 4:30 am. How do I know where I am unless I tell myself that I am in America? It's still cold outside, but inside the room the temperature is moderate. I was surprised to see UG coming to the airport yesterday, and so many others coming with him. Julie's car is big; it's a Dodge Caravan. It can seat seven people. UG sat next to Julie in the front seat. While Julie was trying to drive out of the parking lot, a young lady tried to overtake her. The woman was frowning and signing to Julie with her hand to let her go first. Julie started to slow down to let her pass, but UG shouted, "Don't! Teach that bitch a lesson! Don't give her any room; don't allow her to overtake you!" Julie moved ahead blocking her way. That competitive lady was screaming, pouring abuses on Julie. Julie retorted, "Don't lecture us; go your way!" Apparently, UG wanted to teach that arrogant woman a lesson.[1]

We received the hospitality of the Malladis in the Holiday Inn before we went to Palm Springs. They must have gone to Detroit on the 19th. I phoned Aruna and talked to her.

*   *   *

It's 7 am in the morning now. In the backyard of the house I see a tree with ripe leaves shining in the golden-yellow sunshine. The sun is white. There are mountains all around.

---

[1] Julie's comment: "I think UG was showing me how innately aggressive I was, why would he bother upsetting a woman he didn't even know?"

We made our first visit to Jenson Bakery. I thought the prices there were pretty steep. UG also came with us. From there we went to see Moorty, Mahesh and Ramesh, who are all staying at the Whitewater Club. Ramesh prepared some nice tea for us, which Mahesh praised. UG started his harangue, declaring that that we had now polluted the atmosphere by drinking tea. "Anything from the North is taboo here!" Earlier, I had breakfast with slices of oat bread with cream cheese and coffee. UG ate oatmeal in his cottage.

* * *

Mahesh put UG on the spot by asking him why he had dragged us here. What was the need for it? UG answered, "I won't tell you now. Let Moorty come first. Then I'll tell you." In a little while Narayana Moorty joined us. "Now you must tell us," repeated Mahesh. "No special reason. I wanted to see both of you; so I asked you and Chandrasekhar to come. I am not going to India, let alone Bangalore."

In the evening, when UG was talking with Ramanand and others, I lay down for a little while in Moorty's room. Earlier, in the afternoon, they had driven us around Palm Springs - downtown, two or three malls, and a Pick and Save (it's very nice). We went to an Indian cuisine restaurant called Delhi Palace. The lady there was thrilled to see Mahesh. Ramesh came in his car. Dr. Raj phoned. His website with his internet "Guide" and the site he has built with photos and comments as a supplement to UG's website are nice.

* * *

Lisa took us to her hotel. She showed us the spa in a hotel where she works. We had news from Bangalore that our shoes and clothes were stolen in our house. That caused some disturbance in my mind. Yet there is nothing we can do from here. It's useless to worry about it.

December 21, Monday – Day 2

Woke up early in the morning at 4 am. Julie was already awake. Lisa is in one wing of the house and we and Bob are in the other. In between are the living room and the kitchen. We two (Julie and I) chatted, drinking coffee and reminiscing about past events. She told me her son Justin phoned at 1:00 am last night. He had talked for half an hour, and then she couldn't go back to sleep. His mind is not stable. She hopes that if he visits UG he will get better. But he doesn't come. He is 32 years old now. "If you have trust in UG, he will somehow help you," I told her. That's what I feel. His curses are all blessings. "My curses work, but not my blessings," he says. His curses work as blessings.

*   *   *

Ramanand is a friend of Nataraj. Luna and a couple of others came yesterday at 4:30 pm. We met at the Whitewater Club in the apartment where Mahesh and Moorty are staying. UG's discourse is *Shitopanishad*, said Moorty. His "*Om tat shit*" got further elaborated in my head as follows:

> That is shit. This is shit.

From shit comes all this shit.
Even when the whole shit is cleared
Shit alone remains.
Om tat shit.

*   *   *

Can anyone recognize an enlightened man, I asked UG. "Your question is not correct. What is there in an enlightened man (or in the one you consider to be enlightened)? What do you think there is? You must ask that question. Whatever you have known about it is all that presents itself as an answer. That's what you will experience. There is nothing besides that," said UG.

*   *

The TV news is filled with Clinton's impeachment. All the TV broadcasts are about that. UG's slogan: "Kill Clinton!" "Politics should not be used for personal destruction," Clinton comments. The American political scene is chaotic. People have a forgiving attitude toward Clinton. But this is a golden opportunity for Clinton's political enemies to bring him down. They are keen on getting him to resign.

*   *   *

December 22, Tuesday – Day 3

I woke up after midnight at 1:30 am. I couldn't get back to sleep. Yesterday, I inserted all the postcards I had bought for all the teachers in envelopes, writing their individual names on each of the cards, and got them ready for mailing. The time now is 3:30 am. It's silent all over. The central heater system is making a *'gudu gudu'* noise, and I can also hear the refrigerator sound in the kitchen. Sleep overwhelmed me last night around 9 o'clock. After I went to bed, about half an hour later, I got a phone call from Aruna.

I don't know who will come on the weekend. Perhaps Mr. And Mrs. Raghavendra Rao will come along with Aruna and Venkat. Today Paul is driving in his car from San Francisco.

*   *
*

What all happened yesterday? The weather outside was very cold. In the morning at 8 o'clock, we went over to the Whitewater Club. Everyone gathered there after a little while. In front of the video camera, Mahesh related how the influence of drugs created in him an interest in spirituality, and how Rajneesh exploited that interest, making him his slave with the pretext of saving him. Bob too spoke of UG as he had known him before his Calamity. Everyone left by 11 o'clock. Moorty and I discussed Shamarao's Kannada book and he suggested some changes.

Scott came in the afternoon in his van. Suguna and I saw the inside of the van. It looked just like a house. It has all the conveniences. In the afternoon, Suguna and Julie made couscous and *papads*. We ate them with yogurt. Last night before dinner, UG vented his fury: "I don't want the stench and stink of an *ashram* here!" – the usual song. He wouldn't let

Julie breathe nor would he let Mahesh drink his coffee. Scott was scared and he went out to eat. Moorty ate some pizza and brought the remainder to our house. We all ate soup and bread. I don't know what Mahesh ate. Julie was scolded for turning the house into an *ashram*. UG says everyone must make their own cooking arrangements. He wants all those people around him, yet he doesn't like them to eat, drink and have fun. He can't tolerate it. Especially, he doesn't like everyone gathering around the table and eating like gluttons. 'Why is Luna here?' he asks. He pours more abuse on Julie. The only thing he didn't poke at was Suguna's cooking. UG is yelling again, saying that tomorrow Guha and Lakshmi will arrive; they will cook for everyone, ransack the whole house and turn it into an *ashram*. He warns, "I'll tell them not to come." He says to Julie, "Julie, I don't need you any more. I asked you to come for helping the Malladis. Now you can go."

*   *   *

"Each day there is danger, yet you live to be a hundred years!"

December 23, Wednesday – Day 4

Today too, I woke up exactly at 1:50 am. I didn't feel like going back to bed. I finished washing and have been enjoying a cup of orange juice. Time 2:30 am. Last night, quoting O.S. Reddi, UG said, "The right time for everyone to wake up is between 2:00 am and 3:00 am. During that time the hormones in the pineal gland make all other glands function most effectively."

What happened yesterday? Julie came while I was writing my diary early in the morning. Then Lisa came and read three poems she had written. They're very nice. Needless to say that she has been influenced by UG. Moorty and Mahesh also liked them. I must copy them to some other page in this diary.

It's dawn now. UG stormed into the house like a tornado. UG's room may seem to be adjacent to this house, but it's actually 50 to 60 feet away. No sooner had he come than he exploded on Julie, "I told you yesterday not to eat here at all. Why did you do it?" he roared at her. I wasn't there at that moment. We knew that the UG thundercloud has been building over Julie; but we didn't think that the cracking would happen so soon. UG was in no condition to hear Julie, even when she tried to explain to him that she hadn't eaten there. "Vacate your room immediately and leave. You can't stay here. You must not even stay in town," he said and cast her out. There is no count of how many times this has happened. Julie cried, vacated her room and left. She rented a room in the Ocotillo Lodge.

As soon as Julie vacated her room, UG told Lisa, "Arrange your kitchen stuff as usual in the middle room," Lisa got pretty shook up and said, pitifully, dreading the task ahead, "Why now, UG? Everything has to be changed. I don't know where I left my kitchen stuff and cooking range; I need to arrange them all." "Don't worry; all these people will help you," UG insisted. In his world, things have to be done instantly; he doesn't tolerate any delay. There is no room to think "I'll do it later." Lisa got into action reluctantly. We moved her bed frame and beds into our room. She got busy arranging her kitchen.

UG phoned Lakshmi and Guha and told them not to come. UG believes that if she [*Lakshmi*] comes she will start cooking communal meals; he says you can't have such things in this house. Moorty argued last night, "Why do you take responsibility for everyone? Why do you arrange things for them? Why should you give them hospitality? They should take care of themselves. " But UG is reluctant to let that happen. It would be nice if those who come would recognize his wish and not cause him hardship; it would be nice if they ate and drank somewhere else and then came here. When they come to visit UG, it would be fine if they stayed for an hour or two. Hanging around UG all day long, not caring about the times when people who live here eat their lunches or drink their coffee – this is the tendency of people, not just in this country, but everywhere. That's why UG gets so irritated. Why don't these people understand? Don't they know that UG doesn't appreciate their hanging around him for hours together? But that's the effect of UG's attraction. No matter how long people spend time with him, it's never enough. Some deliberately stay on for coffee and meals. UG doesn't like to eat without caring for them. People like Lakshmi and Nartaki feed them, and they get a joy in such feeding. Such are UG's problems.

That's why UG started the discussion when Mahesh, Moorty and Ramesh came in this afternoon. It's amusing to see UG adopting such roundabout methods in discussions like this, while he is so straightforward, clear and to the point about everything else. Whenever he was straying from the point of discussion, Bob tried with all his might to get him back to the issue at hand.

It's the usual song: "I have given away all I have. I don't have a red farthing left. Who will give me money?" he moans sadly. Mahesh agreed long ago to pay for a ticket for UG to go around the world once a year and also for all his expenses. When UG says, "What do you have to give me? All your money is in my hands. I get interest of Rs. 100,000 a month, $30,000 a year, on your money. You'll get that money only after I die." Mahesh replies innocently, "How long do you intend to live, UG?" That's right. What more does UG want? He said, "I am not coming to India anymore. If I need to, I may pass through India, but I won't come to Bangalore and stay in their (our) house. I am going to be far away from everyone." He is giving us a sign that in the days to come his style of travel is going change in radical ways.

"I am going to tear America apart with my comments. Maybe this government won't give me a visa. But I'm not worried," he says. He is going to severely criticize the policies of the government and the deep-rooted status quo in India. "That's why I am thinking of staying away from them (meaning our family). The troubles the government and police created for Chandrasekhar's family at the time of Sai Baba's murder case are more than enough." That's true. My body trembles with fear when I think of the incidents that occurred six years ago. "From now on, I am going to criticize individuals, institutions, establishments and the society more severely – none of them will be able to withstand my attack. But I don't like anyone to be inconvenienced by my talking," says UG.

All right, what does he want? What should we do? "UG, what do you really want? What do you want us to do?" I put him on the spot. "I don't need anything," he says. Then why have these meetings and discussions? What do you want to do? No one is stopping you. Mahesh says, "You are saved because you don't have an institution or an *ashram*. Or else, governments would have strangled your throat long ago. So, no matter how much you criticize or scold as an individual, it's like rain falling on a buffalo; the world leaders who are entrenched in world establishments don't care." That's true. That's why from the beginning UG has been taking care that no *ashram*-like atmosphere, with its "stink and stench", forms around him. No matter what corner of the world he is in, his manner is the same. This individual called UG has no need to protect himself. He has no shields, armor or cloak. That's why his situation is so vulnerable, a totally insecure state where there is no security or protection.

I feel that perhaps governments of the world tolerate UG for the same reason. Maybe they think: "He is a crazy guy. He blurts out whatever he pleases. Why bother about him? Why drop an atom bomb on a sparrow?" That's why there doesn't seem to be any scope for people at large reading about UG and being influenced by his devastating ideas and rebelling. Only a few people gather around him. Besides, UG doesn't have assemblies, platforms or public speeches. That's why, although he talks about overthrowing governments, those governments consider his talk as childish and do not concern themselves with it. Not many people know that this chatterbox is not an ordinary person but is capable of creating chaos without directly involving himself.

*   *   *

While I was writing this, I lay on my back on the carpet in the hall for a little while. My head felt heavy. I stretched my arms and legs on the floor and lay as if in *Savasana*. Suddenly I remembered UG's words from yesterday. He turned to me and said, "Not many days are left between you and me. What will you do with all those tapes, photos and newspaper clippings? Do something with them. Whatever you want to do with them, do it soon." For a moment I was speechless. "I am ready to let everything go. But my problem is who will do the job? There is no point in just freely distributing them to everyone." "Whatever taped interviews you want to preserve, you preserve them in some form. You keep the stuff you have written and things which belong to you for yourself. Why do you keep the things made by others?" he asks. I don't have any intention of keeping them with myself or earning fame or money through them. Something good must come out of them. Everyone must know about them. There is nothing better than the Internet. Bob says I should digitize the video tapes and put them on CD's. But that's a huge task which involves a lot of expense. I am unable to do that. I have debts up to my brim; how much expense can I bear?

*   *   *

The meeting closed without any conclusion. There will be a discussion again today. Moorty will format my journal into book form on the computer and make a floppy for me. With that the publishing job will become easier. The Kannada book also must be published. Moorty gave some suggestions. "Proofreading is very important in desktop publishing. You must proofread the manuscript at least six times," he said.

*   *   *

The great job Raj has undertaken cannot be completed in a day; it may take a year to get it into some shape. Luna liked his "Essential UG" website very much. Moorty says that the layout must be changed. He says it's more appropriate to have one or two quotes under each photo. If we add a brief introduction and some highlights of UG's life to those pictures, the web page will look very nice. We need some material for that purpose. If we put together highlights of UG's life with the photos then it becomes another biography. Appropriately so. "We can extract photos from the video tapes," says Bob. You need computer literacy for all this. One must know those tricks. Raj is that sort of a man. It would be nice if he could come here. I must talk to Bob and ask him to invite him here. Or I must meet him in India. Raj is coming back to the US in February. Bob is leaving for Bombay on January 5. He is trying to get his book into shape. UG asks him to get Moorty's help. Bob doesn't like that. Moorty is a strict man. If you want to work with him, you must mostly adjust to his likes and dislikes. Things won't get accomplished otherwise. Bob doesn't like to lose his power. He doesn't agree with Moorty's opinions. I think that's why his book has remained unfinished.

I must discuss with UG all the following things:

1) How to bring Bob's book, his memoirs, into some shape.
2) How to make the project Raj has undertaken more attractive and aesthetic.
3) What should I do with all the stuff that is with me? Is it possible to make some kind of documentary with them?
4) What's the way to bring my journal, *Stopped in our Tracks* into a book? When should we publish the Telugu original?
5) Should we publish books at all from now on?

I am trying to figure out what would be my answers if I ask myself these questions. Even though he appears to think with us, UG knows that what is supposed to happen has already been determined. No one can stop it.

The statements Bhagavan had written to his mother come to mind: "Whatever is destined to happen will certainly happen, no matter how much we fight against it; whatever is destined not to happen, will not happen, no matter how much we try otherwise. So, it's best to sit quietly."

How true, this teaching! I must listen to it when UG explains it more in detail. As UG says, my days are nearing. I don't have much time. Should I waste my life running around for the few days I have left on this earth trying to do this and that, or should I sit quietly in a corner and witness everything passively?

As long as I am involved, I must be entangled in the experience of pleasure and pain. As long as I have the notion that *I* am doing things, I must have anxiety in my mind. Unless I realize that "When the notions of 'I' and 'mine' end, I wouldn't have any concern about what happens," my game won't be checkmated.

*   *   *

Yesterday we went in Lisa's car to many supermarkets, in Palm Springs, Rancho Mirage and Palm Desert. We also went into many shops on Highway 111. Suguna bought a leather handbag, the 'world's smallest umbrella' and a clock. UG paid for them. I bought many more picture postcards at the post office. I must write notes on them. Last night we went around the town once again in a car. They have decorated the houses and trees with varieties of lights (for the Christmas holidays). The whole town is decorated with lights. I was falling asleep in the car. UG was also sleeping. Lisa was so surprised to see UG giving up his front seat to Suguna. Lisa says, "She must be really somebody, some special person." UG generally never gives up his seat by the driver's side to anyone. Suguna is an exception.

*   *   *

Aruna and Venkat are coming by car either Thursday evening or Friday afternoon. Her in-laws will remain home. They are doing OK. I asked Aruna to get me a glucometer so I can test my blood sugar level. Palm Springs is a big town. Yesterday afternoon, I, Suguna and UG went to the Albertsons supermarket by walk. There is a small post office outlet there; and also a Jensen's supermarket.

It didn't feel very cold yesterday, but the day before it was very cold. Yesterday, it was so pleasant to walk in the sun at 11:00 in the morning. When I asked him about David Barry, Scott invited us to go to Ojai.

*   *   *

Ramesh Ganerwal left yesterday. He is going to India in January. I invited him to come to Bangalore, if it is convenient for him, and gave him my address. He has a house in a forest near Sacramento. He lives there alone like a natural man, without a worry. He has no itch to save the world. He is not anxious to interact with other people. He lives fearlessly, away from civilization, in the lap of Mother Nature, with minimal conveniences he has created for himself. As I observe his life, he appears to have been some kind of a sage in his previous life. Otherwise, it is rare to have such qualities living in this country.

*   *   *

I was thinking the other night that I don't have a single photograph of myself with UG. Last night Simon took a picture of me and UG together. Let's see how it will turn out. A German '*sannyasi*' called Vibodha has been coming every day. These have all been Rajnishi *sannyasis*, the poor folks that have of late been caught in the net of UG's attraction.

Something funny happened yesterday: as soon as I said in front of everyone, "I have a problem", UG answered repeatedly, "You cannot have any problem. I assure you, you have no problem." I didn't understand why he said that. I then explained to everyone what my problem was. What should I do with all those things about UG that I have collected? I must find a way of putting them to use. Whether they are with me or with someone else, the effect is the same. But what should I do with them? Why, for what purpose have I collected them? So that they may be useful for everyone? How will they be of use? Is it to make people realize that they cannot be helped in any way?

*   *   *

December 24, Thursday – Day 5

"How do I feel here?" I am asking myself. The answer is, I feel very well. I got up early in the morning at 3 am, washed and showered, put cream on my body, drank a cup of orange juice and sat down to write. Both inside and outside I felt peaceful.

I reduced the heat in the house a little last night. When Scott came in the other day, he complained, "It's very hot inside here; it's really hot." (When you come in from the outside cold, that's of course how it feels.) He stopped when UG said, "We feel fine, no one here is complaining about heat." Still, every now and then Scott puts his head out the door "for some fresh air". UG maintains that "this is the only way to drive them out." "If you can't stand the heat in the room, just go," – that's the path UG shows you. If you pray to him, "I've lost my bearings, UG, please show me the way, I'll be so grateful," UG shows only one way – the door! Or, you might not even get that. Then, there will be no way out!

*   *   *

Lisa didn't have many massage sessions yesterday. She stayed home till 11 am. Mahesh and Moorty came. After them, the Germans and Bob and Paul came. Paul has been sitting in the chair and dozing off. Obviously he is tired. At least today I must find time to talk to him.

Lisa is surprised to see me talking to Aruna for a whole hour on the phone, and Suguna and Aruna talking for hours together. "I don't know how to talk to my mother like that," she remarked. "It's amazing how they are talking so nicely to each other, as if they are close friends," she said admiring them. Aruna may come tomorrow with Venkat. UG had the second bed from my room moved into his room. When Lynn comes on the 26th, Moorty will stay in UG's room just for that night. If Aruna and Venkat stay for 26th and 27th, then he will have to spend two nights there. I and Lisa moved the bed into UG's room. After January, Lisa must either leave this house or share it with a partner.

I said, "UG, you keep this room. Don't let it go. It would be nice if the rent for it could be arranged whether you are here or not." The trouble is who would pay the rent for it? Lynn can. But would UG like that?

Narayana Moorty has been declaring his independence recently. "I will take care of my own room and board myself. No one needs to feed me," he said and hasn't been eating here or even touching the coffee here.

Lisa doesn't want to vacate this house. Nor does she want to take in another person to share the rent. UG asked her, "What will you do alone in such a big house?" Lisa said, "I'll convert one room into a massage room, another will be my office, and I'll sleep in the third one." "That's O.K., if you want to do your massages here also, then the whole house will be put to use," agreed UG.

*   *   *

This morning, Moorty has been talking about my journal. Will it be possible to print it through DTP (desktop publishing) if we put it into the Word Perfect format? Or should we publish it through offset printing by saving it as a text file? This is the problem. I asked him to prepare both versions. "I am going through all this trouble trusting that you will surely publish it. Or else, all this effort will be a waste," warned Moorty. "I don't have that much money, but I must get it printed even if I have to borrow money," I replied. Moorty didn't respond. I raised this question with UG that afternoon. "It's a waste to invest so much money on the book. Just drop it," he said. My heart sank. The cost estimate is Rs. 50,000. What will be the Economic Batch Quantity (EBQ)? "How much would it cost if it were published through DTP? What would it cost if we print 250 copies? What would it cost using offset printing? I must find out Shamarao says that for his Kannada book of 100 pages it will cost Rs. 10,000 to print a thousand copies.

*   *   *

Afternoon 2 o'clock exactly. Simon and Trisha came in his car. UG had arranged for this before. He is going to take us to a place called the 'Hundred Shops'. The four of us left with UG. On the way, at the base of the foothills, there were hundreds of windmills, but their propellers weren't moving. When the wind is stronger they start moving and produce electricity. On the way, on Highway 111, UG took us to the Hadley Dates and Nuts Shop. This is the most famous dates shop in this area; here you can find dates grown in the desert. It's a big shop. UG bought us a date-banana drink which was made like ice cream. It cost nine dollars for three glasses. I didn't like it much. The shop is filled with dates, almonds, cashew nuts and other kinds of dried fruits and nuts. Almonds are the cheapest item among desert-grown foods. The tag says it's $3.30 per half a kg. You could have bought a whole kg for that price ten years ago. We drove on further. After going for some distance on Highway 10, we saw a shopping complex which looked like a big town. This is what is called the 'Hundred Shops'. There are outlets here for all the most famous companies in the world. Their opulence is dazzling. Your heart quivers when you look at the prices of things in the shops. Who can buy such expensive things? Can those who have come from India buy such luxury goods even if they are rich? I think it would be impossible. Any item you touch costs thousands and hundreds of thousands of rupees, if you translate the price into rupees. You have the famous clothing store called Barney's. In it, UG bought a 100% cashmere sweater for Suguna. It looks very nice. It cost $130. That means its Rs. 5,800. I felt like, "My God!" when I thought of the price in rupees.

"You shouldn't do that," says UG. "It's the same with everything. That reference point is 'you'. You can't do anything without that reference point. That's why I say there is no such thing as your own experience. If you want to experience anything, you must first have the knowledge about it. You can't experience the present except on the basis of that knowledge. That means the past is transformed into the present. In the same way, the past is also reflected in the future. There is nothing else except the past," says UG

* * *

We finished shopping and returned at 4 o'clock. Mahesh, Moorty and others were already there. UG asked Bob to show us the video album he had put together. It was 18 minutes long; it shows many photos one after another while UG is heard talking in the background. UG's words did not match the pictures, but the pictures in the video were very good. I think it's important to weave a theme around the pictures; otherwise, you can't make heads or tails out of them. Later, I offered to show the "Natural Man" video that I made. Bob first tried to prevent it; he seemed a little agitated. Why? Maybe Moorty wouldn't like it. But why can't everyone else see it? If they don't like it, they could give suggestions as to how to improve it. We watched it for an hour and a half. In the middle of the showing, Mahesh and Moorty got ready to leave. All the while he was there, Moorty looked indifferent. Everyone listened to my commentary and laughed. That was OK. But I wanted to ask them one thing. If you are eager to show UG to the world even a little bit, you can't but sympathize with the struggle and torture I went through in making this video. It's easy to brush it off saying "This is all useless." Is it a big problem that I put Indian music in the background? The tape is evidently too long. I don't deny it. I must shorten it. It also needs some technical improvement. They can tell me about those things and suggest ways to improve it, but it's not fair to brush off the whole effort. That's the question I want to ask them. My original tape has not been returned to me yet. What Bob has given me now is an NTSC copy of that tape.

*   *   *

December 25, Friday – Christmas – Day 6

I woke up early in the morning at 4:15 am. When I was soaping my body in the shower, I was humming *Aditya Hridayam* as usual. After washing, I was sitting at the dining table by 5 o'clock, drinking a glass of orange juice. But what am I? Even though I have come here and am so close to UG, why is there no change in me? The delusion that I am my body has only been getting stronger and not going away. Is there such a thing as destiny? I want to ask UG about the message Bhagawan wrote to his mother. But did Bhagavan practice it in his life? Annamalai Swami made it clear in his book that he perhaps used "Whatever is to happen must happen," as the ultimate weapon, but that he tried at every step to make sure that whatever he wanted to happen did happen. Then what's the point in asking people not to do anything? Must we think that the actions of those realized people are different and that their teachings and actions could be contradictory to each other?

Isn't that clear when we observe UG's actions? If we try to measure their actions using their own standards, they will turn around and knock our teeth out. Do those standards apply just to us, then? I feel that these standards are tricks that are used as brakes to stop our minds from time to time; I feel that it's foolish to think that beyond that these teachings would serve as beacons shedding light on our lives. Then what's the use of all these teachings, books and tapes? Think. You will find out yourself.

*   *   *

Yesterday morning I taught Lisa *mudras*, *pranayama* and 'Salutations to the Sun'. She works as a masseuse. *Mudras* and *pranayama* can be useful in generating more energy in oneself. She has learned 'Salutations to the Sun' to practice in place of her daily exercises.

*   *   *

Five years ago, UG came to this area trying to find a house in Idyllwild. The town is 30 miles away among the forests on the mountains. It snows there in the winter. Today, they took us up there around 10 o'clock in Paul's car to show us the snow and the town. It took us 1½ hours to get up there. UG picked up some snow and gave it Suguna. This is the first time in our lives for us to step in snow and to make snowballs in our hands and throw them. Mechanically, as though we were completing a ritual, we checked out an old house for a couple of minutes, bought some picture postcards and got back into the car. There is a thick forest in this whole area. Evergreen trees and thickly snow-packed rooftops. I was wondering if those were casuarina trees; perhaps they are pine trees. They call them Christmas trees. Paul doesn't know. Poor man, he was very tired after driving the car for three hours. After coming home, we ate the broccoli-couscous Lisa had cooked and went over to the White Water Club where Mahesh and Moorty are staying. But we came back in 15 minutes. Then, until 4:15 pm when UG opened his door to come inside here, I have been napping a little and sitting reading the newspaper.

*   *   *

In the evening everyone came. Tonight is Christmas night. UG says it's a very important day. In 1974, exactly on this day, we two, after we were married, went to Jnanashram upon UG's orders. It was again the day before Christmas [*in the year 1969*] that I had met UG for the first time. On the same day every year, the battery that is running low gets recharged.

Michael, a diamond merchant who lives in San Francisco, came last night. He came just to spend time with UG. He ate with us. He sat in front of UG with closed eyes. Apparently he is a friend of Jack Masson. He knows UG through him. We were informed that he is an expert in recognizing true diamonds, just like the gold merchant Krishnachari in Bangalore. Or else, why would he come this far to see UG?

We've been waiting for the arrival of Guha, Lakshmi, Shilpa and Sumedha. Just as UG was saying "it would be nice if they came," Shilpa opened the door and came running and hugged UG shouting, "UG!" She dropped herself in UG's lap. What a captivating scene! Those children just love him so much, especially Sumedha. Guha came in laughing boisterously and sat down near UG's feet. He said, "They upgraded our tickets to first class, thanks to your grace." Lakshmi looked thin and small. I thought the children resembled her more [*than they did their father*]. Sumedha is especially cute.

The whole atmosphere changed as soon as they came in. Till then our crowd had been carrying on conversation with UG using obscenities. Apparently Larry Morris asked UG to give two sermons in his church. UG chose the topics "The Art of Adultery" and "Halleluiah Prostitution!" A case study for the first sermon is the Clinton-Monica love scandal; for the second it's Kennedy and some other man's scandals. Then UG was elaborating on sex in Hinduism. The Shiva Lingam signifies the sex act. You worship just the organ without the rest of the form of Shiva. People who follow such a religion have lost their right to speak against sex and sexual desires. UG uses the "f-word" pretty freely in his speech.

Aruna and Venkat should be coming in today. "Why couldn't they leave at 4 in the morning? Why wait till 6 o'clock?" he is asking. I didn't feel like phoning Aruna asking her to leave at 4 o'clock. What's the loss in just a couple of hours? But we'll see. I talked to Aruna yesterday morning. Apparently, she could find directions to come here on the Internet. She said that with some software you could find directions to go to any remote place in the US. David says, "If you want, you can see a photo of this house taken from a satellite." He is married to Maria, sister of Nataraj, an astrologer. They all were once Rajneesh's devotees; David had been a close disciple of Rajneesh. Later, at 9 pm, Nataraj and his friend Mitra came.

Nataraj showed me the Jupiter-Moon conjunction in the sky. He predicted that "by the end of this month a lot of money will rain in UG's lap." Guha placed $2,000 in UG's hands. Before that Moorty had given $50. All that money UG then gave to Guha's children. He is so fond of them. Earlier, he had given them each $50,000. Apparently, they invested the money in Resurgent India Bonds. In seven years the money will grow to $100,000 each. UG says it will come in handy for their education. "Where do gods live, UG?" asked Sumedha. "They live in the toilet," UG replied. The girl pinched her nose shut and ran out. We all laughed. She had really been asking about Christmas angels.

*   *   *

Julie came into the house. UG let her come in. She had driven to the airport to bring Guha's family here. Yesterday morning we went to the Ocotillo Lodge and checked out the room where Lakshmi and her family are going to stay. UG is never satisfied unless he checks out for himself to see what it's like.

*   *   *

December 26, Saturday – Day 7

I woke up at 4:30 in the morning today. That means my body is getting back into its normal rhythm. It will be nice if I wake up from tomorrow at the same time every day. Yesterday was Christmas.

After 8 o'clock we all went to the White Water Club. We all met there. Julie gave me the printout she had gotten made from the floppy that Moorty had given me. It's a 230-page book. UG took it in his hands and read out pieces from it. "Valentine's house wasn't her father's; she had bought it. The money she got from selling it then came to you," he said. Since her money went to buy the Bangalore house, it remained in the form of a house. 'Hridaya Vihar' is Valentine's house. It just moved from Geneva to Bangalore, that's all.

*   *   *

Aruna and Venkat Arrive

Many people have assembled. Larry, Susan, Claire, the German group, Michael, Luna, Moorty, Mahesh, Bob, Paul, Guha and his family – if I count all of them, the number will exceed 25. Michael has a Lincoln car. UG thought of going for a ride in that car in the afternoon. But everyone waited for Aruna and Venkat to arrive at 4 o'clock. Aruna just dropped in Suguna's lap crying. There were tears in Suguna's eyes. Mother and daughter have met after six months. Aruna hugged me and cried, crazy girl! She has become thinner. The couple ate as soon as they came. UG gave Aruna a silk slip.

Julie showed a video tape, for awhile, of Mahesh and Bob talking. I didn't feel very cold yesterday. The house was still warm even after we kept the doors open. It wasn't so cold outside either. Lakshmi and Suguna cooked together – couscous, *dahl* and yogurt. Venkat bought wrist watches for Suguna and me. The gifts are very nice. UG expressed his theory that "Youngsters shouldn't give gifts to the elders. They must only receive them." UG sat here with Lisa even after everyone had left last night.

*   *   *

Many people have given money to UG for Christmas. Michael gave three thousand; Guha two thousand. Thousands upon thousands like this. I must see if Nataraj's prediction is going to come true. Yesterday Guha told his whole story. He is always in joy about having met UG

I am noticing how Lisa loves the children. She watches Shilpa and Sumedha and plays with them. And they love Lisa.

December 27, Sunday – Day 8

I woke up at 3:45 am. Last night, after 8 pm, I couldn't keep myself awake. I spent most of yesterday with Aruna and Venkat. Venkat and I went to Walmart in his Toyota Corolla car. We got the engine gear-box oil changed and went around in the store for an hour. By the time we returned home, we learned that UG had come and gone to the Ocotillo Lodge. The rest of them had all gotten together at the White Water Club in the morning for a couple of hours. Apparently, UG had said, referring to us, "Let them spend the day with their daughter and son-in-law."

All four of us ate lunch together in the afternoon. Suguna made rice and dahl. Before lunch the four of us went downtown in the car. After lunch UG came with us to the White Water Club; we said hello to Mahesh and Moorty there and returned at 4 o'clock. Mahesh is alone in that suite. "Please let me go back to India," he begs. "You can go. If you want, I'll take you at this moment to Los Angeles and put you on the plane. But you must give me $3,000," replies UG. "I'm a poor Indian and you are a rich American. Where can I get $3,000? My government doesn't let me take so much money out of the country," Mahesh complains. His movie, *Zekhm*, has been released not only in India but in several other countries. Apparently they banned it in Mauritius. Mahesh looked disturbed. "Give me a trick to use this ban to my advantage, UG," he requested. "What can you do? By banning the movie they are now giving the movie the publicity it needs. On your part, you should never quit the policy of producing popular movies. Don't get involved in politics," said UG in reply.

Of late, Mahesh hasn't been reading books or watching TV. "I don't talk to UG either. I keep silent. Moorty too doesn't talk much. He minds his own business. He cooks very well," Mahesh told me. UG assigned Moorty the responsibility of feeding Mahesh.

*   *   *

Mystical Experiences

UG came and took his seat around 7 o'clock yesterday morning. I finished my breakfast at 7:30. Suddenly he started, "I now realize that Sri Ramakrishna and Ramana Maharshi all stopped with some mystical experience. I had such an experience when I was only a 35-year-old. On its strength I could have started big institutions and dished out that experience to everyone. There is nothing in it. It's very difficult to brush aside experience. Many people stop there," he said.

"Is it in their capacity to go beyond it?"

"There is nothing in their power. Luckily I got out of it. There is nothing you can do to make it happen."

"Human effort works up to the point of having a mystical experience. After that, whatever must happen will happen. Ramana Maharshi too said in his message to his mother, 'Whatever is destined to happen will happen, no matter how much anyone tries to stop it. Whatever is destined not to happen, will not happen, no matter how much anyone tries with all their might,'" I said.

"What's there to happen in the first place?" is UG's counter question. Then did nothing happen to UG? That's strange. The questions UG asks, "What happened? Has anything happened?" – how deep and profound they are!

"These enlightened people, these gurus, based themselves on some useless experience, deceived themselves and misled others," said UG. "Those who have freed themselves from mystical experience don't preach morals. They won't read from books and repeat the *sutras* written in them. It doesn't mean that they will act contrary to morality and preach and incite harm and treachery. They don't do that either," he said again.

The Body will Take Care of Itself

Last night, UG was talking about his travel travails. Shilpa complained from behind him: "You have already told us about all these in Switzerland – the thing that happened to you when you were there in London Immigration with Valentine and Parveen." Sumedha sat at UG's side and was trying to grab his feet. Saying "What are you doing?" he withdrew his feet. "I was trying to look at the cracks in your soles," she replied. "My feet are dirty, don't touch them," he forbade her. A couple of nights ago, Guha tried hard to apply some cream to UG's feet. "I don't need any of those things. The cracks will heal by themselves. You are all anxious people worrying about the body. If you don't interfere with it, it will take care of itself," said UG. Ramana Maharshi said the same thing about the sore on his arm. The doctors didn't listen to him; instead they tried to cut it out, thereby turning it into a huge cancer.

*   *   *

"God is in the Vagina" – Sri Ramakrishna

The other day, Guha was reading the Bengali original of *Sri Ramakrishna Bodhamrtam*, translating it into English for us. "I will remove all my clothes and dance before the women; what do you care about it?" Sri Ramakrishna had scolded one of his disciples. Guha continued, "God is in the vagina. God lets me see him in the copulation of two dogs." Ramakrishna had used much more obscene and vulgar language [*than this*] in his conversations. But Nikhilananda, in translating, had corrected all that, changing it so that people would be presented with the image of a holy man to hold in their minds.

*   *   *

Last night, UG made me call Major on the phone. "You must come here. If you don't, I won't come there," said UG "Not right now," replied Major. "He will definitely come at another time," said UG looking at us. We all said hello to Major. Apparently, the other day he had invited Venkata Chalapati and served him *Upma*.

*   *   *

UG said he will buy swimsuits for Shilpa and Sumedha. There is a nice pool in the Ocotillo Lodge. The children want to swim in it. Last night, the whole UG gang went out to hunt for swimsuits. Seven of us went in Julie's van (Chevrolet) and UG, Venkat, Aruna, Shilpa and Sumedha went in Michael's Lincoln car. We couldn't find swimsuits in any of the shops. But the light decorations in downtown Palm Springs were very nice to see. UG went around patiently through all the supermarkets. At last, we returned home at 8 o'clock and ate our dinner. UG did the cooking himself with potato buds. We ate to our heart's content. We also finished all the leftovers from the morning.

UG was telling– tidbits about his childhood, quarrels with his grandfather, the requirements he set for his marriage – it would be nice if someone wrote a book with the title *The Marriage of UG*. It would be a nice storybook in Telugu. *The Sports of Life* – Rajasekhar gave a nice title to his book. Only the book is too detailed. What you can write concisely he stretches into pages and pages – it gets to be too boring to read.

*   *   *

Strange Business Transactions

December 28, Monday – Day 9

I woke up at 3:15 am in the morning. I started writing at 4:30 am. It has been getting slowly warmer in the last couple of days. I even have removed the sweater I put on when we went to Palm Desert for shopping last evening. How many shops we roamed through! Finally, in a sports shop near Target we found the swimsuits the children needed. UG came in this morning, bringing Paul Lynn with him. It's almost five years ago since I met Paul. He came with his family to Yercaud in 1991-92. He is writing a book called *Male Menopause*. He has found this house and been paying the rent on it so that UG can stay here. Larry bought all the furniture in this house with his church money. To transfer all that furniture to Paul, Larry had to pay UG $1,000! Now Paul Lynn has again to pay UG and close the furniture account! These are all very strange business transactions. They all shell out dollars into his hands without uttering a word of complaint. He took $200 from Julie last evening; that's twice the amount he had spent on the children's swimsuits. And apparently, she had already given him that money that he had spent. On top of it, as soon as she opened her purse and gave him the amount he demanded, he complains that she had shortchanged him. Sumedha ran to UG as soon he called her. UG pressed all those bills into her hand. She wanted to give all that money back to Julie. But Julie did not take it. Sumedha turned it all over to her mother. That's the way!

*   *   *

The Guhas

Lakshmi is a nice woman. She is an unassuming lady. She had helped Guha come to the US while working there. "Now, we have fewer relationships with our relatives and others. UG is the only one we have. We only do what he says," says Lakshmi. Because UG forbade it, Guha didn't even go to India to attend his brother's wedding. "I found UG, what else do I want? The captain of the helm of my life's boat is UG," he says.

You don't even need to mention the kids. They love UG dearly. If the parents start scolding them, they threaten that they will tell UG. When Lakshmi and Guha were planning to go to India, they had said adamantly, "UG said we are Americans and he told us not to go to India. So we're not going." The parents cancelled the trip. These are the only two kids I have seen that take so much liberty with UG and love him so much. Apparently, while he is visiting in Guha's house, when there are no other visitors, these two kids play with UG by combing his hair and braiding it. If there are signs of anyone coming, UG would pretend as if he is going to hit them and say, "Hey, what are you doing? Get away from me." If there is no one else, they have UG all for themselves. UG likes to join them and play with them. They are happy speaking with him in English and playing in his lap. No other kids have come so close to him. They have a fancy for watching the video tape of Archana playing with Valentine when she was little. Perhaps they would like to play like that with UG. When there is a crowd they don't come near him. The other day, when UG was alone, Sumedha was wrestling with him. Of the two, Shilpa looks like the more affectionate type. She wants to be with people and wants their loving attention and favor.

Venkat left yesterday. So the kids got hold of Aruna. "You're here; that's so neat!" Shilpa says and drops in her lap and hugs her. They two look like Aruna and Archana when they were younger. UG used to deliberately tease Aruna and Archana. That's why they were with Valentine more.

*   *   *

Last night, Mahesh and Moorty also ate here. They brought over here the stuff they had made there. UG says, "Moorty is a great editor, but I don't like his cooking at all." Mahesh and Larry both appreciate Moorty's cooking. UG says, "You like it because you don't know what Telugu cooking is like. I don't like it." He degrades Moorty's cooking right in front of him saying he doesn't even know how to cook. Moorty smiles broadly and minds his own business or goes out to do his shopping. The *coottu*-like dish he has made today was very tasty. Suguna said, "You cooked it with *rajma* and other grains. It looks like it has a little garlic in it." Still it was good. Suguna made something like a soup with the leftover *dahl* from the morning and the foods remaining from yesterday and the day before. Everyone ate well last night.

Yesterday, Venkat and I went to Lucky's for food supplies and got whatever we needed. In the afternoon, Suguna made couscous, rice and *dahl*. Venkat ate his lunch and left at 1:30 pm in his car. Aruna will stay here till the 31st and return by air. Apparently you need an ID card even for e-booking. She didn't bring her passport, so Venkat will send it tomorrow by courier. UG arranged it so we could spend the whole day with both of them. He told us, "Don't come to the meetings. Spend some time with your daughter and son-in-law." He came in the evenings with everyone. Venkat stayed here for two nights. "Come as soon as you can, Uncle," he invited us before he left. UG too said goodbye to him on the phone. Aruna looks happy. It's a great vacation for her to come here and spend a few days merrily with everyone. "Coming here and spending a few days here makes her feel like she is visiting her parents' place," says Suguna. There are many relatives of UG in this country; and our relatives too. But Aruna is not close to any of them; perhaps a little with Kamesh. Everyone else lives in their own world.

Last night, Kittu and Sri Valli spoke with UG on the phone. Sri Valli asked for an autographed photo of Mahesh. Even though she knew we are here, she didn't say hello; maybe she was waiting for us to talk to her; I don't know. I have been trying to talk to Kumar, but it hasn't worked out yet. Our friendship with Guha and Lakshmi is very pleasant. Suguna too feels the same way.

"He is my Enemy No.1"

"UG, let the cat out of the bag," said Mahesh last night. He can't figure out why UG fussed so much calling him here. Before we left India, we both felt that there must be a strong reason for it. Although it has been nine days since we have arrived, UG has not broached the 'real' reason yet. What could it be? That day in the White Water Club he had said casually, "I am not coming to India. The Bangalore chapter is closed. Sometime, when I go that way and have to pass through India, then maybe I will stay for a few days; but you must pay for my ticket. How about my travel expenses?" That's the way he has been talking.

He asked me to get rid of the photos and tapes. I don't care now if I have them or not. Does getting rid of them mean that I should pass them out to everyone? Or does it mean that I should donate them to some library? Who will take them? Sometimes he speaks as though we must preserve them. If we have to preserve them, we must transfer them to CD's. That's very expensive. How can I afford it? Who will teach me how to do it? If there is some sort of central archive, I could give them to them.

Last night, when Mahesh repeated his question, UG said, "There is no cat, no bag. You can go back." Then Mahesh replies, "You could have told me that over the phone. You didn't have to get me to come this far." UG said, referring to me, "My photos and tapes are more important to Babu. He may let me go, but he won't let them go. He doesn't realize that he will lose me." I cringed.

Can I bear to lose UG? What good is it to live after that? But if I look into myself, I feel that I can't bear being close to UG for any length of time. My past impressions and my ego rebel every now and then. The ego doesn't go down no matter how much it is hammered. The pride that I have known him for 30 years, the pride that I am the first of his long-standing acquaintances, is turning me into my own enemy. It made UG say, "He is my enemy No. 1."

If he says I am his enemy, his 'Public Enemy', what does it mean? I have always striven to preserve memories of UG for a long time and to make those memories accessible to people, joining them and rejoicing with them when they appreciate the result—that's all I care about. This shows not a simple UG, UG who has no fanfare, that UG who is in the world of Shilpa and Sumedha.

Do I have a hold over that UG? UG is a form which changes from moment to moment. I am trying to fit UG forcibly into a presentation of photos and tapes. Is that possible? The real UG is not the UG I know. Whatever I know, whatever I understand, that's not UG. How can this truth sink into my consciousness? My consciousness only writhes in pain when UG says nasty things about me, but do I ever consider what I am doing to UG? When I get away from the real essence and get caught in a network of delusions, how could I be saved if I get intoxicated with the idea that "this is the real UG?" Suppose I ask him, "So, what do you want me to do?" would he answer? Would he give me some suggestions? UG has been telling me what to do; not suggesting, but clearly ordering me. Still, I can't grasp it. I still need to tune myself. My ego's agitation must subside. Unless the noise of 'this fellow' subsides, I can't hear UG's voice. UG's message is all mixed in with my agitation. "Mahesh, we are not listening; UG has been telling us something!"

*   *   *

While I was drinking my coffee I felt like going into UG's room. I felt like telling him what I have understood: "I am constantly preoccupied with myself. Perhaps that's why I am not able to listen to what you have been saying. This occurred to me just now." It's foolish to expect that UG will tell you something, will direct you or order you. He has been telling what he needed to. It's my foolishness if I don't listen. Maybe that's why Jesus had said, "Let them who have ears listen." I opened the door and walked on the cold ground toward UG's room. Only the night light was on. I didn't have the guts to knock on the door. I turned around.

*   *   *

"You must all be reduced to the level of animals"

"You must all be reduced to the level of animals. Until then you won't understand what I say," said UG yesterday suddenly.

When all our acquired culture and civilization are burned into ashes, when we remain as just us, who are nothing, who don't belong to anything, and who don't think or experience anything – the pure us – then we will understand UG's message. Without that, there is no use in listening to a lot or saying much. "Whether you agree or not, your body lives by itself as an animal. Only *you* have problems. The body doesn't have any problems. It has no worries," said UG

UG is a living example of someone who lives in this world without a worry, like a drop of water on a lotus leaf, living among all these people, yet uninvolved. We give a shape to that form and look it as UG. We dress it up; we take it around in cars; and we feed it chocolates. We think we are talking to it. We pick up quarrels with it. We assume that the sounds we hear from it are words and we try to understand the words. We care. We cry thinking it is scolding us. We are puffed up thinking it is praising us. Very cleverly we whisper, pointing out that there is nothing saying anything, and that whatever is there and whatever we think we know is all a delusion. UG watches all this and keeps laughing to his heart's content and spiting us.

*   *   *

Karma Cards

December 29, Tuesday – Day 10

Ten days have passed in UG's presence. In the beginning I felt like that time had stood still. Why did we come – to do what, to see what? Now I don't have any such questions. I woke up at 4:30 in the morning. We were up last night till 10:00 pm along with UG, till Wendy and Kiran came. They both traveled for seven hours in the car and arrived at Moorty's place in Suite #362 Ocotillo Lodge by 9 pm. UG used to stay in Suite #367 before. Lakshmi and her family are in #354. Julie too stays in #363. Yesterday morning, we all went with UG to #362. The Germans, Stanley and Luna also came there. As usual, UG chatted for two hours. Nataraj brought his Karma Cards and did some Tarot reading again. Two days ago, when UG picked from the cards three times, all three times Venus came up. Once in the 2nd house, the second time in the 12th house and the third time it was in the 1st house. Jupiter and Sagittarius another time. Nataraj's prediction: UG will get a lot of money after 'killing' a rich woman with his 'arrow'. Or he will make her go crazy. Yesterday morning Sumedha asked, "When will the bow and arrow come, UG? When will they be ready?" Nataraj asked UG to pick from the Karma Cards again. The first one was Libra. That's the sign of Sumedha. The second one was in the 12th place. The third was Guru. Nataraj's verdict was that the bow and arrow should come only through Sumedha.

These are some of the amusing incidents that have occurred around UG. But we don't know their implications at this moment. I think that the 'bow' and 'arrow' are symbols of Saturn and Budha. Their celestial powers reside in the form-field. They say that the form-field of Saturn is bow-shaped and that of Budha is arrow-shaped. It sounds as if UG will collect all these powers and destroy the mind, which is close to Moon (Chandra), with one stroke. Perhaps it should be interpreted like this. I mentioned this in UG's presence.

Nataraj's has been sitting for a long time with his eyes closed. Simon also sits silently; and David even more so. Nataraj's sister gave UG some more money – a hundred dollars. "Gifts will only be accepted till 11:59 pm of the 31st of this month. After that, I won't take a penny," says UG. UG's chest of gifts is never full! We were about to give Lisa a small gift and showed it to UG. "You're giving gifts to everyone; what about me?" he says. "What can we give you, UG? You give to everyone. Isn't all this your grace?" said Suguna. He laughed. True, what gift can we give him? If he is taking money, it means those who give it are lucky. He is making some people give. Even those who are in no position to give are stuffing his hands with dollars. Simon feels his pockets sadly and says, "I don't have any money left!"

Kiran

UG detected a great musician in Moorty's son, Kiran. Kiran plays piano and percussion very well. UG decided to buy him a piano. He made an envelop ready with $6,000 in it and handed it to Kiran yesterday. "This is for your piano," he said. Wendy tried to stop him. "This doesn't concern you or Moorty. It's between Kiran and me. Leave it to us," UG said to Wendy. I was right next to her. I said, "It's best not to interfere in such matters; it's better leave things to UG." She showed the photos of the piano.

Yesterday in the evening we went to a shopping mall called 'Perceptions'. UG bought Aruna a microwave oven and a set of utensils in Costco – altogether it cost $125. Suguna has been planning to get them. She wanted to buy them here and send them with Aruna. Her wish has been fulfilled. Aruna bought me a pair of shoes. We went to many other shops.

Claire and Larry

Yesterday, in the afternoon, Claire came with me for a walk. We walked about a mile from the Ocotillo Lodge along the road and came back. She asked a lot of questions about India and about India's poverty, disease and economic conditions. She is an intelligent girl. I invited her to come to India. When I mentioned that to UG, he said, "She will come. But Larry won't, yet." Apparently, Larry hasn't gotten a green signal yet. He met Shau 30 years ago when he came to India with Moorty. He has a great liking and respect for Shau. "I remember that you were there too at that time. You lay in front of her and had her drop *vibhuti* (ashes) in your mouth," he said. I wasn't there then. If I had seen Narayana Moorty at that time, I couldn't have forgotten him. It now occurs to me that Larry is probably confusing me with Mr. Basava Raju.

*　　　*　　　*

Mahesh Leaves...

Today Mahesh is leaving. He must be in L.A. by 1:00 pm. Paul Lynn booked a plane ticket for him from here. UG first planned that all of us should go to L.A. But the 7-seat van will not have enough space for all of us. We needed another car. So UG says, "Why go so far?" Larry reminded him that we should go to Paru's Restaurant. Paru's is a South Indian restaurant which is quite famous in L.A. A Madrasi called Kannan is running it. He is a good friend of UG and Larry. U. G. speaks Tamil with him fluently. He asked Lisa to phone Kannan. "We are not coming tomorrow; we'll come again some other time," UG said to him in Tamil. So the 'danger' of going to Los Angeles has been averted. Today, the main business is to drop Mahesh off at the airport and go around town. Yesterday, when I was about to go with Julie to drop off Stanley at the airport, everyone, including UG, joined us. Stanley was very pleased. He was reluctant to go. He is a confused man. When I look at the way he acts, it looks like he has some drug habits.

Last night, Julie and I dropped off Luna Tarlo also at the airport. She doesn't reveal her true age, says Julie. Although she is not a very rich woman, she made herself a name through her book *Mother of God*. I feel there is something special about her. She read my whole journal. Now Nataraj is reading it.

* * *

Lakshmi and Guha

"Everyone searches for UG, and goes and meets him. But UG came looking for us to our house and became our guru," says Lakshmi. After Guha met UG in New York, when he would go to see UG, Lakshmi used to send with him *idlis* she had made for UG. "I must meet the lady who has made such good *idlis*; let's go to your house," said UG to Guha and went with him to their home. I don't know what auspicious moment it was when he stepped into their house, but he became their household deity and became implanted in all their hearts forever. He built a nest in the innocent hearts of Shilpa and Sumedha permanently. From that day, UG is their God. His word is their law. Contemplating UG is their life. What self-forgetfulness in Guha! If he is around UG he is totally lost. The same is true with Lakshmi. As I watch their family, it's not clear to me whether they were created for UG, or UG has become incarnate just for them.

UG knows very few Indian families in the US. All these years he has known Narayana Moorty in the West Coast. Now, he sees Guha and Lakshmi in the East Coast. Guha was a practitioner of Sahaja Marg before he met UG. He used to be very active in the Ramachandra Mission. Apparently he had heard about my grandfather Kuppuswami (who was also a senior devotee in Sahaj Marg). Guha used to tour Bangalore, Coimbatore and such other places to publicize that institution. He moved away from that ever since he met UG. Now he is filled with UG

* * *

Scott made a beautiful wooden sofa for UG, brought it over in his van and left without seeing anyone. The sofa is very nice. Lisa was happy with it. People's bottoms could fit in it exactly. UG has been showing it to everyone. I want to visit Ojai sometime. I don't know if it will be possible. When all these people leave after their visit, I'll find out. Guha and family will be here till January 5. Larry is leaving on the 31st via L.A. Aruna may leave with them. From there she will go to San Jose by air.

* * *

December 30, Wednesday – Day 11

I woke up early at 4:30 am. We went to bed at 10:30 last night. Aruna got her passport yesterday by courier at 11:30 am. UG got the microwave oven and the box of utensils shipped by UPS to Aruna's address. It cost $35 to ship them. But that saved her the worry of carrying them with her on the plane. Still, if they were bought while Venkat was still here, he could have taken them with him and we could have saved the $35. That's how my mind calculates! It regrets having spent so much money unnecessarily, but it doesn't think that it too is part of the cost of the purchase. If we think that for $35 we could have bought something useful, how about the convenience of Aruna traveling without a bother and not having to check it in and pay for excess baggage? Aren't these advantages? That's how the mind is. It never quits its meanness. It constantly grumbles and complains.

Conflict between Moorty and UG

Last night, there was a minor conflict between Moorty and UG. Moorty told me earlier that he would cook that night for the three of them, him and his family. He thought that it was best that each family cooked for themselves. That's true too. How is it possible to have one person cooking for this many people? Suguna, Aruna and I thought we would cook separately. When we asked, UG told us to prepare food for Guha's family also here. Then, he finally added Julie to the list. Then Suguna and Lakshmi started the inventory: what they have and what they don't and what they needed to bring. Finally, they decided to finish all the leftovers from yesterday; so they just cooked some couscous.

UG didn't like Moorty cooking separately like this. But then, if all of us have to eat together, who would do the cooking? What would they cook? Questions of this sort and of differences in tastes come up. Guha and his family have their own house. They have a kitchen there. They could cook their own meals. But UG doesn't leave them alone. For the last two days they have been eating here, except for the day before yesterday when we ate in their house in the afternoon. The night before the last, yesterday afternoon, and last night too they have eaten here. UG scolds Julie and tells her to cook separately.

Moorty got mad when UG asked him casually, "How long are you going to be in the kitchen? You get out of the kitchen." "I won't come into the kitchen again; the three of us will go out to eat. We won't cook here," Moorty asserted. UG tried to explain himself and probably regretted that he had needlessly hurt Moorty's feelings – all that was funny. It was clear that

UG was upset. Moorty was adamant and said he would stop cooking here and would eat outside from the next day. UG said, "You are guests here; I don't like your eating outside." "Why do you have such a sentiment? This is a decision I have come to after thinking practically. It doesn't matter to me. I am earning money. It's not a problem for me," said Moorty.

UG faltered in his speech and his voice was weakened, reflecting the disturbance in him. "You haven't eaten anything? Why is your voice like that?" asked Moorty. UG had already cooked his oats and eaten them.

I then went to UG's room. "Why should Guha and their family eat here? Why should Julie eat here?" he said. But it was he who wanted them to stay.

I can't wait to see how far this saga of eating will go on today. "I am not going to have any more meetings or talks from now on. I never invited the Germans. They can do what they please," UG said. He turned to Larry and said, "America is finished. This is also the end of the Palm Springs chapter. I am not even going to India." Then he turned to Lisa and said, "Why do we have this big chair here? It's a waste. Return it to the owner. I must vacate this place by the end of January. I'll tell Lynn. There won't be any more meetings. There won't be any talking."

He talked like that, rather incoherently, for a while. This incident is proof that he too reacts to situations by being sorry for what happened and being hurt. Although he says "I never question my actions," it's clear that he is affected by what happens in such contexts. The principal actor of the drama, Moorty, however, sat quietly like a cool cucumber. The three of them ate after we finished.

Aruna, a Hard-Working Girl

Lisa opened her 'sweat shop' in the evening. She went to a shop and brought all the stuff she needed to make two pillows, especially Velcro. Suguna also bought some stuff. Lisa sewed the covers for the pillows with the help of Aruna and Wendy. Aruna and Lisa cleaned UG's room and his bathroom. It was so nice to see Aruna doing everything so briskly. She seems to have turned into quite a hard-working girl. When Julie was putting gas in her car, Aruna got out of the car and cleaned the windshields. She helps Suguna and Lakshmi in the kitchen. She has learned a lot of things in the six months she has been in the US. Last night, Moorty gave her some suggestions that he thought of in regard to her education. He suggested that she should do her M.S. I notice a sort of self-confidence in Aruna now.

UG asked when Aruna will be able to get the money invested in her name [in India]. I answered that she can get it next May. "I will take those Rs. 200,000 and give dollars in exchange. She needs an account here," he said. She has already acquired a lot of credit cards. When Aruna tried to pay for things while shopping, UG prevented her. "I know you are a rich girl, but keep your money," he said, smiling.

*   *   *

Money Due to Mahesh

Mahesh left yesterday morning to return to Bombay. As UG asked him to have breakfast before leaving, he and Moorty vacated their apartment and came early in the morning. "Have you figured out in these ten days why UG has forced you to come here, Mahesh?" I asked him. "Just to tell me that I should stop questioning," he answered without thinking about it. "I learned that questions like 'why', 'what's going to happen', 'what will happen next' should never occur to me," Mahesh said. Then he talked to UG about the money due to him. "You said that I shouldn't direct movies any more; you asked me not to meddle in politics; you told me not to bother with Rajya Sabha and Lok Sabha. But when I ask you about the pension that is due to me, you say it will come soon, but you don't give me a penny. How am I going to survive then? How will I get money?" he said putting UG on the spot. "Your pension is Rs.100,000 per month. But you must go to Bangalore and get it there. That's only the interest. You cannot touch the principal. The pension will start only from August 1999," UG told him.

Mahesh has still to buy UG a business-class round-the-world plane ticket once a year. "Asgar Ali will take care of that. No problem," says Mahesh.

"If that's the case, where will Mahesh get the money when he wants to come and see you, UG?" I asked.

"Why should he come? I won't see his face. This is all one way. When I want to come, he must send me the ticket," UG replied. We all laughed at the exchange between UG and Mahesh.

*   *   *

Lisa's Stay in the House

The weather has gotten warmer. It's quite sunny today. In the nights it's pretty cold outside. If I stay indoors, I feel I don't need to put on a shirt. The number of this house is 2003. The land area is 100' x 100'; and on it they built a long house of 20' x 70'. UG's room, which is a separate unit in front of the house, is 20' x 20' in area. It's very cute and convenient for UG in every way. It has a western entrance like the house in Yercaud. This, however, is more convenient. It would be nice if UG could make some permanent arrangement in this house so that he could come here again and again. UG's worry is that Lisa will have to live here alone. He says it would be nice if she has someone to share the house with. But who will? He says, "She must find some fat cat." If there is such a fat cat, why would Lisa live with UG? "Lisa has orgasms even without thinking about men," UG says. "She is in a state superior to Ramana Maharshi's," he says. Apparently, once when she was making love she got into a state in which she didn't know if she was a man or a woman. When she tells UG such things, he broadcasts them to everyone.

*   *   *

December 31, Thursday – Day 12

Today, I woke up at 4:45 am. That means my body has gone back to its normal routine. By the time I washed and sat down here, it's 5:30 am. I am finding less and less time to write in this diary. From now on, I must try to wake up at least by 4 o'clock.

Yesterday, everyone came. UG told the Germans that he is not going to see anyone from now on. "Hi and Bye" has become his slogan. Those who come cannot stay here for hours. They must see him and then leave. That's what UG wants. That's enough. In those few minutes those who truly want UG's grace will find it. "Don't come back," UG was telling Larry Morris. Isn't it a perversion on the part of people to interpret what Ramana Maharshi says in the vein of Vedanta and say that Bhagavan is actually ordering us not to come back into the orbit of births and deaths?

"Came down quickly!"

There is a mountain called Eggli in Gstaad. It's one of the mountains in the Alps. Once a friend of UG called Henry Dennison asked UG to write a poem, as he considered poetry is a sign of enlightenment. All enlightened people are poets. Poetry pours out of them spontaneously. They don't need to write it down. However, UG agreed and composed a Haiku:

> I went up Eggli
> Found it ugly
> Came down quickly.

It occurred to me that there are great poetic qualities to this poem. The 'Eggli' peak is a symbol for a spiritual peak. After putting in great effort and reaching it, UG realized how disgusting it is, and came down quickly into his natural state. Coming down like that is enlightenment.

*   *   *

Air Museum and War Heroes

Yesterday, I had the opportunity of talking to Paul Lynn for a length of time. At 1:30 in the afternoon we all went to the Palm Springs Air Museum. Arranged there is an exhibition of all the war planes used in the Second World War exactly as they were then. They have arranged them very well. In the WWII, warplanes like P-38s and P-40s created terrifying showers of bombs and decimated strategic locations of Japanese and German armies. Here they have collected specimens of the airplanes and assembled their histories carefully, and arranged the displays well. When we see how carefully they preserved the war memories by setting up this museum, we can understand how people of this country love war. It's not just that they won that war.

We ran into a war hero. He had been an airplane pilot in the war. In his attempt to down a German plane, he got acquainted with an enemy pilot in a short period of time. Apparently after the war was over, the American pilot hero met the enemy pilot once again in Hemet near Palm Springs. Both of them had settled in the same country. Now they are both friends. This incident shows how foolish these wars and sacrificing of lives are.

Karna and Arjuna
> Who fought so long on the screen
> Lie down embracing
> > In the coffin of time. ~ *Sudha*, Chalam

What a great truth! What's real? Setting up boundaries such as "I am this" and "this is mine", marking borders, and fighting and cutting each others' throats – you won't find such things among animals, but only in the human species. Maybe animals too have the fighting quality – dogs fight off neighboring dogs which encroach upon their territory. Men have inherited the same quality.

*   *   *

Larry and Susan

Larry will leave today for Albuquerque with Susan and Claire. Everyday he sits in front of UG with one leg folded around another and keeps saying 'yes', 'yes' or 'no' to everything. UG asks him casually, "What do you preach in your church? Domination, right?" and he answers, "Yes, sir, domination," without hesitating a moment.

"That bastard Jesus, if he had had security men, there wouldn't have been any Christianity at all," says UG. And Larry immediately echoes, "Yes, Sir, there wouldn't have been any Christianity."

"But you are a Jew. You cleverly concealed that fact." "Yes, I am a Jew."

"Jesus provided an opportunity for your living. You made him your living."

"Yes, sir, he is my living."

"You must be grateful and pray to him everyday."

"Yes, sir, I go down on my knees daily."

When you watch this sort conversation between UG and Larry, you can't stop laughing.

*   *   *

You would think that Radhakishan in Bangalore equals Larry, but only to some extent, only to the extent of shouting loudly to justify UG. Larry is more than that. "You are a total goner," says UG. "Yes, I am a goner," Larry joins the chorus. Everyone bursts out laughing.

But Susan doesn't move her mouth. She just smiles and watches the show. Claire knows their relationship. She tells of all the funny things he does in the church. He comes down from the pulpit after the service and hugs and kisses everyone, and he listens to everyone's problems and comforts them. One woman who has been harassed by her husband tells him of her problems and asks him for his advice as to what she should do. Larry's advice to her was: "If you want to live with your husband, live with him; if you want to leave him, then leave him; if you don't feel like doing anything, then don't do anything." That somehow consoled her and she left. That's how it works! But Larry is a great man. He has enormous regard and infinite love for UG. Narayana Moorty says "he's crazy."

*   *   *

There was a sign in the Air Museum which says "June 6, 1944 – Normandy operation." I thought of YNK. Only he can speak of the importance of June 6. When I looked at the date on this page of the diary, I thought of it.

*   *   *

Aruna's Departure

Aruna is leaving today for San Francisco from LA on the 6 pm flight. UG will probably go with everyone in Julie's van. Aruna bought me a pair of shoes in Costco. My left foot is developing a few sores because of them. They need to be broken in some more. Last night, Julie recorded all the Sanskrit, Hindi and Telugu songs that Aruna sang. The recording Kiran played for us of his piano playing was very nice. I don't know how to appreciate Western music. But it was quite nice to listen to. Part of it sounded similar to Indian music. On Christmas night, Suguna and I were also recorded. Suguna recited *Aditya Hridayam*. They asked me too to recite something. That night I recited "*Shannomitra samvarunah*" and also the *Santi Patha*. I recited some poems and devotional songs on Bhagavan. Guha sang a Bengali song – *Rabindra Sangeet*. Everyone sang joyfully in front of UG – it was like a celebration. "UG celebration" – everyone's enthusiasm overflowed; especially the children.

Kiran is a little strange. He doesn't easily mix with others. He is a little shy. The earlier active nature of his has disappeared. He is now 13-years-old. UG says he is a genius. UG says to play on the piano is a very difficult skill. Everyone is praising Kiran saying it's wonderful that he can play on the piano so well at this young age. He can also play percussion instruments. But I don't know where he is now. He doesn't even take liberties with UG as Shilpa and Sumedha do. Claire is not so bad. Occasionally she asks UG a question or two. UG prods Claire to express her opinions about Larry's talks. She complies without hesitation. She has a nice face. It probably resembles her father's.

*   *   *

Paul Lynn and Family

Sophia, Paul Lynn's daughter, has grown up quite a bit. She has a mature face. She is Lynn's daughter with his first wife. Bonnie and Paul have a son called Zack. He is Paul's replica. Paul thinks that Sophia should go to college in Palm Springs.

Currently they are living in Mill Valley near San Francisco. I must visit his clinic sometime. Lynn has a high regard for UG. He lived with UG in Mahabaleshwar [*near Pune*] and also in the house on Vani Vilas Road in 1971-72. We talked about things that had happened then. We remembered Hanumanta Reddi. I must send him a greeting card.

I must remember to write cards to some other old friends today, New Year greeting cards. It's over. With today, it's goodbye to this year. I am saying goodbye to this year, saluting in my heart, with tears of joy in my eyes, to the Primal Energy for letting me start the last lap of this century in UG's presence, and for creating this opportunity.

*   *   *

January 1, 1999, Friday – New Year's day – Day 13

Palm Springs on New Years' Eve

Last night it was New Year's Eve. We two went in Wendy's car with Moorty's family to see the city. When we drove around in the streets of the city of Palm Springs and watched all the decorations the citizens of the city have made to welcome the New Year, I felt as if the whole glory of America is displayed in this one street. Wherever you look, you see electric lights. Crowds of people everywhere, from small restaurants to huge restaurants, bands, dances, laughter and screams. There was a new liveliness among people, and new couples and young men and women were paying their homage to the New Year. After we went around the town and returned home, it was 11:15 pm.

As expected, Paul Lynn and his family came. They opened the champagne bottle which Wendy had bought and gave themselves each a little champagne in glasses. I had some soda in my hand and Suguna had water. Anticipating the New Year, many cakes and eatables were spread out on the table. We ate those and watched the New York Times Square celebrations on a TV channel. The countdown started. We finished eating and at exactly midnight we all said "cheers" and wished each other Happy New Year, sipping the drinks. Lisa joined us. It's almost the same old crowd. The New Year was ushered in this way, in this strange place, among old friends. UG stayed in his room away from all this noise.

Yesterday morning, Larry Morris and others have left. UG has had a hoarse voice ever since he drank the 'Naked' juice. But he continued to talk. The Germans came after a little while. Larry as usual became a chorus of one repeating UG's talk.

Before he left, Larry asked half-seriously, "UG, is there such a thing as perfect justice on this earth?" "If there is such as thing as justice or righteousness, you and I wouldn't be sitting here like this. Creation would have wiped out mankind a long time ago. The only justice I know is the laws created by your men – the laws you have forced on people with not only your army, navy and air force, but also with nuclear weapons. There is no other justice except this. What is man after all among all the species that have come into being in this creation and have become extinct? If we consider the whole span of creation as 12 hours, there is no trace of man in it for 11 hours 59 minutes and 59 seconds. Such a species is arrogantly trying to subdue the whole of creation. Man is plundering and destroying all the riches of the earth with the idea that all other species are inferior to him and that the whole of creation is meant for his enjoyment. Mankind's destruction is inevitable," said UG

That's UG's message, his welcome to the New Year. "I am not worried if my children and their children are all destroyed," he says. This ever-increasing quest for pleasure, this depraved culture which transforms common men into demons and pests (*maricha and mahammari*), must be totally uprooted. Only when this culture and tradition are destroyed without a trace do your bodily organs vibrate with new life. Larry, *you* should go. That's the only way. Everyone must 'go' beyond recognition," he said. This consciousness of 'I' and 'mine' is the coloring that culture has imposed on us. Under the illusion that it's all true, we forget our true nature; and we cry and laugh thinking that our garb is our real essence. The moment that illusion is removed, we will open our eyes to reality.

*   *   *

Lakshmi and Guha (Continued)

Aruna, Lakshmi, Suguna and I went in Julie's car to L.A. at 2 pm. It took 2½ hours to get to the LA airport. As a 5 o'clock flight was ready to leave, Aruna left on it an hour early. Using Julie's cell phone, she phoned Venkat and told him of the change of flight. They both called from there last night around 8 pm. By that time we had gotten back home. The house looks deserted after Aruna has gone. Archana is alone in Bangalore. This time the New Year's is strange. But we have UG's company.

On our return trip from LA in the car, Lakshmi got into the mood of telling her whole story. As she related the story of how Guha had suffered with the problem of gurus before he had met UG, how she and her children had to suffer its consequences, how the problems all got cleared [*with UG's acquaintance*] like layers of fog being burned off by the morning sun, emotion choked her voice. "We'll walk the way he will lead us."

Guha had gotten acquainted with UG in December 1995. "I didn't meet UG until six months later." She was so sorry she had lost so much time. After Guha had come under UG's spell, his former guru once called him on the phone and asked him to see him. Guha agreed. But he was reluctant to go. When he asked UG for advice, "That's something which concerns you. You must decide for yourself. But why do you want to go there?" UG asked. That question burned away the indecision that was raging in Guha. He immediately called his former guru and made it clear to him that he wasn't going to see him and that he wouldn't have any more relationship with him. But things didn't end so simply. People close to the guru started giving Guha moral lectures. Once these people had been his and Lakshmi's life. But he pushed them away. Now Guha is alone, just like me. Lakshmi on the one hand, and children and family on the other, created a chaotic situation for him. But he has been managing nicely.

Lakshmi has an *idli* connection with UG. UG said once, "I must see the lady who prepares *idli* so well and sends them to me," and went to her house on his own. She thinks that this is all due to the merits from her good deeds in her previous lives. "It was different with the previous gurus. They acted as if it was our privilege to serve them. UG is different." Lakshmi couldn't contain her joy when UG came to her house so affectionately and appreciated her *idlis*. Since then she has been feeling like Yashoda who had found her little Krishna.

I noticed that her voice had become hoarse when she mentioned things about UG and the changes he had brought about in herself and her children. She quit her job before she met UG. Guha works in the university. UG commanded him saying, "You must earn with both hands. You must work days in the university and nights somewhere else, and earn money for the sake of the children. These children are my friends. They must not lack anything."

They have not been to India in two years. But UG is not letting it happen. He made Guha obtain a green card. Guha hadn't wanted to get a green card before. He had let go of all his past chances to get one. But soon after he returned from seeing UG in Palm Springs, he talked to his professor and applied for his green card. The professor tried to bend the rules for Guha's sake. He was able to get a green card for Guha in three months. All this wheeling and dealing annoyed the authorities. Becoming suspicious, the authorities decided to investigate the professor. Meanwhile, certain unexpected developments had taken place as a result of which the whole department of which the authorities were part got reshuffled and Guha's green-card affair receded into the background, just like magic. Guha and Lakshmi say, "It is all due to UG's grace."

*   *   *

Narayana Moorty has been working on my journal on the computer. Yesterday, we combined our efforts and brought it into shape. We must work today too. I must record something more in the context of writing things about Lakshmi – it's about all of them becoming friends with Julie. The whole family loves Julie. "She is our elder sister and an elder who takes care of us," says Lakshmi. The whole family delights in watching UG videos and learning things about him through her. Shilpa and Sumedha know by heart all UG tapes and his quotes.

*   *   *

Moorty Walks Out

January 2, 1999, Saturday – Day 14

I woke up early in the morning at 4:45 am. I came here to the table at 5:30 am.

Who are UG's friends? Who is close to him? Who is dear to him? Whom does he not like? I have been thinking about these while I was taking my shower. Suddenly yesterday morning, Moorty announced to UG, "I am going home today; I am leaving with Wendy this morning." For a moment, UG was stunned along with me. He said, "All right." He didn't say anything more. I didn't understand why Moorty came to such a sudden decision. It's disturbing that the thought of moving away from UG occurred to Moorty on New Year's Day. Has Moorty remained hurt so long by UG telling him jokingly two days ago "Get out of the kitchen?" Doesn't UG tease everyone in so many ways? I asked Moorty when we were both correcting the journal on the computer, "Why did you make such a sudden decision?" "I am not expecting anything from UG. I don't want anything from him. He knows that. So, when he has no respect or recognition for my words or actions, I don't feel like staying here anymore. When there is a lack of trust in me, I don't feel at peace in that place. I'm like that. He knows that," Moorty said.

Why did Moorty feel this way about UG? Does he find it objectionable that UG repeatedly refers to him saying "He is my guru"? "What's the difference between you and J.K? If you want to establish a fund with all that money, what's the difference between you and J.K.? If you want to simply give it away, do so; but why do you make arrangements for bequeathing your money?" When Moorty criticized UG like that that summer in Switzerland, U.G distributed all that he had to whomever he had been intending to give it to. He hasn't kept any money for himself. UG tells everyone that Moorty has inspired him to make such a decision. Before that he had wanted to discuss with university authorities at MIT about setting up a scholarship fund to help Indian girls to do research on inventing a virus which will wipe out the entire human race. He also discussed the matter with MIT lawyers.

At first he thought of giving the money to Aruna to take up research in Genetics and help invent the virus. But apparently

Aruna had said, "We're just starting our lives. It's not fair to nip them in the beginning." "What she said opened my eyes. Aruna taught me a great lesson," said UG. So he abandoned the idea of setting up a scholarship in a university. All this happened in August 1998.

Then what's the real meaning in Moorty's being mad at UG? Why did he become so angry? He said, "This computer is also a burden to me. I don't need it. You keep it," and pushed away the Toshiba Libretto laptop computer which UG had given him. "I have no use for it. You keep it. It's useful for you," said UG. "I don't need it; it will be a burden. Give it to someone else." "No one else needs it. If you don't need it, give it to Julie or throw it away," said UG. The computer ended up with Julie.

We were working on the computer till 12:30 in the afternoon. Moorty completed the job by breaking up the whole text, putting headers on it and formatting it as a book. When he tried to copy it onto a floppy, the computer didn't cooperate, I don't know why. He tried for 45 minutes and quit. That job Julie will do on her computer. Thanks to Moorty's effort, my journal has the good fortune of coming out as a DTP product with all the paraphernalia.

After the job was done, Moorty left with Wendy and Kiran in Wendy's car. Wendy cried without stop in front of Suguna. UG didn't say anything. It looks like his voice gave in a little. When he learned that Moorty was going to leave in the afternoon, UG ordered Guha and family to vacate the hotel room and move into Moorty's room. Guha, Lakshmi and the children came over with all their baggage. They will stay here for a couple more days and leave for New Jersey on Monday. Then Julie will take that room. We all must vacate and leave by January 15. We go our own way to Aruna's place.

But where will UG go? We don't know yet. I don't think he knows either. He keeps saying, "I will know it when the time comes. Why should I think about it now?" The jungles of Brazil are still beckoning to us. "Let's all go to the jungles in Brazil in search of UG. Then UG won't move out of Palm Springs," I said. UG didn't answer. Paul Lynn is leaving today with his family. He is thinking of moving with his family to Palm Springs this year. "Sophia must continue her higher education; Palm Springs is convenient for that," he said. But his wife Bonnie doesn't seem to favor that idea. We must wait and see what happens. Perhaps Lisa might have to vacate the house under these circumstances. Or Paul might fix another house. He says that anyway this house is not adequate for him; he wants a four-bedroom house.

*   *   *

Indian Canyon

In the afternoon, around 3:00 pm, we all went to Indian Canyon in Julie's car. It's about 15 miles from here. From there begins the Red Indian Valley. I felt, "Why have we come all this distance to see this valley?" What's there? Some date palms, thickly grown brushes and a small stream. They have made a trail to walk down from the top. There is a trail on top of the mountain leading to Murray Canyon. In that canyon there are some ancient dwellings of the Red Indians. Even now, we can see two or three houses on top of the mountain. I asked, "Who lives here?" Paul answered, "Red Indians." Americans drove them all away or massacred them and occupied their territory about two centuries ago. Now the whole canyon belongs to Red Indians. "Some of them are very wealthy. They hire non-Indian Americans and put them to work. All the income that is generated from this valley goes to them," said Paul. You have to pay a toll of $6 per person to see this valley. It was nice to climb the mountain. Shilpa and Sumedha were able to hike on that trail just as well as I could. We all returned by 5:00 pm.

*   *   *

Last night we saw a video made by Kelkar, a friend of Sri Ram. He is an American citizen. He lives in Atlanta. Ever since he met UG, his interest in UG has become more intense. His wife is American. They have children. He likes America, but he doesn't like its ways of living. Although he doesn't hate it, he doesn't seem to like it.

*   *   *

January 3, Sunday – Day 15

The December routine hasn't gone yet: I wake up at 4:45 early in the morning. It's two weeks since I have set my foot on this land. The last time, we came to the west coast via New York. This time we came with the idea that we would come to the west coast and spend all our days here and return. But I don't know what will happen.

Yesterday, Kamesh, Kittu, Shailaja and others called and talked to us. Kumar did too. They asked us when we will be visiting the east coast. We said it won't be possible this time. It does occur to me that it's too bad that we will return to India without seeing any of them, after traveling all this distance, especially after I talked to Lakshmi and Guha last night.

Working at a Job

I don't know why, but when I talk to them both, I feel like I am talking to people very dear to me. Guha appears to me to be my alter ego. He doesn't care to work at his job. Like me, when he sits down to work, questions come up in his mind such as, "What am I doing? What do I care about this work? Why am I wasting my time here?" But he too must find another way of supporting the household if he quits his job and remains jobless.

UG had asked me then to quit my job. That was O.K., but I lost my peace of mind with headaches from involving myself with other activities. I don't have the disposition to just sit in a corner telling myself I shouldn't do anything. It's all the same what you do so long as you could say that I want this and I don't want this. To have a delusion that everything is due to my greatness, that it will all happen because of me, makes matters worse.

Working at a job, in my view, at least as far as I am concerned, is purely a result of past *karma*. As soon as the *karma* wears off, then going to some place mechanically every day, thinking about one's prospects at some institution, having to make unnecessary conversation with colleagues, acting and thinking contrary to one's nature, and fighting constant battles while making the efforts to climb the ladder of success – all these are gone. But in their place, I got involved in the school, its prospects and its future. Thoughts about the school haunt me. When I think about why I got so involved in it, it's clear that it's not the fault of the school. It's my nature. If the school wasn't there, something else would be in its place to occupy me.

This *karma* is inevitable as long as the mind has the tendency to always struggle, to be stuck with something like this and not be able to get out of the snares of thoughts. I can't but laugh when I think about this mess. The first delusion is to think that I am. If I stop with the idea that I have a body and that this body has some necessities, it would be fine. But as soon as thoughts such as "I live in this body; I have some duties, obligations and responsibilities," start piling up, I sink under my own weight. These are not thoughts one can easily avoid. It will not do to just give myself a command "Don't think like that!" This is all a mysteriously complex tangle. Thought gets caught in a thousand more tangles as soon as you undo some of them. Is thought something that exists separate from me? The more I think the more tangles there are.

This is the current situation with Guha. What can I do for him? UG is there to take care of everything. Lakshmi has a lot of courage. Guha is lucky to have her as his life-mate. She takes the responsibility of raising the children. But it's not as easy as we think to live anonymously like someone who has no place in society. These concerns are all the result of past impressions we have acquired over many lifetimes. They don't break up so easily. They won't ripen. When they are ripe enough, they drop off by themselves. Then they won't bother us. They won't even leave a trace of their falling off. It will all happen so easily. Everything will disappear as if one woke up from a dream.

* * *

My Writing

Guha finished his washing and came and sat with me. He says, "I won't disturb you." Writing this is not such a big job. But it's as essential as breathing to me. There is no purpose or higher aim in doing this. I am writing this because I can. Just as the air from outside goes into the lungs and goes out as soon as its business with the body is finished, these thoughts go from my head, via my hands and fingers, take shape on the paper, express themselves and disappear. These are not my thoughts. The individuality called "I" is a delusion in the first place. I am not just looking at it from the Vedanta point of view. Who has ordained me to write this? Have I planned ahead about what I am going to write? As soon as I sit at the table and pick up my pen, thoughts flow on to the paper.

What are these sounds? Am I reading what I have written or am I talking to myself first and then putting those words down on paper? Which comes first? How could it be sound if I don't talk to myself?

But this 'I' is tied up with this body, these organs and this form. Where am I in this body? What's my role in the mechanical activity that is happening at this moment? What's my true existence? Am I deluded in thinking that I am thinking? Could it be that I am actually doing nothing? Do these thoughts all happen by themselves just like my breathing movements? Is breathing in and out something in my control? I am not even conscious that I am breathing unless I pay attention to it. The most important activity in the body occurs mechanically without any involvement on my part. How foolish it is to be deluded that my thoughts and other activities happen as a result of my willful thinking!

Here there is a break. "This is all nothing. There is everything. Still, there is nothing." How can I grasp all this? Who can teach me? Who can help me? Who can teach me to stop anywhere and everywhere? I need a support to walk with, I need a guiding light and I need strength. Still, why do I need anyone's help to stop taking steps and stand still?

*   *   *

All yesterday we spent five hours in Julie's car on a trip to Laguna Beach. That beach is south of Los Angeles. There was fog there; it was so thick that we couldn't see the vehicle in front of us. Then what would we be able to see at the beach? While we were in a store there, UG bought an alarm clock for Suguna. He had bought ten such clocks before and then had distributed them to everyone. Now, when UG asked the shopkeeper for more watches, the shopkeeper said he only had one. We bought it and started on our journey back home via the towns of Peris and Riverside. On the way, there were mountains, valleys, a big lake with boats in it, and there was greenery everywhere we looked.

There were many interesting places to see in Los Angeles. Aruna said we should see Universal Studios. Apparently it's quite interesting, but my interest in such things has dried up. Even when I go to a new place, I feel like "What's so new about this place?"

Today is the last day for Guha and his family. I could see on Guha's face his dread of resuming his routine life, "My mechanical life, my life in the mill will start tomorrow." There is nothing more. That's all there is, that life in the mill. If one hand is aching, you use the other; if one leg aches, you stand on the other. That's all you can do. I felt it was a boon to spend these few days with Guha, Lakshmi and the children.

* * *

We think so many things are our duties, and take burdens on ourselves and suffer in life. We can't see anything else. We know that in the subtle [*principle*] there is salvation, but that 'subtlety' doesn't always stay. Stuff gathers on it like onto a rolling snowball. Until the sun of knowledge melts the ice with his rays, those things gathered won't go away. When darkness comes again, the snow gathers as usual. It's inevitable. The sun will rise and the snow will melt again.

January 4, Monday – Day 16

The old habit hasn't gone yet. I still think it is December now. Guha and his family are leaving today. It is 15 days since they have come here. I am very happy to have made friends with such a nice family. I feel as if I have known Lakshmi and the children for ages. I don't know why, but yesterday UG suddenly said to Guha, "Take these people also with you." Guha was overjoyed. He said, "You too come with Chandrasekhar and Suguna, UG" "I won't come if Julie is there. She is the big obstacle in my way," said UG. Just as he said this, Julie came in. Lakshmi was asking Julie to remain here. "Julie, if you don't come, UG says he will come to New York. So stay here. I even have the key to your house with me. So we will take care of it," she said.

*   *   *

We have two seats reserved for us on an Alaska Airlines flight to go to San Francisco. But Malaysian Airlines operates to Madras only from LA; their planes don't leave from San Francisco. So we must return from San Francisco to LA on the 29th. That means it won't be possible for us to make our return journey to India from San Francisco. I talked to Venkat and Aruna. Julie and I went to the airport and enquired about all the airlines. Round trip tickets to San Francisco from LA are cheaper than from Palm Springs. Airlines like Reno Air are charging $108 round trip. We must let go of the Alaskan air ticket completely. We will lose $108. So, UG asked us to keep the same ticket. Meanwhile, he is talking about making a trip to New York.

I am not worried about how it all will turn out. First, I must get my journal printed with Julie's help. I need photos for the cover page. Julie took a photo of me with UG. She will get it developed and printed tomorrow. She took many pictures with her digital camera. One was a picture of me, Guha and UG. Another picture – of Suguna and Guha's children outdoors under the tree – came out very well. Julie delights in taking pictures and printing them from her computer printer.

UG has been teasing Nataraj everyday saying, "Nataraj, I will kill you if I don't get the money which you predicted about. I will take your life with this spear."

Lakshmi and others must be leaving now. I will stop for now.

*   *   *

Julie and I have returned from the airport. Guha and his family have left. On our way back, as soon as we turned onto the road leaving the airport, you could see the high mountain before you. The morning sun's pink rays were illuminating the mountain and making them look red. For just a moment, I had the illusion that I was viewing Arunachala. It looked just like Arunachala. However, here there are mountains all around. They appear to be holding the city with outstretched arms. I don't know what this mountain range is called. You don't find boulders or vegetation on them. All the mountains here look barren, like heaps of ashes.

The longer I stay in Palm Springs the deeper the beauties here sink into my consciousness. In less than five minutes, the morning sun has become more intense. The sun is rushing forth over the treetops. There are date palms everywhere around. There is a street called Palm Canyon Street. On it they have planted rows of date palms on both sides of the street. They put lights on those trees. In the nights, the houses, shops and trees all glow in those lights.

I would like to collect more details about this town and write an article. I must also collect photos for the *Inadu* Magazine. Lisa was telling me that I could get all the details I want at the Visitors' Center.

* * *

Julie vacated her room in the Ocotillo Lodge and moved to UG's house. Lakshmi said in the airport, "I feel as if I am visiting my parents' place whenever I come to this town." UG had been going to receive them at the airport every time they came. This time he has sent his 'eldest son' (referring to me) to see them off. As Lakshmi was telling me this, I could sense enormous affection and fondness in her voice. I told Lakshmi, "Bharati named me UG's 'child of the mind' 25 years ago." Sentiments such as these don't touch UG. But you can see great compassion and affection in his actions. His just doesn't talk in those terms. That's the difference between ordinary men and UG.

UG has been considering moving the dollar fund from the Swiss bank to Canara Bank. Today, I phoned the manager of the Canara Bank and talked to him, telling him that we need to deposit $250,000 there. But whatever UG does, he takes care that no one will have any trouble after him. It's UG's wish that whoever inherits that money should have easy access to it. There is a chance that the Indian government might object if foreigners are designated as heirs. That's why he asked me to talk to the manager to find out about all those rules and laws. The manager will find out in a couple of days. I will call him again.

*   *   *

January 5, Tuesday – Day 17

All of us went to the Visitors' Center yesterday. I couldn't find the stuff I wanted there. There was only a very brief history of Palm Springs in a small book in a bookstore. Trisha said I could find the details I wanted in the local library. Then we all went with UG in Julie's van to the Sky Jordon Inn. Nataraj, Mitra and Trisha are all staying there in separate rooms. Simon was living there before, too. Mitra served coffee to everyone. Even though the Lodge is small, it's good-looking. There is a swimming pool on the premises located in front of the rooms. The owner lives in the two front rooms. She rents out all the other rooms cheaply to people; it's $25 per day. You can say that's pretty cheap in America. Thirteen years ago, when I was in Indianapolis, I used to pay the same rent in the American Inn. Nataraj's friends came also in the evening.

Why Did Moorty Get Mad at UG?

Today the discussion was mostly about Moorty. Why did Moorty get mad at UG? I would not have been surprised if anyone else had gotten angry and left, but a guy like Moorty, who bragged, "There is no distance between UG and me. I don't even have the consciousness that I am separate from him"— what's the reason for his moving away from UG? The reason may be anything. It may be related to the eating issue, as UG says. "He is a glutton. He thought I said something, and with that he refused to eat here. It's not practical to live here and eat outside. So, he left," says UG. However, Moorty wrote in his e-mail to Scotty Scott, "I said the final goodbye to UG and left to live my life alone." Scott disappeared strangely, without saying goodbye to UG. He has done the same thing several times before. Then he suddenly reappears.

It's strange that a person like Moorty, who I thought of as a patient man who doesn't react quickly, has broken up with UG and left. It's hard to imagine what happens inside a person, what sort of changes take place.

How many times did such extreme thoughts arise even in me? When I think about it now, it's all accumulated filth and mud. Even if we try as hard as we can to push it down to the bottom, it comes up to the surface in UG's presence. He brings it out deliberately. He sweeps and cleans up all the mud and trash that is caught in the depths and crevices inside us unbeknown to us. In those moments, we don't have any good feelings about UG. We don't have any understanding of him. The mind closes to itself. A person loses his power of discrimination in every way, as in the saying. "A person nearing his death doesn't listen to his friends, doesn't see the star Arundhati[2] or smell the odor emanating from a lamp that's being put out." That's the beginning of the fall.

But I didn't imagine that this would happen to Moorty. I wonder how long he has been holding such thoughts in his mind. What does UG have to lose? He said, "What do I need the computer for? You can toss it on the rubbish heap." "What do I lose if you remove the whole webpage? Do you think I will care if I don't see his face again in my life?" says UG. True. None of this touches UG

*   *   *

Kinkos

Julie and I made a copy of my journal. Last night with Lisa and her computer we went to the copy shop. There they bound the copies nicely in spiral binding. We don't yet know how to print it in book format from the computer. A lady in the shop gave Julie some hints. But I don't have confidence that Julie can do it. Lisa made some enlarged prints of the color pictures she had. They look very nice. Although they look like big

---

[2] A star in the cluster Pleiades, named after Arundhati, the wife of sage Vasishta, known for her virtue. The star is shown to a couple during their wedding ceremony as an auspicious sign.

posters, they do look attractive. It's amazing that they came out so wonderfully color Xeroxed. They looked just like photographs.

Guha and family phoned UG after they had arrived in New Jersey. The house is quiet after the children have left. It looks like Julie woke up early in the morning at 4:00 am. She can't sleep in the nights. It seems that Suguna has been sleeping too much.

Yesterday, we faxed UG's letter to Sitaram to RK Enterprises from the copy/mail center. Last night, I called him again and told him to get the fax. In it UG had written in detail all his ideas of investment. Sitaram is supposed to phone back after collecting all that information, the answers to the questions UG has asked.

* * *

Last night, I read to everyone some excerpts from my journal – the memories of Purnananda Tirtha and the story of Hyderabad Shanta. UG said that he didn't like the subtitle for the book, *Stories of UG in India*. Even the title *Stopped in Our Tracks* sounds too high-flown to my ears. Nataraj and others have suggested various alternative words like "events", "incidents", "occurrences", and many others. UG didn't respond. When the time is right, he comes up with the right word.

* * *

Today, we will go to LA leaving at 10:00 am, three of Nataraj's group and five of us. I don't know how all of us will fit in Julie's van. Nataraj says he will stay back. There is an Indian restaurant called Paru's. Its owner Kannan is a friend of UG. Lisa made a reservation there for lunch. Both of Julie's sons are in LA, but they are scared to come to see UG.

*   *   *

January 6, Wednesday – Day 18

Scotty's E-mail

I woke up at 5 o'clock. Julie is still sleeping. Last night, on top of being fatigued from driving the car for about five or six hours and UG's banging her till her head hurt because of telling UG of the e-mail which she had gotten from Scott, she caught a cold and a headache. She took one of the Sinarex pills I gave her and went to bed. Running away from UG suddenly and then coming back repentantly, wagging his tail, is nothing new to Scotty. Apparently he wrote to Julie yesterday asking her to write to him of the goings on here. "What did UG say after reading my letter? How did he react? Write to me about it," he wrote to Julie. UG had flared up when Julie told him about it. "He thinks he is great and better than everyone who gathers around me. If he has left thinking he doesn't need me, why does he need to know what's happening here and what I have said or what my reaction is? Does he think that only he is clever and everyone else is stupid? Why did you tell him about Moorty going away in the first place? You are showing your usual traits. Julie, you can't stay here anymore. Get out! Do you want me to kick you out again?" UG roared. "Please, don't," pleaded Julie pitifully. "What else? If I am tolerating you, it's not for my sake or for your sake. It's for their sake (meaning me and Suguna). I know very well that you and your mentality will not change in this lifetime. You can't play your games with me. Why did you have to tell Scott?"

Julie didn't say a word in response. UG calmed down after a while. After she went into her room, she was still afraid that she would be thrown out. She just can't imagine being away from UG. The very things, words and actions which irritate him simply slip out of Julie without her knowing it. Then the casting out begins. This is the routine that has been going on for the last ten years.

*   *   *

99-Cent Market

Yesterday Lisa was off from her work. Eight of us left for Hollywood in Julie's van. On the way, we bought some clothes in the Burlington supermarket. From there we went to the '99 Cent Market'. There whatever you buy costs 99 cents. Suguna and I freely bought things which you can't get or are rare in India, as well as many gift items for people close to us. UG too bought several wrist watches and gave them to us. About 90%

of the stuff in that shop seems to have been made in China. Whatever you see, it has 'Made in China', marked on it. My head turned. The Chinese are making so many things of so many kinds; I was impressed by the amount of progress they have made in the world of technology. We didn't see Indian made goods anywhere except some stainless steel glasses and some Rajasthani skirts in a shop or two. Wherever you look in the shops, you find clothes of silk and wool, all made in China.

*   *   *

At Paru's

From there we went to Paru's Restaurant. As soon as he saw us, Kannan darted out to receive us with his broad face showering smiles on us. Although we haven't met before, he recognized me by my name. He happily said hello to UG, and in Tamil, "It's has been so long since I've seen you." He knows each one of those who came with us by name. He said hello to Julie calling her, "Julie dear!" "Where is Larry? Have the Malladis left? The man who came from San Francisco, Douglas, is he O.K.? UG, how is your health? Lisa, how are you?"

He was dancing around in that small hall, moving the tables around while greeting us, without stopping for one moment. Meanwhile, he had also been greeting customers at other tables, filling them with his smiles as well. He was saying goodbye and thanks to those who were leaving. At the same time he was welcoming those who were coming in and finding out what they wanted to order.

Then he rushed over and sat next to me. "Hello, Chandrasekhar. I am so happy that you have come. Are you from Madras or Bangalore? Everything is OK for you here? How long has it been since you have come to LA? Is this your first time?" Thus he made me answer in my broken Tamil while he happily chatted away in his mother tongue. I was very much impressed by Kannan's friendly manner and his style of hospitality.

I have read recently about Paru's restaurant in the *Hindu*. Well known Indians from LA frequent this restaurant. The place is filled with many colorful decorations. Kannan has hung pictures of almost all the gurus currently in the holy business. "I want to see where he hung UG's picture," interjected Suguna. Kannan answered, "If I put up his picture, UG will kick me out. That's why I have to keep it safely hung in my mind." We couldn't but laugh loudly at his smartness.

He served the 'Tanjore *tali*' to all of us - two *idlis*, a *vadai*, *masala dosai*, *upma* and coffee. But he served UG three *idlis*. He knows that UG doesn't eat anything else. He first asked the waiter to bring some hot water for UG.

It looks like his business is thriving. Not just Indians, but Americans as well come here to taste Indian dishes. Before we left the place Julie took pictures of all of us. Kannan walked us to the car and said goodbye with a smile. He said goodbye to me cordially: "Please make sure to come again before you leave, Chandrasekhar!"

* * *

From Hollywood we went to Beverly Hills. We had been to Barney's there before. Next to it is Sak's Fifth Avenue. This is the place is where wealthy people, the richest people in the world, go shopping. Money is no object for them. But our eyes first look at the price tags. A sweater costs $65. Suguna bought hair clips for Aruna and Archana. From there we headed back to Palm Springs. On the way we stopped in two clothing stores – Ross Dress for Less and another one. It was 7:30 pm by the time we arrived home. Suguna made angel's hair which we ate with cheese and yogurt. It was 10:00 pm by the time we put away all the things we had bought.

* * *

Shopping is a hobby for UG. He especially goes into clothing stores a lot. He looks for cashmere clothes. In Beverly Hills we had gone up to the fifth floor in Barney's. When he saw us, the supervisor came over to us asking, "Can I help you with anything?" I replied smiling, "I came to buy this whole shop. I am taking my time looking at everything. He understood my joke. He said smiling, "Please look around; there are many things on sale."

The whole of America looks to me like a big supermarket. Many different kinds of things. Many different kinds of people. And big businesses. UG says, "America is a banana republic." There are so many supermarkets here. So many people are pushing their carts and buying and eating. Still the shops look deserted. Everyone says that Christmas buying has been slower this year.

The Euro currency was inaugurated in Europe on January 1. Many economists believe that it will have a serious effect on the dollar. The dollar may go down in value. Some others prophesize that the 'great depression' is not far away and that it might start in March or April. "Do you think there will be an economic crisis?" I asked UG "Everything depends on Japan and its economic condition. The world economic situation depends on its health," said UG. If the dollar falls, then the whole world will be topsy-turvy.

*   *   *

Lakshmi and Guha phoned separately. It doesn't look like UG has picked up the phone in his room.

January 7, Thursday – Day 19

Woke up at 4:30 am. I woke up so early even though I had gone to bed late at 11:00 pm; yet I am not tired. Julie and I phoned and talked to Guha and Lakshmi. It's cold and snowing where they are. Here it's hot. In the afternoon the sun scorches like in hot summer till about 4:00 pm. Then the weather starts cooling off. In the evenings we can't go out without a sweater. It's very pleasant nonetheless. People in this country like to go out in the evenings. Almost all the shops are open not only the whole day, but also in the nights. When we drive by in the car, you can see the cities illuminated brilliantly with colorful electric lights. The three cities, Palm Springs – Rancho Mirage and Palm Desert – run into each other. There are supermarkets everywhere. They all compete with one another. Each shop is a world in itself. Yesterday, when I took my suitcase with me to get it repaired, the shop assistant in a shop called 'It's Your Bag' demanded $40 to fix it. You can buy a new bag with that much money. I have to buy a new suitcase anyway. "Let's go to Marshall's," said UG.

Clinton's Son

This morning Nataraj and his friends will be coming. Maybe we will go out with them. Yesterday afternoon, Lynn called to pour gossip about the latest Clinton scandal into UG's ears. Apparently, it has become known that Clinton had a son with a black prostitute. The boy is now 13 years old. Clinton had a relationship with the woman. He took her to his mother's house (when the mother was not in town) and had sex adventures with her there. When once she told him "your image is making a home in my womb," he apparently said that it couldn't be his child. But the Clinton baby was born and he resembled Clinton closely. Now at 13, he looks even more like a replica of Clinton. It's not just a rumor if responsible newspapers like *New York Post* are also writing about it. There must be some truth in it. Apparently they are performing DNA tests to verify that the boy is indeed an offspring of Clinton. With those test results Clinton's true colors will be revealed. So what if Clinton had relationships with several women? Isn't that common with people in this country?

UG says that every American home is a brothel. There is no distinction between what is moral and immoral in people's minds here. They talk to each other about the things they do in bed as freely as they talk about brushing their teeth. On the Internet they describe their sex activities to each other in public. It's common in India for people to look at and talk about sex stealthily, drooling over it; but then in public they pose as if they are chaste saints. "India decrying pornography? That country is the birthplace of pornography! Search through any temple, listen to any hymn, examine any icon; you can't but notice the enormous amount of sex and libertinism. People of such a country have no right to condemn pornography," says UG. True. Our ancestors tried to satisfy themselves by sublimating their sexual desires into their gods and goddesses. What is there in classical poetry except pornographic descriptions? Plain obscenity and sex. It doesn't make any sense that such a country criticizes foreigners' less hidden pornography. Old proverbs, riddles and folklore, all prove how obscenities are an important part of our culture.

In UG obscenity takes a very natural form. Here in this country everyone uses 'fuck' as a catchword. In earlier days, I used to have difficulty listening to UG use even words like 'bitch' and 'bastard'. Compared to the obscene words he is currently using, they would sound holy.

UG stopped calling Julie a 'bitch'. How puffed up she looked when she reported that in anger UG roared at her, "You are such a dunderhead!" Crazy Julie! She doesn't mind when he calls her names in front of everyone. But she can't stand it if he keeps her away from him.

Yesterday, UG was asking Julie questions about her financial condition. Besides her own income, she has spent in these past four years all the $180,000 she got from selling her mother's house. Apparently, it costs about $5,000 a month to take care of her mother. Add to it the money for her travels and the money she spends on people who come to visit UG. Her capital is dwindling slowly. "At this rate you will soon become a beggar," warns UG. When UG asks her, "How rich are you?" she used to say, "As rich as you have made me." "Hereafter, she will say, 'As poor as you have made me,'" says UG.

*   *   *

Attempts to get my *Journal* printed are bearing fruit. Yesterday, Julie talked to a DTP publishing company and got the whole thing printed in a book form. We even added some photos. We went to Kinko's last night and got the copies bound. We must show them to UG. We can correct any errors in one copy and get two or three more copies printed on Julie's printer.

*   *   *

Why indeed am I writing all this? I can't hold all the thoughts that run around in my head; so I am putting them on paper. Or else, what's their point? Who needs the stuff that I write here? Even I don't need it. These pages are worth less than toilet paper.

January 8, Friday – Day 20

I didn't wake up till 5:30 in the morning. I don't know why I slept so long. Last night, I went to bed before 10 pm. Yet, I don't know why I didn't wake up. Julie spilled some hot coffee on herself in the morning while making it. All the milk is now gone. There were no blisters on her hand, but her skin turned red. She continued regretting her spilling of the coffee for half an hour. Today it took me 45 minutes to finish washing and showering and sit down here to write.

Last night we went to K-Mart and the Dollar Store in Desert Hot Springs. The shops there looked like shops in Bangalore. K-Mart was no good. All in all, Palm Springs, Palm Desert and Rancho Mirage – these three towns are the best in the desert. These are the rich towns. All the rest of them are poor.

* * *

As soon as Nataraj came in yesterday UG asked, "What do the planets say, Nataraj? When is the money going to rain?" "The planets Venus and Neptune are in conjunction. There must be a lady coming before the 10th," says Nataraj. What lady? Some very wealthy woman somewhere must have been counting currency bills just waiting to give to UG! In the meantime, UG has been cleaning up all the money that is with him and giving it away. UG asked Nataraj to invest 10,000 francs in our

Finance Corporation as a fixed deposit. I couldn't believe my own ears. That means almost Rs.300,000. UG asks me, "How much interest will you give?" I said, "He will get Rs.4,500 per month. We are paying 18% interest." "Nataraj, what else do you need? I will guarantee you the principal, OK?" assured UG. UG making someone invest in my finance corporation took me by surprise. Trisha has left.

*   *   *

After we leave on the 18th, Nataraj and Mitra will stay in this house till the end of the month. UG is asking them to stay in the north wing so that Lisa won't have to be alone. Lisa will have to make a different arrangement starting February 1. For these ten days, UG will go somewhere. "If I remain in America, I'll return in February and stay till March 15 and then go to Australia and New Zealand. Or else, I'll disappear into the jungles in Brazil. No more America," UG says. He doesn't think about what he should do next. He appears to makes plans, but he doesn't think at all the way we do. But something will happen in these 15 days. I strongly feel that he will make some very important decisions. Astrologers predict that there might be a very rich woman coming into his life, but I don't see any signs of it. Julie must win the lottery and become a millionaire; that's the only way.

*   *   *

The Future of America

The future of America is going to be terrible, says UG. Economic experts predict that because the European nations got together and instituted their Euro currency, the American dollar will go down in prominence. "Why didn't Britain join the European Commonwealth? They are worried that the British pound's domination will be lost. But England must become part of the US. England is not compatible with the European nations in any area. The English used to say, 'The Channel divides us from Europe.' Instead, they should say, 'The Atlantic Ocean divides us from America.'"

UG praises China a lot. "There is a lot India can learn from China. Like Russia, India is also a nation of slaves. Their people are slaves. They only serve in their jobs and are devoid of independent thought and effort. From the start, the Chinese have been freedom lovers. England tried to destroy China by supplying opium and getting its people addicted to it. But that did not succeed. Chinese philosophy is superior to India's. In that country spiritual philosophers abound. India is inferior to that country even in that respect. Ancient Indian philosophical thought is like a lamp before the sun when compared to Chinese philosophical thought," says UG. "Can India produce one person like Mao Zedong?" he asks. He attacked Nehru's useless arrogance and egotism, and also his policies which, according to him, drove the country to poverty. "Nehru was more egotistic than Julius Caesar. He caused the downfall of India in his fifteen years of rule."

What will be the future of the world? "Other countries must put a stop to America's monopoly and arrogance. All other Muslim countries must join hands with Iraq and stop exporting oil to America. The world's future won't get better unless America is destroyed. The American economy is dependent on the Japanese economy. If Japan goes down, America will be totally destroyed. Who is America to drop bombs on Iraq? Who gave them the authority? In China, 21 missiles are set up aiming at various American cities. If there is going to be a year-2000 (Y2K) crisis, in that crisis the computers which control those missiles might also go berserk. Anyone can imagine what would happen next." UG has been talking in this vein. Yet he asks those in India who have any talent to go to America. "India is a useless country. It has no future. There are still opportunities in America for individual talents to flourish," he says.

*   *   *

January 9, Saturday – Day 21

It's exactly three weeks since we have come to visit UG. Today, I woke up at 5:30 am. That means my body has gone back to its routine. Still, when I sit quietly in the evenings in some place, I can't keep my eyes open. Yesterday, we were watching news and special items about Clinton. I sat in the chair next to UG and dozed on and off. Suguna was smiling, watching my plight.

*   *

*

Pleasure-Seeking and the Continuity of the 'I'

Man uses his every action, thought and experience to seek pleasure. The search for pleasure has the only aim of maintaining the continuity of the 'I' without a break. When we notice that our attempts are, even in sorrow, worry and depression, to make the 'I' continue, we must also count them as part of the search for pleasure. It is as much a pleasure movement when the devotee pines for God's mercy, when the spiritual aspirant yearns for oneness while struggling in duality, unable to achieve unity with the animate and inanimate world, as when the lover trembles in eagerness for the bliss of his beloved's embrace. We seek pleasure especially in the food we try to find, prepare and fill our bellies with. The body doesn't know what we eat, nor does it care. The body doesn't know hunger. Hunger is a chemical event. If thought does not translate the chemical event that occurs when the blood glucose level drops to a certain level as 'hunger', we wouldn't be anxious to fill our stomachs; and in that condition there wouldn't be any debate in the body about what to eat and what not to eat. The body grabs whatever is within its reach. It won't be eager to hoard for the next day. All that food worry is only for the false, delusional individuality, for the separate identity called the 'I' that this culture and civilization have created in the body. That individuality constantly – every moment, day and night – fights with the mechanism of the body to assert its separate existence. It needs permanence. It must always survive. It must live higher and higher, wealthier and wealthier, happier and happier. Even if one's body is in ruins, is decomposed or dead, it must continue to live at least in another body.

Immortality and permanence, living forever, these are the primary goals of this 'existence'. It is thanks to these goals that man has become a pleasure seeker. By trying to plan every action based on wanting to secure his happiness, his pleasure, his satisfaction, he becomes a poisonous worm, destroying the whole of creation which supports his body. The body tries to shake off this poisonous worm with all its might. It's this struggle which the 'individual' experiences as fear, anxiety, disease and psychosomatic illnesses.

When the struggle with the body stops, the individuality called 'I' will disappear. It will appear only when it is necessary for the protection of the body. At other times, it is merged with the mechanisms of the body with no separate existence of its own; and it does not separate itself from this creation and struggle in duality; it lives quietly, united with life. In that state there is no 'pleasure movement'. There is no search for pleasure. That's the natural state of each one of us. That's what I feel UG is saying.

"The guy called Chandrasekhar is a squatter there [*in that body*]; he is an alien. He is a thief who is trying to appropriate [*that body*]. The body mechanism tries with all its might to expel him. From time to time, human culture and civilization pour life into him, seeking to maintain him permanently. What you call life is only the struggle between these two conflicting goals. The body is not concerned about Chandrasekhar's likes and dislikes. In fact, whatever he likes are like poison to the body. Still he imposes them on the body. He wants to impose them forcibly and lock in his experience of pleasure permanently. The body pushes it all out as shit. The thoughts that come into his head, it throws out through the mouth as verbal shit." This is why wise men command us to sit quietly shutting up both the top and bottom orifices. Yesterday UG demonstrated this truth so forcefully that it has left a deep and lasting impression on our minds.

*   *   *

Clean-Up Time

Julie went in the morning to Lucky's for shopping at 7:30. She walked in with all the stuff in heavy bags; she bought all the things we needed in the house, different kinds of foodstuffs for cooking and for snacks. UG was sitting in the chair next to the TV. He just came out of his room into this part of the house. As soon as he saw Julie with the bags, he pounced on her: "Why did you buy all those things? To eat like a pig? What business do you have in the kitchen? If I am tolerating you, it's only for the sake those two. Not for your sake. No one needs your help. Get out, right now!" he yelled at her. Julie was paralyzed. She couldn't say a word. "Throw all that stuff in the garbage! Get out! If you don't, I'll push you out!" he roared.

Julie instantly ran out, carrying all the bags to her car, and drove away and dropped them off at the garbage bin near the store and returned. UG's anger hasn't subsided yet. He asked us to pull out all the foodstuffs accumulated in the kitchen cupboards and refrigerator and throw them away. "You keep only what you need for cooking. That bitch can't eat here any more. She wastes all the food like this," he said to Suguna. As I watched, all the cupboards were emptied. Julie stuffed all those things into garbage bags and took them out. The kitchen became bare. Suguna couldn't find sugar for her coffee. But all the stuff that has been left over – the stuff that Lakshmi and Narayana Moorty had bought during the last month and used, as well as the stuff that some others brought and has been sitting rotting – has been thrown out.

"Who are these fruits for?" asked UG, noticing some apples and bananas in a corner. When Suguna said she wanted them, he relented. "You keep just what you need for today. You should throw away in the garbage what you don't need," he warned. "Julie, you are not needed here. You can't play your games with me. Your friends are deluded in thinking that some change has happened in you. The only change that needs to happen in you is to move away from here permanently."

July was terrified. She slipped into her room and didn't come out for a long time. Meanwhile, while this Daksha sacrifice was going on, Nataraj and his friends came. UG's mood was still ferocious. He talked about how mean man is, how he destroys the whole of creation for his pleasure and for continuing permanently. There was a Creator's fury in UG's outburst. The whole universe belongs to the Creator. If man, who is only one among the millions of species in creation, blinded by his arrogance, thinks that he is in charge of the whole of creation and that the whole world exists only for his enjoyment, and acts without any respect for life, exploiting and plundering the resources of all other living species in creation for his own selfish enjoyment, truly all that must bring forth the wrath of the Creator! Yesterday morning, that wrath was reflected in UG.

"Why should you eat fruit? They are meant for the animals. Grains and seeds are food for the birds. Why should man eat any of them? That's why he has all these diseases. Eating is a great pleasure. That Ramana Maharshi who renounced all other pleasures ate like a pig! Why did that 'gentleman' who had the habit of quoting, 'There is no father, no mother...' get a temple built for his mother? Why did he pass on the *ashram* to his younger brother?" thus UG attacked Bhagavan for some time. I don't know what world he might be in now after he died, but yesterday UG blew away in one minute all the teaching that old man put out for fifty years, lying on a sofa with his legs stretched out, feeling his belly.

"The *ashram* people fabricated stories that Ramana Maharshi had undergone surgery without an anesthetic. One of the members of the team of doctors who had performed surgery on him, my brother-in-law, Dr. Seshagiri Rao, is still alive. He will tell you how many times he had administered an anesthetic to him. What they tell you are made-up stories. J. Krishnamurti drank gallons of whisky before he died because he couldn't bear the pain of his cancer. He cried, 'Why do I have this cancer? I can't bear it.' No one writes about these things. These things must be brought to light. I am not sure if he cried, 'What sins have I committed?' He surely must have cried so," this is how UG continued his tirade against Ramana and JK.

*   *   *

Moorty Phones

Narayana Moorty phoned UG last night. He apologized for his behavior. I think he probably said something like "There were many reasons why I had go away. But it wasn't because of you. UG, you shouldn't take it any other way." UG was saying in reply, "I told you that you are my 'guru'. You don't need to explain about what had happened. I have never had any misunderstanding about you. I thought you were probably enlightened when you said you were leaving me." My mind felt relieved. I knew that Moorty would fall in line again. I can imagine the hell he has gone through for the past one week. "The whole atmosphere inside and outside froze like ice. I couldn't breathe," Moorty apparently said. Now the ice curtain has cleared for Moorty.

* * *

January 10, Sunday – Day 22

Today I didn't wake up till 6 am. I stirred in bed around 5 am, but sleep rushed in again. If I get up late like this, I may have to write this diary in the afternoons also. Yesterday morning, as UG walked in, I said, "I am getting another evil thought." Half-curiously he asked, "What is it?" "That I should stay in the US longer," I said mischievously smiling. I elaborated on my and Suguna's thoughts. If we are going to stay with Narayana Moorty for three days, we could postpone our journey for another week. Then we could stay with Aruna for ten days. By that time Raghavendra Rao and others will have gone to Bangalore. Aruna's apartment won't be too crowded.

UG replied that it's a good idea. Then, right away, Julie called Malaysian Airlines and changed our tickets. We will now leave on February 6, Saturday. We will arrive in Bangalore Tuesday morning, around 9 am. On the way we will have a layover in Kuala Lumpur for a day. The airlines will arrange for our stay in a hotel. After we completed the ticket change business, I informed Venkat and Aruna of the changes in our plans. When we talked to Archana and others last night, we told them too. Archana said sadly, "You won't be here then when I get the results of my examination?" I comforted her and said not to worry.

       *   *   *

Nataraj and friends are coming everyday both morning and afternoon. Yesterday, Nataraj seemed ill. Perhaps he has a fever. He doesn't take medicines. He says it's nothing. When UG asks, "Then, why do you look like that?" he replies, "You know very well what it is. You know what's happening in my body better than I do." He says that it's some sort of energy attack all over his body. "It's not fever. Some energy is agitating my body. I know. I am fine," he talks mysteriously. Apparently, things calm down a bit when he sits in front of UG. What are all these changes? I hope they are not signs of some craziness. UG asked Nataraj to eat here. They both ate here.

Last night, I, Suguna and Lisa went with Julie to the Rock Garden Restaurant. There, after we finished, we had a lot of French fries and ice cream as well as a veggie burger left over. We had the food packed in doggie bags and brought it home. Today, we consumed all of it. Suguna made *dahl* and rice. We ate that as well. As a matter of fact, during our stay here, we have no thought of what we eat or what we cook. At each time, on each day, we eat whatever there is to eat. In the stores they sell ready-to-eat *chapattis*. They too taste good. We can buy buttermilk. Last night Suguna made couscous. And she made *idlis* for UG.

*　　　　　*　　　　　*

I found a nice, cheap suitcase for $28 in Wal-Mart. In other shops suitcases like that cost at least $50. Lisa took me to Dollar Shop. There too, we bought a few things. I hesitate to buy anything valuable, anything which costs more than ten dollars. So, UG bought us all the things we picked for our personal use. UG is spending a lot of money on us. To add to it, through Guha he also gave us $1,150 in rupees to pay off Major's loan. Our travel tickets alone cost a total of about $2,500. In addition, he is buying us many things. He spent $160 on a microwave oven and kitchen pots and utensils for Aruna.

*　　　　　*　　　　　*

Yesterday morning, I was reading aloud from a page in my journal. It was called "My approach ...," the first of the excerpts I had extracted from UG's tapes: Lisa was very much moved by it. They were the words UG spoke when he talked to Adamar Math Swami in 1972. It's hard to describe how he had expressed his opinions in such elaborate detail. Why he was talking; if he had a thing like his own philosophy, how it would be; what he intended to communicate through his speaking –

all these UG had mentioned very poignantly. He hasn't done so anywhere else. I too like that piece very much.

When I read the second part of the journal, it seems so eye-opening even to me. I selected those pieces very carefully for my own use and transcribed them. How good they sound! Is this also pleasure-seeking? Listening to tapes, chewing on old written and spoken pieces like this and relishing them with associated memories – these too are pleasure movements. If they are not there, where do I exist? They create me.
Yesterday, Suguna said to UG, "After my wedding I came here to Bangalore, and I can't forget the first handshake you gave me at the airport while saying goodbye; I can never forget the feeling of your touch." "Did I shake your hand?" UG asked surprised and smiling. "Yes, you offered your hand first. I was surprised and hesitant. Something like that happened. I don't quite remember. But when you stretched out your hand I took it. How soft and smooth it felt! I'll always remember that feeling of touch," said Suguna. Normally UG doesn't shake women's hands, but he shook Suguna's hand at the end of their very first meeting. In unimaginable contexts UG brings us under his influence without even our knowing it.

*   *   *

UG reminded us of something else. "You remember, when you [*Suguna*] first came to Bangalore, before your marriage, Valentine asked me to call you so that she could see you? Your parents hesitated because you were in your period and they thought that was an inauspicious time. We asked you to come anyway, vetoing their opinions as mere superstition," said UG. Even I had forgotten about it. "Yes, yes," agreed Suguna shyly.

January 11, Monday – Day 23

A Near-Miss

I didn't wake up early in the morning. It was 5:30 when I opened my eyes. I had various dreams before I woke up. I can't remember them even if I want to. They were not nightmares, however. A couple of days ago, Lisa dreamt that she was traveling in the back seat of a car. Suddenly a fire broke out in the engine. It was enveloping the car in circles. She was terrified that the car might explode. Then she woke up. That day she left a pan with some milk in it on the stove and by mistake turned the stove down but left without turning it off. Then she forgot about it. By the time she returned the pan was all warped and bent. She barely escaped a fire accident. The house was filled with heat. That was the same day on which Julie spilled hot coffee on herself and burned herself. It was also on the same day that UG had flared up on Julie, making her throw out all the stuff she had bought, and then having us collect the stuff that was in the house and throw it away too.

Punit and Family

Yesterday, a man called Punit came from San Diego with his family to see UG. Once upon a time he had been a devotee of

Rajneesh. His parents, his sister and wife came with him. I didn't ask his father's name [*his name is 'Satyapal', the world famous dealer of 'Satyapal' brand designer saris*], but everyone, including me, appreciated his father's personality. Punit is a handsome man. And he has wealth that surpasses his looks. He has a millionaire father who gave hundreds of thousands of rupees to Rajneesh. It was his father who had arranged for Rajneesh to fly from America to India on a chartered flight. He has huge properties in Delhi. Punit's uncle once came to Yercaud to see UG.

This is the first time for his father to see UG. They brought many foods they had prepared. Ever since they arrived, UG talked constantly about money matters, repeating the word 'money' many times; he talked about sex matters, discussed sex and commented on the sex scandals of Clinton and Monica. He talked only about such things; he did not let people's attention be diverted to spiritual matters. He brought out the 'porno album' of sex games and pictures of Clinton's sex mess printed from the Internet for him by his friends.

What's surprising is that you don't notice any expressions of disgust or shock on even the women's faces. Punit's father kept laughing. UG narrated in detail, on purpose, once again, the story of Buddha's birth. Everyone listened with keen interest about his meeting the 95-year-old Zen master in Kyoto and the mystery behind Buddha's birth and then broke into loud laughter.

He introduced me and made me read three or four verses in Telugu. I read the poems translating them and explaining them in English. They seem to have enjoyed them.

Lisa is an old girlfriend of Punit. Punit's family are all Jitendra Baba's disciples now. Punit has created a webpage for him on the internet. Apparently, Reshanwala Baba will come to America in February. Baba venerates UG as a guru. They say his blood cancer has stabilized.

Nataraj felt that UG has been fooling them with his words; he has been suggesting to them off and on to ask some serious questions. "There are no serious questions and there are no answers to them either," said UG. He asked Julie to play the video tape of Mahesh and Bob talking here on Christmas Day about their respective experiences. Mahesh had spoken in it about his friendship with Rajneesh, his breaking away from him, and about Rajneesh's condition in his last days.

We all ate together. There were six of us and five of them. We all enjoyed the meal which included the rice pudding made by Suguna and the various food items and fruit they brought with them. Then UG fell into his real groove. He recited his Veda to everyone while they were all dozing on and off with heavy stomachs. Punit's father, Satyapal, was the only one who listened with rapt attention. I can't remember exactly what UG said. Whatever it was, it was great. Everyone was content. They sat here till the evening. The father had no choice except to get up when Punit signed that they should go now. Satyapal suddenly tried to reach and touch UG's feet. UG prevented it by grasping Satyapal's hands and bidding him goodbye.

* * *

Today, I must go with Julie to the DTP Company to proofread the book. Punit had talked about a software called Page Maker. He didn't know about Word Perfect, he said. He is also in the DTP business in San Diego. We thought that he might give us some helpful hints, but he doesn't know about Word Perfect. We'll see how the DTP lady will be able to help us. UG says that when this job is finished we must go to Las Vegas. I don't know who all will go.

UG appeared weak by the evening – perhaps from those people's visit and his talking so much. He says he will eat his normal oatmeal. Earlier this afternoon, he ate *idlis* with us and a bit of a *chapati* they had brought. That *chapati* was hot. They brought stuff like sesame meal, three kinds of *chapattis*, a couscous dish, stuffed bitter melon curry and fruit – they brought so many things.

*   *   *

Last night, UG and I talked to Rajasekhara Reddi. UG decided that the UG devotee Rajasekhar had mentioned – Sharmila – and the unknown devotee whom Bharati had mentioned in her astrological reading are one and the same. Rajasekhar talked emotionally and said that something is happening to him, and it's all leading to a big change in him. "That old Raja is dead, Chandrasekhar; the old Raja is no more," he says. Something is happening to him.

*   *   *

January 12-13, Tuesday and Wednesday – Days 23 and 24

Las Vegas – Palm Springs

Trip to Las Vegas

Yesterday about this time, we were sleeping in the Holiday Inn Hotel in Las Vegas. Such a sudden decision of UG's! After he talked Monday morning with Lisa, that same afternoon he decided to go to Las Vegas. Lisa was off on Tuesday. It's possible that UG might have thought that the trip to Los Angeles wouldn't be as much fun without Lisa. In America, he makes a pilgrimage to Las Vegas at least once in a year. Sometimes he went to Grand Canyon, and from there to Las Vegas; another four hours of travel in the car. UG doesn't like the Grand Canyon very much. "What is there in the Grand Canyon? It's a big hole in the ground." In the same stroke he asks, "What's so attractive about any woman? Any hole is the same." Apparently, he used to talk like that to his wife! "What kind of love is there between us? Where is love in the first place except [*an exchange of*] fluids? You are a just a woman with a hole in the middle. I agreed to marry you with the idea that it's easier to marry one hole instead of looking for a hole every night" – only UG can speak bluntly like that!

Before we left we had an appointment with the DTP computer company at 1 pm. Just one lady manages that company. She is very active and intelligent. She could easily grasp what our problem was and how we had gotten into a jam. She told us she would fix the book and get it ready for printing by Thursday. Right after we got back from there, we, seven of us, left at 2:15 pm in Julie's car.

Although it's still winter, it's very hot in the sun. The sun shines brilliantly in these areas against a clear blue sky. You don't sweat a lot because the atmosphere is not polluted and there is no humidity in the air. If you move into the shade it's cool and nice. People keep all the doors in their houses open so that fresh breeze can come in. In the nights it's cold. You must turn the heater on in the house. Apparently, it rains three or four times a year in these areas. There are tall barren mountains all around. Sometimes you have very swift winds. But there are no rain showers. That's why they set up hundreds of windmills on the hill slopes here. It looks like they produce electricity from them. The mills have huge propellers. Those wheels turn slowly even with a small breeze.

*   *   *

Julie, UG, the Germans, Suguna, Lisa and I – we all left for Las Vegas. Because we are going to stay there for one night, we packed the necessities in a small bag. Nataraj's friend Mitra drove.

Mitra used to be a receptionist in the former Rajneesh Center in Cologne. Currently, he is going around in the UG orbit. He is probably about 30 years of age. When Lisa told me that he has a seven-year-old son, I was surprised. His girlfriend has been pining for him in Cologne; but he is stuck here with UG. The man is very gentle. He knows UG's moods and doesn't talk much. Unless there is a need, he doesn't open his mouth. I thought he is a sensitive and cultured man who can understand others' problems. Last Sunday, he was the only one who noticed that Punit's pregnant wife had trouble sitting in the chair and also on the floor because of her huge belly. He got up from the sofa and offered it to her. Two days ago, when he drove us to Las Vegas, we also learned about his driving skill.

American highways are a standard for the whole world. In no other country do you find such nice highways. Besides, this is a vast country. It is three times bigger in area than India. But the population is about a third of that country. You see more cars here than people. Standing in front of the shopping malls and pointing at the cars parked there, UG says, "They don't belong to the buyers; they belong to the employees who work in those shopping centers. Visitors seeing those cars are fooled into thinking that business here is booming."

*   *   *

Mitra showed us Joshua trees in Las Vegas. There is a street in Las Vegas called Joshua Street. There is a national park of these trees on the mountains. Nataraj says it's beautiful. It has a forest of Joshua trees going for miles and miles. I remembered Gurram Joshua. When I was mentioning him to Nataraj, UG said from the front seat, "In my childhood, we read Joshua's poems in our textbooks. His poetry was great." The collection of his poems *Firdausi* is like a flower that never fades in the garden of Telugu poetry. Driving a car on American highways and traveling in it are a pleasure. Besides, Julie's is a rental car, a navy blue Chevrolet. Seven people can travel in it comfortably. Mitra was driving at 80 miles an hour; still the car didn't feel like it was moving. No one talked much on the way. Without stopping anywhere Mitra drove 300 miles straight through and finished in 3½ hours. By 6 o'clock we were parked in front of the Holiday Inn. On the way, we saw the sunset in the western sky; the sky was covered with many colors. We were driving east. The highway was straight for miles at a time without a curve or a bend.

UG rented four rooms in the Holiday Inn – one for Julie and Lisa, another for me and Suguna, a third for Mitra and Nataraj, and the fourth for himself. On the weekends these rooms are rented for $80 a night. But because UG has a Preferential Card, we are only paying $45 a night for these rooms. The rooms are very nice. By 7 am everyone got out of their rooms. We bought whatever we needed in a Lucky supermarket, especially cream for UG.

The glory of Las Vegas can only be seen at night. Colorful lights illuminate the whole city. There are casinos everywhere. When a person steps into this world he will forget his own existence. But you must have money in your pocket. The more money you have the more entertainment you will get. So much pleasure! But people like us don't have money.

There are light shows of dazzling electric lights flashing in various shapes, appearing very high as if they are touching the sky – a thousand eyes are not adequate to behold a city like Las Vegas. There is a big lake in front of the Bellagio Hotel. In it they have a water fountain show once every hour, in which they make the water fountains dance to the music played on the loud speakers. It's a scene that everyone must see. The water rises high suddenly from those fountains, along with some flood lights, each jet dancing beautifully in its own way – that's a kind of entertainment. We have had something like this in the Mysore Brindavan Gardens for a long time, but that's nothing compared to the water fountains here.

As soon as we went into a casino from the Bellagio Hotel, another magical world was waiting for us. The description of it as Maya's court [*the architect of Devas is Maya; he created a magnificent court for the Pandavas in the epic Mahabharata*] is not adequate to capture it. In the middle of the lobby there is a glass frog; around it they created a pond with colorful leaves, flowers and vines. Lights shine from within these things.

In this huge casino there are different kinds of gambling machines. You hear the sound of coins in machines everywhere. The jingling of coins sounds like music to the players' ears. All of a sudden some fellow becomes lucky. You hear the sounds of the coins dropping into the winner's bucket. There are hundreds of game machines there. Some are $5 machines, some $1 and some others twenty-five cents machines. These machines are everywhere. There are counters where you can get change. Besides these, there are different tables where there is gambling with cards. There is a crowd around each table.

The gambler in a man jumps out in this environment. You hear nothing but sounds of coins rolling. In the game machine, you insert a quarter and turn the wheel. It's enough if you press a button; the wheel turns by itself. When the wheel stops, the machine gives you coins appropriate to the numbers that come up. Those who are lucky win hundreds and hundreds of dollars. There is a gambler in everyone. That gambler possessed Dharmaraja and made him lose the shirt on his back, his wife and his brothers. Here you see many such Dharmarajas. You see different varieties of people: those who lose a hundred dollars in half an hour in front a game machine and then despair, those who go into ecstasies when there is a shower of coins, and those who struggle looking for ways of finding more money after their money has disappeared into those machines. I felt that these vast gambling houses prove that a gambler and a debaucher are hidden within every person. We get to experience here what it means to look for easy ways of making money, and, trusting our luck, lose whatever we have.

We must pay homage not only to these games, but to the glory there. We can never say we have seen enough. You feel that man cannot create any more than this for his entertainment. You can spend days upon days going around shops, eating snacks, having drinks and worshipping the goddess of luck in front of these game machines. This whole world is different. You don't have a worry. It's another world. I felt [*the illusion*] that Las Vegas is the city which hands out pure entertainment to thousands of people without giving way to bloodshed, crime or deception.

Caesar's Palace is another hotel. If you want to see all the hotels completely and in detail, it would take hours upon hours. You can witness the glory of the Roman times here. You have the experience of standing in the middle of a crossroads in Rome. They decorated the ceiling with lights to look like the evening skies of Rome. It's a very unique sight. And there is no count of the number of shops. You will see and hear all the world's famous names here. The whole splendor of America dazzles in Las Vegas.

It was 1 o'clock in the night by the time we had finished our touring and got back to the hotel room. We went to bed and were ready again the next morning by 8 am. This time it took two hours for us to see two casinos called 'New York, New York' and MGM. A pair of eyes is not enough to see these places and a pair of legs is not enough to walk these distances. And a pair of hands is not enough to buy in the shops and to play the games. 24 hours are not enough hours for a day. You can't sleep. Suguna won $30 playing the games there. Mitra gave UG the $20 he had won. An old rule is that whatever anyone wins, he or she must give the winnings to UG. UG's rule is "What's lost is yours and what's won is mine." Suguna also gave him her winnings. UG gave it all back to Suguna. Julie spent a lot of money on us and on our entertainment. She must have spent at least a $100 that night for entertainment.

*   *
*

We vacated the rooms at 11 am and left on our return trip in the car, arriving home yesterday around 2:30 pm. Suguna made couscous and we all ate. UG ate *idlis*. This time, it's surprising that although she traveled such a distance, was awake all night and again traveled in the car, Suguna was not tired. Then, last night, Lisa, Julie and I went into town and brought some veggie burgers and French fries. We went into a bookstore. I was looking for detailed information about Palm

Springs. I haven't found the right book yet. Last night, Lisa started playing a game with cards. The numbers on the cards in each hand must add up to 21. Any number of people can play the game. Four of us played for an hour for money. Lisa gave us the change she had, pennies, etc. How many games there are in Las Vegas! It's all over now. UG's pilgrimage has been completed in a day.

UG thinks that a visit to America is never complete without seeing New York City and Las Vegas. The last time, he showed New York to us both; and this time he has shown us Las Vegas. Last evening, we went to Pick & Save and bought several small items. Now we have to transport all these back to that country [*India*]. That's the biggest burden.

*   *   *

January 14, Thursday – Day 25

The counting of days for our return journey has begun. Four days remain until it is time to go to San Francisco. I woke up this morning at 6:00 am. I wondered how I could have slept so long. I went to bed at 10 o'clock. Why am I spending so many hours in sleep? I don't know. We spoke to Archana yesterday. We tried so many times to call Venkata Chalapati on the phone, but no one picked it up on the other end. We remembered that it was Sankranti yesterday in India. It was Dakshinamurti's birthday. All of us called him on the phone and talked to him. ... Last night we talked to Sitaram. He said he didn't get the money from the Swiss bank yet. He said he will invest it as per instructions as soon as receives it.

What's There to be Proud of?

We have been looking for the history and legends of Palm Springs. Yesterday, we went to the Visitors' Information Center and to the City Library. I copied material from four or five books to bring home. I would like to prepare an essay on America in general and another especially on Palm Springs. Many writers write appreciating the American way of life, the people's economic status and their entertainment needs, and criticizing our country and its conditions. But UG talks about how many atrocities are being committed in this country, and how many horrible things are imbedded in its history.

* * *

What's there to be proud of
In the history of any nation?
The entire history of humanity
Is [filled with] the exploitation of others.

When I look into American history, I feel that the above is literally true. In olden times, Red Indians lived in Palm Springs. They had their own ways of living adapted to the desert life. While Mexicans invaded them, occupied California and destroyed some of them, a hundred fifty years ago, Americans hunted them, tortured them and slashed their throats, and destroyed about 90% of their population. The slogan was "A good Indian is a dead Indian." They were killed for no particular reason. On such a blood-soaked land present-day Americans have built a heaven on earth.

When we speak of Americans, who are these Americans? What is their race? It's not one race. All those unwanted rogues from the dominant European nations like Germany, England, Italy, Spain and France planted themselves here. Theirs is a mixed race. They didn't come from one country. They fought among themselves and destroyed about 6 to 7 million Red Indians. When they formed the United States, the question arose as to which language was to be the national language. English and German competed for that status. They polled everyone. English won by one vote. "Otherwise, German would have been the national language of this country," says UG. At the time of the Second World War, all the scientists in Germany ran for their lives. They were all Jews. As Nazis were killing the Jews, they escaped to Russia and America to save their own lives.

Later, probably in 1955, the news that Russia sent Sputnik into an orbit in the sky amazed the world. The then-President Eisenhower was envious of Russia's glory; so he commented: "Russia is bragging about throwing a tennis ball into the sky." The Hollywood actor living in Palm Springs called Bob Hope said on TV: "Half of the German scientists escaped to Russia after the Second World War. The other half found shelter in America. The ones who got away to Russia proved themselves superior to the ones that had come here."

How have they come to dominate the world in this fashion? Asians – Vietnamese, Japanese, Chinese and Indians – are far brighter than the average American. When America imposed sanctions on India, our leaders must have warned the American government that they would withdraw Indian electronic engineers from America. In the electronics field in America, about 50% are Asians. Hundreds of thousands of Indians are working here. They are all working to benefit the progress of America. If they all go back, what will happen to this country?

As a matter of fact, Asians are able to find admissions more easily in colleges and schools here. In years to come, the US government may need to reserve seats for the local citizens.

The world population is five billions. What a small part 300 million from America are compared to that? However, 25% of the world's resources are in America. It's a land of plenty given by God. But they are plundering all that (on this planet there are enough resources to feed 12 billion people). So much of the world's wealth is accumulated in the demonic hands of arrogant wealthy nations like America, reducing the rest of the earth to poverty. As long as Russia was strong, it acted as a goading hook so that America could not wag its tail. But with Russia's fall, America is no longer answerable to anyone. China is the only country which could perhaps pose a challenge.

People in America are abusing the world's natural resources. They have a 'throwaway' mentality in regard to everything. It's a 'throwaway' culture. It's a culture in which people use everything and then throw those things away. How much paper is wasted! Still, these gentlemen who use tons and tons of toilet paper, throwing it away, talk about ecology and protection of the environment! For them wasting is a hobby. Now Asian countries are also mimicking this behavior. Unless this mimicking is nipped in the bud, man cannot survive on planet earth.

*   *   *

People here think that America is the whole world. There is an International Film Festival in Palm Springs this month. It's still going on. There is not a single film in it from India. There is not even a mention of the name of that country. Doesn't it indicate the arrogance of the people of this country not to take into consideration a country in which a fifth of the world's population lives?

It was Hollywood actors who made Palm Springs famous. There is a close link between Palm Springs and movie actors. An actor called Gene Autry built the Ocotillo Lodge; he also built the Givenchy Hotel. There are many other places with his name. There is also an important highway with his name.

*   *   *

"Bob Hope made more money on real estate here than he did in his films," UG observes. Bob Hope's mansion is located on the hill east of Palm Springs. He and his wife have just celebrated their 65th wedding anniversary.

*   *   *

Elvis Presley used to live here. This city once used to be a honeymoon resort.

*   *   *

When we go into the shops in this country, we learn how little technical and industrial progress our country has made. Wherever you look in the stores, you find "MADE IN CHINA" on all kinds of things. In earlier times, about fifteen years ago, you could see "Made in China" only on small electric gadgets and nail clippers. It's not an exaggeration to say that now about 90% of the things sold in American stores are Chinese made. You don't even hear the name of India. All the electronic manufactured goods are from China, Japan and Taiwan. You hear the name of India, especial of Andhra, only in the software industry. The iron manhole covers (inspection covers) over the sewers in New York City are made in India.

*   *   *

"Water shortage on this planet is going to be a more serious problem than the shortage of gasoline," says UG. Even now you can see the signs of it everywhere. Even in America.

*   *   *

This is a land of entertainment. It invests heavily in the entertainment industry. Hollywood movies, theaters – people invest millions of dollars and make movies.

*   *   *

Only those countries which have 'economic power and military might', what UG calls 'the two weapons', are the topmost countries. If India cannot obtain them, America wouldn't care. The same advice that UG has given to Lisa applies to India: "You must prove yourself needed and indispensable. You shouldn't find fault with the management and criticize them."

* * *

January 15, Friday – Day 26

I had several different dreams as I was waking up around 6 am – a dream that I was still hungry and eating and a dream about jubilation over meeting my uncles and aunts, and so on. Why doesn't UG appreciate the joy of letting everything go? In one of the dreams I had thoughts about asking him and finding out about it. Thus I woke up. Yesterday morning when I was on the toilet seat, I thought, "I must give all the money I get from the books to UG. He must spend it and I must not have anything to do with it."

When UG came in this morning he spoke about the exact same matter, "Julie gave me the money for the books. I'll pay it to you in rupees. If you want, I can give you dollars." "No, no, I wanted to tell you that I don't need that money at all," I answered. I was very happy when UG said, "OK, I'll take it then." In some way, a burden has been lifted off my chest. How light I felt when I thought that "that money is not mine, and I don't need it!" Apparently, Julie gave $60 to UG. Mitra gave $10 for a copy. I gave that money also to UG. He took it.

We spent all yesterday shopping. The handicrafts shop in downtown called "The Alley" was very nice. We went out again in the evening, this time to visit a place called "El Paseo" in Palm Desert. That's a street name. All the shops on it have been opened recently, that is, in the last month or two. That street is wonderful! When I look at its glory, I feel like going there every day. Sak's Fifth Avenue was there. All the shops were neatly organized. They compete with each other in decorating. The wonderful buildings which contain them looked very pleasing to the eye. UG calls some people "stinking rich". Only those sorts of people can buy in these shops. UG bought a top in one of them.

* * *

Julie has been taking pictures of UG and me for the last week or ten days for a photo for the back cover of my book. Not a single one was satisfactory. Yesterday, I put on Julie's glasses and got a picture taken by Lisa. I thought it was OK. Or else, my black frame glasses cover my whole face and would not let my eyes be shown in the picture. I must change my glasses after I go back to India.

* * *

'Public Enemy No. 1'

Unless the agitation in my mind subsides, I can't hear what UG says. The more distracted I am the more distant I become from him. When the agitation subsides, I see the truth in what UG says. I used to ask myself why UG calls me 'Public Enemy No.1'. I would give myself different explanations. But none were satisfactory. Finally, yesterday the answer dawned on me. UG tries to wipe out all the memories, traces and signs of himself from the earth along with his actual self. He says forgetting him and his 'teaching' completely is the greatest favor we could do for him. He says it even now. However, every thought of mine, every action and every word – they are all contrary to his wishes. My attempts are centered on making people remember him for a long time. That's why I feel that he calls me 'Public Enemy No.1'.

*   *   *

Fair in Palm Springs

Every Thursday night (like last night), there is a street fair in Palm Springs. There are stalls set up on both sides of Palm Canyon street. Last night the street looked very busy. I asked Julie to write the names of the foods we ate last night. It was a Middle eastern mixed plate containing: *falafel* (deep-fried cakes like *bondas*), stuffed grape leaves (like stuffed eggplant), *tabouli* (some kind of leaves [parsley] chopped finely and mixed with pasta [*cracked wheat*]), *hummus* (with a cream-like sauce on top of it– I felt it had a bit too much salt) and *pita* bread (these are thick and round, like *chapattis*; one of them is enough to fill your stomach).

There were many other stalls in the street fair. One musician was playing on the guitar. He was chatting and playing it wonderfully at the same time. Julie bought me a CD of his. In another place, they were cutting marble-looking stones into thin slices and selling them as cutting boards to cut vegetables on. Julie bought one for $15 and Lisa another for $10. I was surprised when the sales person gave Suguna a heart-shaped Corian slate wishing her "Happy Valentine's Day." When Suguna mentioned to him that she was from India, he acted surprised and, making theatrical gestures, said he thought she was from China. Lisa told us that he knew that she was Indian.

* * *

January 16, Saturday – Day 27

There are two days left for our departure. I woke up at 5 am today. But I didn't feel quite like getting up, so I lay in bed till 5:15 am. Yesterday afternoon, Mitra phoned saying that since the central heater had been making noise, he had removed the plug to it. Without the heater on, the whole house felt a little cold. Right away I plugged the heater back in. The heater is now working and the heat in the house is increasing gradually. In the nights and early in the morning, it gets pretty cold here. In the town where Aruna lives it's many times colder.

* * *

Photos for My Book

The efforts to get photos suitable for my book haven't borne fruit till yesterday. Julie and Lisa together took dozens of photos of UG and me together. My glasses are the big problem. As soon as the sun or light falls on them, they turn dark and my eyes won't show through. My face comes out terribly in the photos. Julie took a lot of pictures with her digital camera. As we didn't like even a single one of them, UG scolded her for her ineptness. "This idiot doesn't know how to take a picture for a book. She lies and says that she had worked for the *Time* magazine as a photographer. She is a dunderhead. She has clay in her head!" so the badgering goes on. I thought that one of the close-up pictures which Lisa had taken was all right, but UG didn't like it.

While the sun was setting, last evening, Lisa took another series of pictures, making UG and me stand outside on the street. Not one of them came out satisfactorily. When each of them was commenting, "This is good, that is good", "None of you really understand that on a cover picture the features of the person must appear very clearly. Who cares about the mountains and the trees in the background? I am the one to select a picture, no one else!" UG blasted away.

He asked me to take all the videos that were in the table drawer. He also asked me to throw the file of Clinton's 'sexcapades' into the wastepaper basket. I arranged all the computer photo prints which Julie has taken in a file. UG flipped through those pages and said, "This photo looks good for the book," pointing to the picture taken of me, UG and Guha. He advised, "You just have to cut Guha out of the picture, that's all." Julie printed the photo on the computer within minutes. It really looked good, I thought. UG was sitting back in a relaxed fashion. I was sitting on the bench next to him, matching his height. Julie printed the cover page with the photo.

Last night we took all that stuff and went to Kinko's at 10:00 pm. In the afternoon, in the hot sun, we went to that Sushi DTP publishing expert and picked up the book and the floppies. When we went to Kinko's in that sun, they told us to come back at night. So last night, we waited there for half an hour. The guy made four copies besides the original. After so many days the book has finally taken a complete shape. Suguna got the photos of both of us together blown up in Kinko's to A4 size. They can be enlarged into even bigger, poster size pictures. The color Xerox pictures came out pretty well. Kinko's is a leading copying and book-making store. There are many automatic Xerox machines in it. The man there made four copies of the book and spiral-bound them for $45. They look very good. We should see what UG says.

*   *   *

UG's Kuja Stage

Nataraj is saying that we must see Joshua Tree and Bear Lake national forests. That was the big discussion yesterday morning. "Nataraj, you are not saying anything. What else must they see here? There are just two days left," UG kept asking again and again. And then he would veto, saying "No" to whatever Nataraj suggested. Finally, he said that they should take us to Joshua Tree. But he himself wouldn't come. "It's not fun if you don't come," said Suguna.

"I'm fed up with these two guys. They are leaving," he was telling Moorty on the phone. Moorty seems to have said, "You are fed up with all of us." If we go to San Francisco, UG will go somewhere else. Larry is coming in his car on the 19th. They both will probably run away somewhere. He is not mentioning the topic of the jungles of Brazil nowadays. "I will stay here if they start a Senate investigation of Clinton. Watching that will be a nice pastime," he says. UG comments that every home in America is a brothel. He criticizes Clinton saying, "It's not enough to condemn Clinton's sexual promiscuity. What's worse is that he has tried to deceive so many people with his lies. Behaving in such a base fashion being a President is an insult to the office of the President." "It would be more honorable and sensible to resign. Being attached to the seat of the President, he got stuck and got buried in the mire. It's entirely his own fault," he says. UG's slogan: "Kill Clinton!"

It's sometimes frightening to see UG throwing his criticisms and opinions about so candidly, fearlessly and freely. He is warning us again saying, "It will be a lot more horrible when the Kuja stage begins." "I don't know how it is going to be; it will be completely contrary to my past life," he says. "It's not correct to say it will be completely opposed to it, but there will be a complete change," he expands further. Why just countries, their leaders, scientists, the innovations in technology, the protectors of the environment, psychiatrists and educators, even the thought trends of those who have made these human skeletons into great people – each model that the culture follows and each great soul that it imitates – he tears them apart one by one. "Gandhi too exploited the Harijan problem and the problem of poverty and used both as pawns in politics for his own grandeur," he says.

"You are using the misery of the people to show in your films. Why should I see them?" UG asks Mahesh. He attacks every politician, writer and artist, everyone, the same way. They want to share their feelings of misery with everyone; so they highlight them in their works; other than that they have no altruistic motivation. That's the way the world is. It's all pretensions. Compassion, sympathy, pity, empathy – are all cover-ups. UG reveals before our eyes such cruelly selfish beings with their horrible fangs and devilish laughter. All our thoughts and experiences are crooked; they are all deceptive. We don't think of it until UG shows us the reality hidden in them. Our culture regards mother's love as divine. When UG remarks that "mothers are monsters with respect to their children," not only mothers but even their children pounce upon UG. But how many can see the destructive nature of mothers who, with their first kisses, ignite the debased idea of the 'I' in their children for their own self-satisfaction? Some ask the question, "So, we shouldn't love our children?" They think they are arguing very cleverly. "What do you think is love? Who are you to show love?" – these 'loving' people don't ask such questions.

Lisa's Gift for Mario

The other day, Lisa was mentioning an incident in relation to her lover Mario who lives in a foreign land. UG doesn't let the two get together. Lisa has been learning to live independently, under UG's oversight. He puts Mario down in front of everyone saying that he can't do anything and he doesn't deserve Lisa. But Lisa likes Mario immensely. She constantly dreams of her future with him. UG knows all that.

Once, Lisa bought four different kinds of articles of clothing to send to Mario. UG told her, "I want all of them." Lisa gave them to him without question. A few days later she again bought some nice jackets that would fit Mario to send to him. UG showed his liking for them this time too. "I want this particular one," she said, and gave the rest reluctantly to UG. The next day, she walked into UG's cottage and Nataraj was there at the time. All the things she had wanted to send to Mario with all her love were lying there on the table. Nataraj was trying them on. In a moment Lisa realized that UG had been giving them to Nataraj. The next moment, all the frustration and anger she had been holding within herself broke loose. "He can't, Nataraj can't wear these, I bought them for Mario!" UG was right there. "Once you have given them to me, you don't need to know to whom else I will give them away," said UG. He had a big package in his hand. He was asking Nataraj to mail it to Mario. The package was filled with several beautiful pieces of clothing, more valuable than the ones Lisa had bought; the clothes stared at Lisa, mocking her. She almost collapsed at UG's feet. She felt like pulling her own tongue out for hastily questioning the love with which he had been collecting the clothing more carefully than she ever did to send to Mario. That's how UG's grace is!

*   *   *

January 17, Sunday – Day 28

Today is Suguna's birthday. It has been four weeks since we came here. I woke up at 6:00 am, early in the morning. After washing and showering, I demonstrated to Lisa the 'Sun Salutations'. She too did them. I wrote down some *mantras* for her. Julie videotaped it all for Lisa. I showed Lisa some tricks. I also taught her *mudras* and *pranayama*. She believes that these will help her in her massage practice.

*   *   *

Yesterday at 12 noon we went to the Joshua Tree National Forest. UG didn't come. Lisa went to work. The trip took us four hours. We rode about 150 miles and saw different sorts of hills, rocks and skies of various colors. We saw the ocotillo tree. We came across a coyote on the road, an animal which looks like a jackal. Julie took a video of it. UG stayed here all of yesterday until 8 o'clock.

*   *   *

Last Day in Palm Springs

Today is our last day here. Last night, we packed all our suitcases. "It feels like we have settled down here," Suguna said to UG. UG laughed. There is no count of how many times he has moved or to how many places. I don't know where UG will go after we leave on the 18th. "What I shouldn't do is clear to me; I know that well. I won't come to the Bay Area. I won't go to New York. But I don't know what I *will* do," he says.

While UG was talking yesterday, I thought I should note down several things. But when I actually sit down to write, I can't remember them. That's how it goes. He certainly poured abuse on the Buddha: "Buddha was the first in human history to start *sannyasa*. He is the first rogue who initiated it as an institution. He is the first advocate of the doctrine of illusoriness [*of the world*] (*mithyavadi*), who arrogantly said that 'As long as a single soul is caught in the snare of delusion, I refuse to enter the gates of Nirvana.'" Who else in this world except UG has the guts to pour all those abuses on the Buddha? He can pour abuses upon abuses without repeating a single one of them.

* * *

UG is worried that Lisa will remain here alone. He thinks it's not safe for her to live in this house alone. He asked Nataraj and Mitra to stay in one of the wings – in the wing in which we are currently staying – till the end of this month. The whole house will be under Lisa's control after February 1. I feel that UG will continue to stay here. The weather is very nice. It's suitable to UG in every way. He likes dry weather. Anywhere else in the world right now it's cold and snowing. Even the weather in San Francisco is not so good. But it's heavenly here in Palm Springs.

Aruna phoned. The time is 8 am. I must put a stop to this writing now. If I have the time, I'll pick it up again later today. Or else, who knows when?

* * *

Afternoon, 2 pm. Everyone has been sitting here a long time and dozing off. UG went into his room. "You finished all your shopping?" he asked Suguna. Today, it's Suguna's birthday. It's going on smoothly without much fanfare. We ate the *idlis* she has made today. I don't know what we'll eat tonight. UG is blasting away at Julie.

I must read Julie's journal. UG asked me to look into what she has written and how she has written it.

*   *   *

We talked to Archana on the phone; we also spoke to Aruna. There is no news except that Henk is in Bangalore. Bob and Raj are in Bombay. Apparently, Mahesh got some awards for his films. Tanuja's movie got three awards. Mahesh's article has been published in a newspaper. I don't know which newspaper. This morning, Guha's family sent birthday greetings to Suguna over the phone and on the computer.

The sun is very hot outside. It looks white; it looks as if melted silver has been poured over it. It's over: our ties with Palm Springs end today. Tomorrow we go to San Francisco. We'll start a new chapter from there. We will travel to Seaside tomorrow night. Narayana Moorty phoned saying that their bathroom is being repaired and that we should come a day later. UG said no. "It doesn't matter. Go on the 18th," he said. He told the same thing to Moorty.

*   *   *

January 18, Monday – Day 29

Julie's Diary

The alarm went off early in the morning at 4:45 am. I finished the morning rituals by 5:30 and sat down. All yesterday we had discussions about Julie's book. Julie read some pages to UG. I read another twenty pages. Suguna also read some. Nataraj read some parts of it and started laughing. Unable to contain his happiness, he said, "I feel like dancing," and hopped around. I said, "I'll sing if you dance." Nataraj says, "We will dish out some entertainment for everyone on Suguna's birthday." The things Julie has written in her book portray UG as a different sort of person. She used to be associated with a teacher called Andrew Cohen before she met UG. Her getting disillusioned with him after she had met UG, getting attached to UG, trying to get close to UG, UG spurning her, and finally asking her to get out – all these are steps in Julie's dance. "But if you show those steps again and again, the reader gets bored," UG comments. That's a fair assessment. That's why she must condense her 1,000-page story. She should cut out about three quarters of it. Julie has the problem of what and how much to cut. She can do that job. She said she will send me a copy. I too promised to help her.

*   *

*

We finished packing. It's time to leave. We must leave at 6:15 am. Our time is up in Palm Springs. Last evening, we went on a car ride with UG one more time. We went via Indian Canyon Road to downtown on Palm Canyon Road. On the way we saw some historical monuments. The Starbucks coffee shop was packed with people. We saw the Desert Museum from the outside.

It looks like UG has come in. I must close this now and sit with him. I don't know when I will be free again.

*   *   *

Yesterday morning at 6:15, we took leave of UG. Julie took us to the airport in her car. We checked in around 6:40 and went into the airport restaurant. Julie looked sad. She is going to LA from here. "You can't come back here. You must leave directly from the airport," UG ordered her. She doesn't know what to do. Without UG she has no world. Her son Justin is mentally ill. He calls in the middle of the night. He wants to see her. He says he will come. Then he says he won't. "He is mad," says UG. Julie is anxious that he should see UG at least once. Her older son, Marc, is married and has a family.

Her daughter Sasha is an opera singer and has her own apartment in New York. None of Julie's children need her. Julie's mother, however, lives nicely in Julie's apartment under the care of two maids. Her mother is getting pretty old. It's easy for Julie to take care of her. But if you just sit idly and spend the money, even mountains will be reduced to small heaps. It's not new to her to burn thousands upon thousands like this.

*   *   *

En Route to Seaside

In the airport they told us that Alaska Airlines departure is at Gate 6. We talked a bit with Julie at the gate. Finally, we said goodbye and sat down in the Boeing 737. The plane left exactly at 7:35. It was 9:00 am when we got to San Francisco. Aruna and Venkat came to the gate. It took another half hour to get the baggage. And it was 10:00 am by the time we arrived at their home. On the way, they both showed us several things. I figured that Foster City is not even 10 miles from the airport. It was raining outside. The sky was heavily overcast. "What's the point in going to Seaside in this weather? You can spend the night here and we'll go tomorrow night in the car," said Aruna. Venkat said the same. We agreed. I phone UG before I called Moorty and told him that we are staying here for today. Then I told Moorty that we will come there tomorrow.

It has been raining lightly all day long. We chatted with Raghavendra Rao and his wife. We saw a video and ate lunch. Then I read for a little while a novel by M. V. Krishnamurti, '*Nattalostunnay Jagratta*' [*Beware, The Snails are Coming*] and dozed off. In the evening, around 7 pm, after Venkat returned, we went out for a car ride for a little while. We shopped in Safeway and K-mart and then chatted again. That's how we spent all our time. ...

This trip has worked out now after ten years. Aruna and Venkat living here on the West coast, Venkat's parents and us coming to America before the end of the year after Aruna and Venkat got married, meeting them here and having a good time – all these happened in a strange fashion. Whoever thought we would come here in this manner?

* *

*

I woke up today at 7 am. After finishing the morning rituals, I called UG at 9 am. I told him of the details of my conversation with the manager of the Canara Bank. Just before then Julie called from Santa Monica. She said she is going to New York today. UG said that he is going to LA and meet Julie there. He will probably take Mitra and Nataraj with him. Lisa is also off today. Perhaps they have all left by now. Around noon we all went up to the San Mateo Bridge and came back home, having taken videos and photos.

*   *

*

Outside, it's cloudy again. The sun came out for a while in the morning. We thought that was not bad. Before long, however, dark clouds covered the sky. When it is sunny, the whole apartment has a lot of light. It looks nice.

*   *   *

Yesterday, someone called Harry phoned me and said he wanted two copies of *No Way Out*. I gave him Chrystal's phone number and told him to ask her. He reserved two copies in the Quest Bookstore. He called me again to tell me that. He said he wanted a copy of my journal. He also wanted the audio tapes. I took his address. I could send him the galley copy I have with me. I must phone him and ask. I don't know what UG's plans are yet. Apparently, Dr. Lynn is coming to Palm Springs in February. Will UG also be there till then? He asked Larry not to come. He said he was going to LA to confirm his tickets to New Zealand and Australia. I don't know when he will travel there; perhaps in February? Nataraj and Mitra will be there till the end of the month.

*   *   *

Outside, clouds are gathering heavily. It's dark already at 4:30 pm. In the last 30 days, I haven't seen this kind of weather even once in Palm Springs. In India I blamed UG for being so unkind to ask us to come to the US in winter. "Why did he call us to come to America in the winter cold weather? Why didn't he let us remain happy in Bangalore and why did he cause all this hardship to us?" I had complained. But when I set my foot in Palm Springs, I realized what sort of a heaven he has invited us to. When I think about how he didn't cause us the slightest inconvenience, how he had called Aruna and Venkat too and created an opportunity for them to spend some time with us, how he bought a microwave oven for Aruna and thus fulfilled Suguna's wish, and how he had tried to remove my anxieties in so many ways, my heart is filled with happiness and gratitude. He saw to it that my book got into a shape. How many hundreds of dollars he has spent on us! At last, the book is ready. Moorty will put the final touches to it. UG is paying off the Rs.50,000 that I have borrowed from Major. It must all be due to the merits of my past karma, I thought. Moreover, he is asking Nataraj to invest Rs.300,000 in our finance company. I will look and see if it is possible to invest all of it in one person's name. I must ask Gururaj about it.

*   *   *

It's almost 5 pm. Venkat should be coming about now. We should leave for Seaside as soon as he comes. By the time we return from Seaside, Raghavendra Rao and his wife will have gone. Ten days after that we too will make our return trip to India.

* * *

Seaside

January 25, Monday (San Francisco)

I had to look up in the calendar to find about today's date and how many days have elapsed. Although it's a week since we have come here, I haven't had the free time to touch this diary. I thought it had been just three days.

That's right, we arrived here Tuesday, the 19th. That day, by the time we went out with Raghavendra Rao and his wife in the afternoon for an outing and returned, it was dark and cold. It already starts getting dark here by 4 pm. Venkat came around 6 pm from his office in a hurry and took us to Seaside in his car after taking some photos at 6:30 pm. Aruna also came with us. It was raining and cold outside. We had to travel more than a hundred miles in this sort of weather. In India people wouldn't dare to do that. Here on Highway 101, many cars were darting very fast, competing with us to get ahead. No one seemed to mind the weather. The car was warm and dry. The roads were shining, reflecting the lights. Because we took a wrong turn on the way, it took us half an hour to get back to the highway going to Seaside.

It was about 9 pm by the time we got to Narayana Moorty's house. We ate quickly and Venkat and Aruna left to return at 9:50 pm in the rain. Although they knew their way back, apparently it was 11:30 pm by the time they got back to their home.

In Moorty's house, they arranged for us the bedroom adjacent to the kitchen. It was very cold. The heater did not make much difference. Wendy was getting tiles put on the floor in the bathroom. Moorty said it was impossible for us to take our baths here as long as the work was not finished; so he said he would arrange for our showers in his friend Murali's place. I asked myself why we should go to his friend's house just for a shower; so we quit taking showers for a day. The second day, I had an idea: I thought we could take our baths sitting in the bathtub without the water spilling on the tiles. So I talked to Wendy and when she put up a plastic sheet on the wall, the bathroom became available for a bath. For the next three days we both had our baths that way. We brought hot water in buckets, sat in the tub and poured water on ourselves with a tumbler. Except for this inconvenience, we spent the three days (from 19th night till 23rd morning) in Moorty's house pleasantly. For each meal Moorty cooked a variety of foods with his own hands and served them and made sure that we ate well. I felt that in Moorty's house we have eaten again to our heart's content after a long time. Wendy spends all her time, ever since she gets up from bed in the morning, with Kiran – looking after his needs, taking him to his music lessons, taking care of the house cat Whitney, shopping and bringing the stuff they need at home. On workdays, Moorty cooks half the time. On holidays he takes over the cooking responsibility completely.

*   *   *

Kiran lives in a different world. He wouldn't come into our world. If we said hello to him, he would come down from that world, as if he is coming out of sleep, mumble a couple of words, smile within himself and slip back into his world again. School, study, the piano which UG has bought him, and other percussion instruments and his mother Wendy – Kiran has no other world except these. He is not bothered about who is visiting, why they are here or what they need etc. When Moorty calls him five times, one of those times he responds smiling. No one can hear what he says. He loves piano. Everyone thinks he has gained proficiency in piano. Moorty says he is very skilled in percussion instruments also.

*   *   *

The very next day after we came, on Wednesday the 20th, Moorty and I sat down and completed whatever we had to do for my book on his computer. He too liked the book cover. Neither of us liked the photo of both UG and me on the back cover. Moorty's friend Sajid came with us last Saturday to San Mateo and took some pictures of me with UG in the Holiday Inn. Moorty believes that we can find at least one or two of them which will be suitable for printing. Sajid lives in Santa Cruz. His wife is Laura. They are quite amicable with each other. Sajid is also an engineer. He is currently not working. Computer graphics is his hobby. The walls in his living room are filled with his drawings and paintings of nude models in various poses.

*   *   *

The weather was beautiful for the three days we were in Seaside. The first day, we went to Carmel. From there we went on the coast, on the 17-mile drive, in the car. You have to pay a $7.50 toll to get in. It was great. We stopped at places and saw the sea lions and birds on the distant rocks in the ocean. The Pacific Ocean looks spread out in blue in any direction. Natural scenery – it looks like the ocean is incessantly working hard to wash away all the filth which man has created.

*   *   *

It was probably in 1993 that Mahesh wrote UG's biography in 30 days; he had written it in Carmel. Moorty showed us that house. From there we went to a bookstore called Pilgrim's Way on the main street. It was there that Julie had first bought UG's book. Luna too met UG through the manager of that shop. His name is Paul. I felt like I could spend hours in that shop. How many different books, it's like a library! The store is famous especially for spiritual and religious books. I bought a used book on palmistry and an astrological calendar. The latter is for Vedam Satyanarayana. From there we returned home via Monterey by the evening. We had a feast of music in Moorty's home, music from old records – Pankaj Mallik, Dilip Kumar Roy, Balamurali, Ali Akbar Khan, Amzad Ali Khan, Dwaram,

L. Subramaniam, Lalgudi Jayaraman and Lakshmi Shankar – music of many voices and instruments. We heard till the rust in our ears was cleaned out. Moorty gave me a copy of his book of Vemana's verses. He also gave a book each of Chuang Tzu and Allan Watts. Very generous man, he has a tendency to give away whatever he has without considering it his. He constantly seems to think about what else to give next.

*   *   *

January 26, Tuesday – Day 37

With Aruna and Venkat

Woke up at 6:30 in the morning. Last night, after Venkat has returned from his office, we went for a drive at 7:30. By the time we finished the shopping and got back home it was 10 pm. N. Moorty and Sajid have sent photos of me with UG by e-mail. Moorty has selected one of them for the cover page. I thought I couldn't imagine anything better than that, although I was wearing glasses in it. Sajid had taken that picture. Yesterday, at 12 noon I sent e-mails to Moorty and Sajid. All the fine details needed for the book are now worked out. The Word Perfect CD disc which Julie sent has also come in the mail. We talked to Julie on the phone yesterday. I also spoke to John Allen. He said he will come on Thursday and take us in his car.

*   *   *

Slowly my mind is getting crowded with thoughts of India, thoughts about all the issues there, one after another – the future of the school, our future activities, financial issues and such. My mind was quieter when I was around UG. I wondered if I even had a mind. There were no anxieties. Now waves of thoughts are rolling in. That's the way it goes. This writing will turn out like Julie's journal. Last Saturday night, there was a talk about that journal in UG's presence at Holiday Inn. "There is nothing interesting in it. Everything in it is repetitive," UG had said. "That's not true," said Moorty, "not all of it is like that. Those thousand pages have to be edited into a book of about 200 pages. But until UG gives me a clear sign, I am not going to touch that manuscript. If he asks me to, I will." UG didn't respond. When the time comes he will make the decision. Till then it has to wait. If Moorty could polish the crude material written by O. S. Reddi and turn it into something readable, it's not hard for him to work on Julie's journal. He never bothered about it because sometime ago in the past UG asked him not to. It looks like Julie's journal might see better times now.

*   *   *

Livermore Temple

The four of us went to the Siva-Vishnu temple in Livermore last Sunday. It's about an hour's journey from here by car. The temple is built in a large area. The main temple top is taller than the Bangalore Banasankari Venkateswara temple. In the compound there are temples of Shiva, Parvati, Ganapati, Subrahmanya, Venkateswara, Sri Devi and Bhu Devi. They have installed some very good-looking images. There are also images of Radha and Krishna, Sita, Rama and Anjaneya as well as of the nine planets. Apparently they had the Kumbha Abhisheka in 1996. There is certain peacefulness in the atmosphere around the temple. As we walked into the temple, the priest was chanting the *mantra pushpa* and was presenting the *aarti* to everyone [*to receive gods' grace*]. We too received grace. We learned later that it was *Ratha Saptami* that day. But by that time it would be Sunday night [*in India*]. Still there would be a remnant of Saptami [*the 7th day of the lunar month*]. *Ratha Saptami* was precisely the day eight years ago on which we immersed the ashes of Valentine in the Kaveri River. This year it falls on the 24th. Valentine died on January 20th. I didn't remember it this year. That was the day that Moorty and I completed the work on the book in Seaside. Valentine, you are secure in my memory. Now you are taking a concrete shape in my book. I must dedicate this book to you. It would be nice to insert a picture of UG and Valentine in the book.

*   *   *

It's colder here near San Francisco than in Palm Springs. Besides, it's always cloudy and raining. For the first time, we stayed indoors all day, packing the suitcases. We have filled the large suitcase I had previously sent with Aruna with the stuff we have bought here. If we take stock, the things we have bought are all trifles. Half the space in the suitcase is occupied by tablecloths, videotapes and books. Now we will need another suitcase to carry the things we have yet to buy. To transport them all to India is the big task now.

* * *

Aruna took us to the public library of Foster City. It's two blocks from here, that is, from the Water's Edge Apartments. There is a lake next to it. Surrounding the lake there are clubs and playgrounds. When I entered the library, I felt like never leaving. Besides books, they also have CD's. They let you borrow books free of charge. There are many magazines as well as numerous books. There is also a children's section. Anyone can surf the Internet on the computers. Aruna goes there almost every day. She reads the books right there. All these past days, Raghavendra Rao and his wife have been here. Now we two are here. A year ago, I never gave a thought to Aruna's family life. They had just been married and were setting up their family. It's uncanny how UG called us both here and saw to it that we are with them. Things are happening at an unimaginably fast rate.

* * *

Chinatown in San Francisco

In every big city in this country there is a Chinatown. There are many Chinese in America. They have been here for a couple of centuries. They are good in business. Mainland Chinese have trade relations with many countries. Now, when you look in any supermarket, 50% of the merchandise is marked "Made in China". You would wonder what it is that they don't manufacture. There is a Chinatown in the middle of San Francisco.

On Sunday, after we left the temple in Livermore, we went to see the Golden Gate Bridge. We drove around downtown San Francisco in the late afternoon, ate French fries in the Burger King Restaurant, also had some coffee there, and then started walking from the gate of Chinatown.

From there we went all around Chinatown returning home by 10 pm. All the shops there are run by the Chinese. Different kinds of toys, electronic goods, curios, gold jewelry, jackets laced with expensive diamonds and other colorful precious stones such as gems and topaz, pearl and coral bead chains – are all sold in abundance. If you don't bargain with them, you can easily be taken in. We bargained a lot in a shop called Pearl Bazaar and told them we would come again, and we did go there again today.

John Allen

Unexpectedly, John Allen came this morning with his mother-in-law who is visiting from England. She is over 80. She still looks healthy and active. In downtown San Francisco, in the Union Square, there is a shop called Needlepoint and she wanted cross-stitch mats there. That's why John took her with him, came to our house on his way to San Francisco and took the three of us with him.

It has been many years since I have seen John. He lives in Palo Alto. He has two sons going to school and his wife is Margaret. He works in computers in Stanford. We went all around downtown San Francisco in his Volkswagen car. We went to Chinatown and went back to the Pearl Bazaar shop. Aruna bought pearl necklaces for Suguna, and emeralds and jade for her friend. When we all returned home, it was 3 pm. John dropped us off at our home.

*   *   *

Nataraj has not phoned yet.

*   *   *

January 27, Wednesday – Day 38

Telugu Language and Telugu People

It was Republic Day in India yesterday. There probably was a celebration in the school. They would have hoisted a flag under the supervision of Venkata Chalapati. I need to find the exact equivalents of English words in Telugu. I don't know enough technical vocabulary. If an idea cannot be expressed in a language precisely, then it's either the fault of the writer or the fault of the language. Chalam has expressed all sorts of emotional ideas in Telugu very precisely, so there is no dearth in the language. In the Telugu vocabulary there are many words. We can easily express our ideas. But we have to look up the Telugu equivalents for some technical terms in English. One's style, one's way of writing, however, is purely personal. Different writers can express the same subject matter in different ways. Chalam's writing style is different from R.V.

Sastry's style. Kutumba Rao's is different from either of them. If we compare their styles, we understand their personalities.

All the Telugu people in this city celebrate Sankranti under the auspices of BATA [*Bay Area Telugu Association*], Aruna told me. "We saw such things celebrated by Kannada people before. They weren't very good. Once we go there, the whole day is filled with events. They arrange for meals there. If you like, we can go," she said. The admission is $15 per head. That means we have to pay $60 for the four of us. I thought that would be a waste. We wouldn't know anyone there. As a matter of fact, it would be nice to meet with one or two Telugu friends, but I can't stand Telugu groups. The pettiness of Telugu people comes through when they are in groups. That's why I try to keep away even from celebrations of annual Telugu gatherings called Melukalayika in Bangalore.

Everyone tries to show off a greatness and brilliance which they don't really have, and no one appreciates the nobility apparent in the person in front of them. They can't honor true art. That's why Telugu people cannot succeed in their own Telugu land. Other Telugus won't let them. If they want to get themselves known to the world, they must go outside the borders of Andhra and settle there.

UG's case is proof enough for us to feel ashamed. Telugu people don't take the initiative [*to recognize him*] even after several of his books have been published in English, even after he has given four interviews in Delhi Doordarshan, and has a lot of stuff published in newspapers and magazines in English and other languages. They haven't even given him one TV interview. Not a single important Andhra newspaper has published news about UG. They only publish news of useless scandals. In 1980, *Andhra Prabha Daily* did publish a long essay. After that, no press correspondent from Andhra has ever written on him in Telugu and none tried to meet him. These people don't realize how proud they ought to be that a seer like UG, a candid man, a philosopher and a world traveler, is Telugu. The Telugus don't know how to honor and celebrate their own great people while they are still alive. Then after they are dead, everyone starts praising them. It's only the Telugus who fear that their own greatness might be diminished if they admit the greatness of another. That's their bane.

*   *   *

UG's Friends

I am noticing a peculiarity in UG's friends and people who are close to him, especially in this country. When UG is here or comes here, everyone gathers around him. Everyone says hello to each other and chats about this and that. When UG leaves, each goes his or her own way. They don't meet again unless they need to. They don't talk to each other for months. When UG comes again, they all reappear. It's different in India. Once they become close, people make it a point to meet each other, or at least phone each other, even after UG leaves. They write to each other. They talk to each other about various things that UG says. You don't see any of that here. They don't say hello to each other, even though everyone has a phone, a computer and other modern tools and conveniences.

When John mentioned this to me yesterday, I was surprised. He is not in touch with anyone.

For instance, everyone knows that Douglas is in financial troubles. No one tries to help him. Even UG did not let him come near him this time. He helped Douglas with what he needed before. UG says it is Douglas's own doing. Nonetheless, when there is a need, UG will certainly help.

*   *   *

Today it's very sunny. It's now 8 am. There is a canal flowing behind the house. Its waters join the ocean. There are ducks and cranes on the water. People have built houses on the canal's banks. Some people have small boats and in the summertime they go around in the water rowing them. Now it's winter and the cold is bone-biting. Even if you are clad very warmly, you still feel cold. Even though I am indoors my fingers freeze when I sit here writing early in the morning. The ducks gliding on the water are making noises. But the cold here never freezes the water. When you go north from here, you notice a change of weather every ten miles.

It was extremely cold yesterday in downtown San Francisco. When we were walking along the streets, John's mother-in-law – an English lady – was also shivering. I must wear thermal underwear. Even when wearing two sweaters and a jacket, because I don't wear gloves, I feel cold in my palms. If I don't wear boots to cover my entire feet, the cold creeps in from under my feet. In this cold, Venkat puts on a single jacket and walks around comfortably without even any thermals.

Yesterday, Suguna had hard time moving her feet with the weight of the things she was carrying. We can't tell when the clouds will gather or when it will start raining. Even though it's sunny, it's only warm in the car. It's only cold when we walk. I think that UG is fulfilling my hidden desire that I should experience the weather in this country in wintertime.

*   *   *

January 28, Thursday – Day 39

We should be leaving tomorrow according to the plan we made two days ago. But we have postponed our departure by a week. If we were leaving tomorrow, then our stay would have been 'forty days and forty nights' exactly. It's now 7 am and it's cold. It's still cold even if I wear a sweater on top of the thermals and close all the doors. There is central heating in the house, but Venkat is allergic to its heat. Apparently, he will start sneezing and go on sneezing all day. That's why Aruna doesn't turn the heater on. That's why it's so cold in the house. It was quite sunny yesterday. There was not a single spec of a cloud and the entire sky was blue. When I put a chair out and sat in the sun for ten minutes, the sun began to scorch my skin.

*   *   *

Yesterday, Aruna took us both to the Foster City mall. We went on the city bus. A bus company called Santrans runs the buses in Foster City. There are many routes. One route takes us from their apartment to the mall. The fare of $1.10 is the same for any destination. The buses are very convenient, but they seem empty whenever you look in them. They are not crowded like in our country.

In the mall we went around for three hours. We went into Sears and Nordstrom and many other stores. We couldn't find anything to buy anywhere. We had coffee in Burger King and headed back home in the bus around 5 pm. Yesterday UG was in New Jersey; he spoke to us from Guha's home.

     *   *   *

Aruna has turned into quite a hard-working girl. From the time she gets up from bed in the morning till Venkat leaves for his office she keeps herself busy. She is completely occupied with taking care of his needs. She packs his lunch box. She makes a different dish every day – normally foods like *upma* and *chapatti*. Venkat eats his breakfast here and takes the lunch with him. He eats something light in the canteen in the afternoons. He has coffee when he comes home. Meanwhile, Aruna takes care of all the household chores. She keeps the house tidy. And she visits the library everyday.

     *   *   *

January 29, Friday – Day 40

Today it has been exactly 40 days that we've set foot on this soil. This is the first time that I have been in a foreign land for such a long time. On our last trip, we stayed in Switzerland for a month and in London for a week.

Suguna just brought me some hot coffee. The weather was good yesterday too. There was bright sun all day long. The sky was plunged in blue color. Yesterday at 11 am, Suguna and I visited a school here, an elementary school called Kids Connection. There was a lady administrator at the front reception desk. We explained to her our background and asked if we could see the school. She asked us to check with the principal. We talked to the principal for about 15 minutes. She said she would call us on Wednesday or Thursday. They don't allow stray visitors into the school here. In view of the children's safety they don't allow photographing or filming them. You can take a video of the school facilities. Still, if we can take some sort of video, we could show it in India. We'll have to see what the principal will allow.

We walked from the school to the beach park on the sidewalk next to the San Mateo Bridge. We walked a long time. There we got acquainted with a young Telugu woman with a two-year-old daughter. Her name is Anuradha and her child is Anjali. Her husband, Rajesh, works for Oracle. Venkat says that the majority of people who live around here work for Oracle.

*   *   *

Yesterday we started editing and copying old videotapes from the handy cam camcorder onto a VHS tape. We completed one tape. There are four left. I must finish them. Last night, there was a message on the answering machine that Julie had called. She said she would call again tonight.

I talked to Moorty yesterday. He has a fever. It hasn't come down yet. Yet, he sits in front of the computer and works. Moorty is a real *karma yogi*. Nataraj and Mitra must have left yesterday in their car. Apparently they spent some time with Paul Lynn and Michael.

Paul Arms called. He hasn't come here from San Rafael nor have I gone there. We must meet him sometime. We'll see. If we go on the train to downtown, it would be nice, if he could meet us there. Or else, Venkat must take us on a Saturday in his car. He can't take us on workdays. There is only the next weekend remaining to spend time with these two.

Venkat is very amicable. He is quite capable and knowledgeable. I must say Aruna is lucky to have someone like Venkat as her partner.

This is the third day this week that the sun is shining brightly in the sky. But unfortunately, we don't have a car to go around town.

* * *

Just a while ago, I had a call from Julie. UG, Lakshmi and Guha spoke. Hearing Guha's laughter, I said, "I hear a sad undertone in your laughter." True, today, UG is leaving for Palm Springs. I could hear the disappointment in his laughter. Guha is inebriated with UG. UG is saying, "You are a crazy guy," in the background. I said, "May your tribe increase," from my end. Guha laughed again even louder. He said, "Chandrasekhar is asking to include him in the 'goners' list," repeating to UG what I said. UG said, "Aha!" Tonight, by 9:30 pm, UG will be in Palm Springs. He will probably come to LA on the day we will be leaving; that will be exactly next Saturday. Last Saturday, we were with UG in the Holiday Inn. Julie said she will call tonight at 6 pm from New Jersey.

*   *   *

Venkat will leave for his office at 8:45 am. Every morning Aruna walks him to the car. Raghavendra Rao can't keep himself from praising her for such niceties. Venkat doesn't return until the evening. In between, he phones Aruna at least three times.
When I watch Aruna's family and think of UG's grace my eyes become moist.

*   *   *

January 30, Saturday – Day 41

Gandhi Worship Day. Does anyone think of Gandhi today? I doubt it. Is there anyone who thinks of the horrible incident which had occurred 51 years ago? The public sector, TV Doordarshan and All India make a lot of noise, but that's because they are obliged to do that. Other than that, is there the slightest sympathy in anyone's heart for Gandhi and his self-sacrifice?

Chalam's *Sudha*

> Gandhi, who tried to put out hatred
> In restless violent hearts;
> Ravi, who tapped at the doors
> of impenetrable hearts;
> Jesus, who came down pleading,
> Promising the fallen ones to redeem their sins
> With his own blood;
> Mohammad, who chopped off people's
> Heads and peeped into their souls;
>
> Today all these are mere names
> In religions, fights and passions

said Chalam in *Sudha*.

'How true!" I feel. It is to Moorty's credit that he has translated such a poem. He told me the story of Motilal Banarsidass's publishing the book and the troubles they had caused him. Whatever might have happened, the book is brought to the English reader's notice. But how much and to how many? Who thinks of that book even among Telugu speakers? Can people appreciate Chalam's *Sudha* as much as they chow down Yandamuri's novels? Everyone gobbles up Chalam's stories like *Maidanam* and *Brahmaneekam*, but how many can appreciate the nectar of passion in *Sudha*. There are only two or three others who can appreciate the poetry in that book as well as I can. Sundar, Hanumant and now Narayana Moorty. When I first read the book, I was breathless with its poetry. The arrangement of words, the composition of phrases, the music that the words sing – they all work together to beautify the poems. Whenever I think of the poems in *Sudha* my mind becomes lighter.

Chalam's and Dhurjati's Writing Styles

Chalam's translation of Ravindra's *Gitanjali* is also brilliant. The poetry of Dhurjati called *Sri Kalahastiswara Satakam*, written four hundred years ago, is great poetry, too. Its poetic style is unforgettable. Whether he used complex Sanskrit phrases or expressed music in his words with light Telugu vocabulary, Dhurjati's style is unique. What's striking in both these poets is the concise use of words. They use just those words that are necessary and to just the extent needed. Not indulging in showy vocabulary is a sign of great poetry. We can perceive such a characteristic in UG's day-to-day conversations. He uses words in a balanced fashion. Try as you may, you can't find alternate terms for his words. Other words don't have the same sharpness, force and intensity. The arrangement of his words appears to compete with the energy behind them. Everyone knows that he doesn't think about what says before he says it.

*   *   *

Yesterday, I sat with Aruna and copied all the videotapes onto one big tape. Only one tape remains. I wrote "American Sojourn of Father and Mother" on the tape. I don't know if Aruna liked my label or not. She tries to look at her likes and dislikes in the mirror of Venkat's tastes. She wonders if he will like something or not.

    *   *   *

Today the weather is foggy. I don't know if it will be possible to go out or not. We thought of going to San Jose or Santa Cruz. If the weather is like this outside, perhaps it's better to stay home. You can't even hear the noise of the ducks on the water in the stream. They must all be taking shelter in a corner from the cold. Venkat got up and talked about old things for a while and is now phoning to India. Every Saturday and Sunday they both phone to India. Their phone bill altogether runs into more than $200 a month. That means Rs. 9,000. In India we get Rs. 3,000 phone bill per month on an average. Still, if we compare, they are better off.

    *   *   *

January 31, Sunday – Day 42

My mind is like, "Even if you wash a mouse's tail for a whole year...."[3] No matter how much it learns, how much experience it has gathered, indeed, it doesn't quit its worries. As soon as I heard early in the morning today from Archana that they have kept the school application pending, my mind collapsed. How terrible, I thought. Immediately, I had my fears and anxieties; I worried about what I should do next. Who will help? Why

---

[3] "...it won't be straightened...": allusion to a verse of Vemana, a 17th Century Telugu poet and philosopher.

have I been so lazy for so many days? What will happen now? How much longer will the application process take? What will happen to the kids' future? Thoughts spring up like mushrooms in this fashion. Just as I watch, they take over my entire mind and kill my joy that Archana has passed her Inter CA examination.

Last night, Aruna and Venkat got Archana's examination number from her and looked up her results on the Internet. Archana's name is included on the 'passed' list of both groups. We were very happy. We phoned her this morning and she spoke in detail about everything.

That's when she also gave me the school news. My mind has become all chaotic ever since I heard the news. That's how mental states are. My mind has not yet developed equanimity of facing everything bravely or remaining indifferent, saying, "what do I care what happens?" It won't happen before I die. But why should I be anxious that this [*agitation*] should go away? What if I do have a disturbance in my mind? If it makes trouble on its own, why should I bother to try to distract it, console it or cheer it? If it is not this, it will get hold of some other thing and worry about it, plucking its feathers. If it quits one, it picks up another. Even after I have seen its ways for so many years, why hope that it will be straightened one day? But can I survive without hope? I have an attachment to my mind. I try to somehow keep it cheerful and happy forever. What do I care about what happens around me? What are all these people to me? What do I need?

Eddy's Prank

Just a while ago, Eddy and Lulu phoned. Eddy wanted Henry Dennison's number; so he phoned Julie and she gave it to him. When I told him that UG is still in Palm Springs, he felt like teasing UG a little bit. He likes to make practical jokes. He phoned UG. When UG picked up the phone, he assumed a Texan accent and said that he was a 90-year-old millionaire and urged, "I must become enlightened; I must be enlightened before I die." UG couldn't detect it was Eddy by his voice. "You go to whoever is promising you enlightenment. What's the use of asking me? As far as I am concerned there is no such thing as enlightenment," he replied. "I know you are the only one who can give it to me. If you want me to come, I can put on wings and be there instantly in your presence. Please grant me enlightenment," Eddy begged. "I spent all my three-qaurters of a million dollars without a second thought. That's all I can do. I don't have any enlightenment to grant," said UG

"Then you must have one-quarter of a million dollars still with you. What did you do with the rest of the money?" asked Eddy. "What do you mean a quarter million?" asked UG. "The Bible says donate a tenth of your property. So, you must still have some millions left." While Eddy was saying that, Lulu was laughing listening in on another phone. After teasing him for a while, "If I come, you may ask me to donate my millions. I don't like that. So, I'm not coming," Eddy said and hung up. Eddy says UG couldn't identify his voice. Then when Suguna and I called UG a while ago and talked to him, he told us, "I knew that it was Eddy talking to me; I heard Lulu laughing in the background."

Apparently, Shilpa and Sumedha called UG. Sumedha apparently asked UG, "You say that you are not educated. Then how come so many people come to you and ask you questions? Tell us the truth. You are not a drop-out. You're not illiterate, right?" "The reason why you are asking me this question is the same reason why everyone else is asking me questions," UG said. Sumedha hung up the phone. Yesterday, Lakshmi talked on the phone joyfully for half an hour about the time they had spent with UG and about other news.

*   *   *

February 1, Monday – Day 43

Tranquility of Mind

New Month. The second time a new month has started in this country. The counting of the final days has begun. We will leave six days from today. We haven't finished shopping yet. Our days here have been spent in an interesting and jolly fashion. We have had a pleasant time. When we get back to India, the usual rut will begin.

Why should I get the feeling of "what am I doing all these things for?" These fifty years, or at least forty years, I have been struggling in my life; I have been trying to keep my mind in a tranquil state. My whole life has been spent in trying to control myself by turning my mind away from disturbance, anxiety, sadness, worry and such. I have taught my mind not to lose its equanimity; whether I taste the frontiers of joy or delve into the depths of sorrow, I have learned to stand firm. I persuaded it. It listens to everything. But then when it meets a similar situation again, it collapses. Is this what I have learned in so many years? Why doesn't the truth work?

I know that my efforts – my efforts to see that I should never be sad, or that I should never cringe, and that I should always be jumping with joy – are futile. Yet I can't help but make them. Must this go on for the rest of my life? Is life nothing but this constant wrestling with air? There is no end to this except in death.

But what do I know about death? I can't experience 'death'. How can I experience my not being at all? I can't, even in my dreams. If anything comes into the realm of my experience, that has to be something I have imagined. I am only imagining as death the lack which I feel when I watch people around me die. But what do I know about 'death'? Who knows? How does he who says he knows know? It's all a grand deception. No one knows. How can there be something which no one knows? There is no death.

But then is there birth? That's the problem. Was I born? When? How did I know that? Was I there on March 26, 1945? How come I don't remember it? I don't have that information in my head, do I? If my being born was in fact an event, how am I concerned with events that I can't remember? How come my mind thinks about everything else, but lets go of such an important issue without resolving it? If I can't resolve the question of whether I have ever been born, who cares about all these other botheration?

In the very question, "Was I born?" is hidden the answer that I wasn't. There is no birth and there is no death. This is all old hash. Haven't I been listening to this philosophy for eternity? How do you think you are alive without being born, you fool?

How do you know that you are alive? Why do you want to separate your life from yourself and look at it? Do you know every moment that you are breathing? Do you know it in sleep as well? Even when you think you are awake, how much are you conscious that you are alive and that you are breathing in and out? Was that awareness ever constant? Then, where is the certainty, what's the proof that you are alive?
The feelings, thoughts and ideas that go on in you become known. They are reflected in you like in a mirror. If I say that you look at yourself in that reflection and assume that those actions are yours, and are thereby deluded into thinking that you are living as a separate being, how would you respond?
You dumb head, none of the thoughts, anxieties, emotions and feelings are yours. They belong to the image reflected in that mirror. Those are changes occurring in the image on the movie screen. It lives by itself. Without keeping that reflection in your mind, could you still grasp the truth that you are alive? Doesn't whatever you know pertain to that reflection? It's indeed not yours.

This tranquility and this anxiety are, indeed, not yours. Why, then, are you concerned with them?

What's the guarantee that you were born? Don't try to convince me with logic. If I don't accept the basis of your logic, what happens to it? So, first you don't know whether you were born or not. As a matter of fact, you don't even know whether you are alive or dead. You don't know at all for sure the truth that there is no possibility of knowing. These are the truths that are going to enlighten your life. Why do you hanker after truths which you don't know? What a waste of effort! Let it go.

Can you let it go? Can you just be without doing anything? "Without movement or vitality, paralyzed and untainted" – don't just repeat those words. It's not just recalling UG's and Chalam's words. Every place, every moment, every minute, every hour and every day: can you stop and remain in that aloneness where only you exist and nothing else remains? Don't try. You crazy fool! That's the mistake you have been making. You just stop where you are. You can't do it? Just collapse. Struggle like this.

Stopping doesn't mean doing something. It is stopping all doing, as an unwound doll stops all its movements, at any minute and any moment. This is the secret of Vedanta and the essence of all religions and all paths. There is nothing else. Whether you realize or not that there is nothing else, the truth won't stop. It says hello to everyone on the way and moves on. In the meantime, you stop. You stop wherever you are.

*   *   *

Outside, the young sun is crawling upward brilliantly in the sky. He is brightening the earth with white light. The sun's rays, reflected on the ripples, are spread along the waters in back of the house. You can hear the cries of the ducks from a distance. There is not much noise anywhere around although it's past 8:00 am. I am trying to turn my mind away from my philosophical reflections.

*   *   *

Yesterday we went to the Exploratorium science exhibition. It's near the Golden Gate bridge. The admission is $9 a head. There are nice exhibits of physics experiments in light, sound and magnetism. Completing the tour took about four hours. By the time we finished shopping at K-Mart and returned home it was 8:00 pm.

*   *   *

February 2, Tuesday – Day 44

The Struggle

It's no wonder that Tyagaraja lamented once: "No matter how much you have learned or experienced ..." That's the nature of the mind. Wherever it is, it gets stuck there. I wonder where it got all these past impressions from; it doesn't let go of them so easily. Even when it knows that they afflict it, it still hangs on to them. "O my mind, how can I bear this, please listen to my request...." Tyagaraja pleads plaintively, poor fellow! He despairs, saying, "If I can't hold my mind steady, what good is it to have or achieve anything?" No matter how much he struggled, it doesn't look like Tyagaraja himself had his mind under control. He was wailing like this all his life. Poor fellow, did his mind cease to be finally? Did only 'he' remain while his existence was gone? Who knows? Suppose that Rama, to whom he was so devoted, had appeared to him, so what? Then his mind would get tangled in Rama. Tyagaraja's agony occurred whenever his mind strayed from the thought of Rama and moved on to something else. Why? He had the crazy desire that he should have only that one thing and not anything else. Aren't we all doing the same thing – struggling with the same craziness?

Every living thing is eager always to live happily and not have a single moment of pain. How many struggles we go through to keep these shadows of happiness permanent! If we can't hold on to happiness in this moment, it seems to move to a distance, egging us on to come towards it. With the hope that we will be able to find it in the future, we agonize day and night, unable to stay in one place – this is life. The moment we become weary, our body is in ruins and we collapse, incapacitated and unable to move, Then It [*death*] takes us into its arms, and then it's too late. The mind that has agonized so much, this individuality, subsides, becomes dissolved and goes into a long sleep. Perhaps it will wake up again, sometime, some place. Then it will start all over from the beginning. The old memories warn from a distance. But the past impressions drag us on forcefully. That's all. That's all that remains in the final analysis.

Meanwhile, how many deceptions, how many illusions, how many fabrications, how much arrogance that everything is due to my greatness! How we fall, get hurt and get bumps on our foreheads! No matter how many times the head gets bumped, it never learns. It never drops its foolish desire for capturing happiness in its grip permanently. Once in a while, a great soul like UG comes down and bangs on our heads. A fellow like me keeps striving futilely for that happiness in the midst of so much pain. This fellow can't just be. He may become unconscious with the hammer strokes that fall on his head; nevertheless when he regains consciousness he will resume his struggle as usual.

Is it in my power to keep quiet? Isn't keeping quiet another trick to sustain my happiness? The logical mind is again raising these thoughts. If I say, "I should keep quiet," that too is another kind of movement which is opposed to the original movement. In its background there is greed prancing around which whispers that if we stay quiet, then we can gain permanent happiness. In that case, how could it be called "being quiet"? What's the difference between that and running around? Whatever I try to do, I am still in bondage. In the final analysis, running around and being quiet are one and the same.

Otherwise, it may be somewhat better to shut up and sit quietly. "What's better?" asks my logic. Compared to what is it better? Does being quiet mean falling asleep? If I can spend the rest of my life in sleep, what more do I want? There won't be any of these worries in sleep. But there will be dreams. I will be woken up from my sleep. No use. None of these will work.

Whether you like it or not, to stop making an effort is not in your hands. The effort will keep on going as long as you breathe. You can't but both suffer and enjoy because of it. If you don't try to escape from it, pain is not so painful. It's not that it will go away completely, but it won't have that intensity. If the struggle to sustain happiness is diminished, then the intensity of happiness it delivers is also diminished. It's wise to live reducing the intensity of both as much as possible. Neither will go away completely, no matter how great a person is. But you are not really concerned about anyone else. As far as you are concerned, that's the way. This balancing game is nothing new to you. Don't complain, saying, "After all this, am I not starting all over?" You haven't moved one step forward!

* * *

Last night we had dinner at Deepak and Renu's home. After coming home, we went to bed after I copied the data from the floppy I had into the computer. Venkat said he would make a CD out of it in his office. Moorty also had said that would be better. I called Sajid and asked him to send the TIFF file again. He said he will.

* * *

February 3, Wednesday – Day 45

During the night I woke up a couple of times and checked the clock - it was 1:00 am and then 4:00 am, so I went back to bed and finally got up around 7 am. I have the same routine everyday: By 7:30 am, I finish the morning rituals and sit at the table to write.

Yesterday, we went to John's home. We have been friends for 25 years. Back then, when UG lived on West Anjaneya Street, Volker, John, Lynn and I lived there also. None of us were married at that time. We used to cook together. After so many years, John and I have both grown older; we have families, children, and their problems.

*   *   *

At John's home, John and I made *masur dahl*. On the spur of the moment, we went to a shop and bought some tomatoes and cucumbers. He had bought cilantro before. He had already brought mustard seeds, cumin seeds, asafetida and ghee. Apparently, he cooks rice and *dahl* like this occasionally. With Suguna's help we finished cooking basmati rice and *dahl*, while John and I remembered the old days. I was happy to see John being jolly. How much of those days he remembers!

*   *   *

Coming back from his office, Venkat arrived at John's at 6:30 pm. After dinner, we all left for home at 8:30 pm. We bought the things we needed in K-Mart and Target and got home by 10:00 pm.

*   *   *

Today also it has been nice and sunny. I now worry about how the weather will be tomorrow. This is the sickness of the mind.

It doesn't remain in the present moment. It always thinks about the past or about tomorrow. Its attention is always on what's going to happen; and it also thinks about what has already happened. It cannot stay on what is currently happening. What's the use writing like this so many times?

The white sun is coming through the Venetian blinds, spreading on the table and moving on the wall. The waters are still in the canal behind the house. There is no noise of the ducks. If I push open the pane on the glass window, there is a cold breeze. The air outside hasn't warmed up yet. The sun's rays are slanted even at noon. That's why the sun is not very hot. Even after walking in the sun, it feels cold when you get in the shade. Still, in wintertime, this Bay Area is like heaven compared to other places.

* * *

February 4, Thursday – Day 46

I think that UG will perhaps come to India even this month, maybe because of Malladis' pleadings, or for some other reason. Yesterday, he said he will go to Australia for a week and then come to India.

On the one hand, I am happy that UG is coming now; on the other hand, I am worried that the school business will take a back seat. Why do I worry about it? Is the school more important than UG? Why does my mind get involved like this?

When will I open my eyes? What do I really want? As long as UG is there, what does it matter if the school is still there or it closes? Business? Why do I pay attention to the school business? Whatever will happen will happen. Why worry about things before they happen? Who has been taking care of them when I am not there? Has it not been working out? It will work out even if I don't do anything about it. Why worry? Will my anxiety remove the obstacles in the way? Isn't UG coming to set everything right? It can't be a sin to chop this mind to its roots.

*   *   *

I have time to write for one more day, i.e., tomorrow. I think we will be in LA by this time the day after tomorrow. I must phone UG and tell him. How is UG going to come there? He has to start early in the morning in the cold weather, in order to see us off. I don't know what he will do.

*   *   *

Return Trip

February 5, Friday – Day 47

It's all over. This is our last day in the Bay area. Tomorrow by this time we will be on a plane flying to LA. I have been amazed at how fast the days have passed, and we have just now adjusted ourselves to this place. Today also it's nice and sunny. The sun looks a like red globe in the sky. The sunrise here is not like in India. The sun is bright here.

Julie called while I was still washing. Since we are leaving tomorrow, she called to say goodbye. She hopes to come to India with UG. Doesn't he know that? He knows everything. When the time comes, he grants to each what he or she needs.

Some good fortune from our past lives is standing by our side and filling our lives with joy in the form of UG. How many people have this opportunity to know UG? How many people have the unique opportunity of spending even a few moments with him? I cannot be grateful enough to him for sponsoring for so many years a guy like me who is an idiot, a useless fellow, someone who didn't have any talent in any area, one who is totally worthless in looks or riches, and for rekindling the light of my life which was about to be extinguished and making a place for me amongst people.

*   *   *

Last night, Aruna and Venkat took us to K-Mart. There, in the photo studio, we had portraits and group photos taken. Venkat also gave me prints of the photos taken with his parents. The photos cost $40. If I translate that into Indian currency, it would be Rs. 2,000. You feel like screaming, "My God!" All right, I must quit. Ever since I sat down to write this, I have been getting phone calls. Aruna and Suguna are sitting across the table. Suguna says, "I am sad that I have to leave now." Aruna answers, "Stay here, then." That's how it goes!

*   *   *

I took my shower, ate Raisin Bran with milk and phoned UG. He says he is leaving for Australia on the 20th. He will come to India two weeks later. Mahesh told him that if he doesn't come to India he will pay him Rs. 50,000. UG said he will think about it if he offered the money in dollars. In any case, he is not going to China. Perhaps he will stay with the Malladis in Madras for some time. At this time Krishnamurti needs some direction from UG.

UG is not coming to LA tomorrow. He wouldn't be able to spend even an hour or half-and-a-half with us, if he came. That's why he must have given up the idea. Besides, to be in LA on time, he must leave Palm Springs early in the morning in the cold. And then he must go back. In some ways, it's better for UG not to come. It won't be a problem for us. We are going to see him in India again in another month. Meanwhile, I must take care of many things there.

The time is 10:40 am. It feels like time is moving at a snail's pace. Ramesh Ganerwal said he will call again. I don't know when that 'again' is. Moorty talked on the phone. Soon today I must close this diary and open it again in Kuala Lumpur, or else, finally, when I get to India. "Pleasant journey and safe landing," said UG on the phone, using JK's phrases.

Yesterday Aruna and I recorded on the video the environs of Aruna's apartment and the apartment complex and the facilities in it and transferred the recording onto a tape. The sun has become suddenly intense. It's very pleasant as long as it is sunny like this.

Ramesh phoned a while ago. Apparently he is trying to go to India in March. He says Raj got involved in many complications in Bombay. Raj tried to bring the money he got from selling his factory into this country. Perhaps the authorities got wind of it. These complications are bound to happen. That's why I asked him to talk to UG and put the matter into his hands. He didn't listen to me. Who can help Raj better than UG? Mahesh has put everything into UG's hands and has indeed remained worriless.

What more does one want? But you must trust him. The feelings of 'I' and 'mine' must end. When UG tries to make them cease, you must submit yourself. I am telling this to myself. I must listen to UG; I must submit myself to him. I must let him bang me on my head. I must accept his abuse. The 'I' must be suppressed. Whatever I do, the pride of 'I' and 'mine' must disappear. This is my meditation. This is my *sadhana*. I have Julie and Guha as ideals in front of me.

I wonder if UG will let Julie come to India. If he lets her, she will grow wings and fly there.

*   *   *

February 8, Monday (Kuala Lumpur)

Yesterday morning, that is, on February 6, we left for LAX on United Air. It was still Saturday in San Francisco. The air travel is 20 hours long from LAX to Kuala Lumpur. We arrived here early in the morning at 1:30 am. On the way, when we got to the Tokyo airport, it was Sunday 6 pm. It was sunny the whole time we were flying in the air. It never got dark. I don't know how Saturday night has disappeared into the dark. I don't know when it has become Sunday morning. This is all a mystery. It's Monday here today and almost 4 o'clock in the afternoon. Right now, it's Sunday 12 midnight in San Francisco. They must all be sleeping there. Earlier, we called Aruna on the phone to talk to her and tell her that we arrived here.

We are guests in the Renaissance Palm Gardens Hotel. For this one day, a Malay taxi driver called Deno took us around in his taxi, showing us all the important places and helping us shop. He charged $30 for it. Compared to American costs, that was cheap.

By the time we returned to the room today it was 4 o'clock. Deno showed us many things today. The 421-meter-high tower, Menara KL, looked great.

* * *

February 9, Tuesday, Madras Airport

Last night, we left from Kuala Lumpur at 10 pm on flight MH180 for Madras. By the time we arrived here it was 11:15 pm. We finished getting the baggage and going through immigration and customs by 12:45 am. We confirmed our tickets for Bangalore on Jet Airways and collapsed on the cushion seats arranged around a post in the waiting room. Now it's 4 o'clock in the morning. I phoned Archana last night and also Aruna. Aruna had fever and cough yesterday. She must have been very tired, poor thing. I don't know if Archana can come to the airport. She has to work today. I could breathe the Indian air after so many days. The body felt happy sitting on the Indian toilet in Madras. All last night I was dozing on and off sitting in front of the trolley on which we had placed all our baggage. Suguna found a convenient place where she could lie down. She said she couldn't sleep. I just finished washing and shaving and sat down refreshed, to write in this diary.

The whole airport looks empty. There are a few people here and there who have to catch early morning flights like us. I must have some coffee. Then I will be revived. I have been sitting here reading the *Time* magazine. I didn't like the food on the Madras flight. I felt very weak. On top of it, I am worrying about tomorrow. Thoughts about the things I have to do are swarming like bees. My mind has been quite upset for a little while and now it has settled down. This whole ordeal will come to a close when we get home in a taxi after taking the 6:45 am flight to Bangalore in Jet Airways and getting off there at 8:00 am. It would be nice if Archana could come to the airport. Maybe she will go to her office, instead.

* * *

After Getting Back to the Nest

February 10, Wednesday (Bangalore)

I woke up before 5 am, but got up at 5. Now it's 5:30. Yesterday we arrived at home at 8:30 in the morning. It only took half-an-hour to get out of the airport. Archana hugged me in the airport. I was worried she might break into tears. Sai came in a taxi. All our bags reached home safely.

I will stop here.

The End

Chandrasekhar and Nataraj in Palm springs

Chandrasekhar and Suguna with Mahesh Bhatt in Palm springs

Chandrasekhar, Suguna, Guha and Family with UG in Palmsprings

Guha and Chandrasekhar in Palmsprings

Suguna, Chandrasekhar and John Allen at Stanford

UG and Chandrasekhar in Palm Springs

UG in Palm springs

UG and Aruna in Palm springs

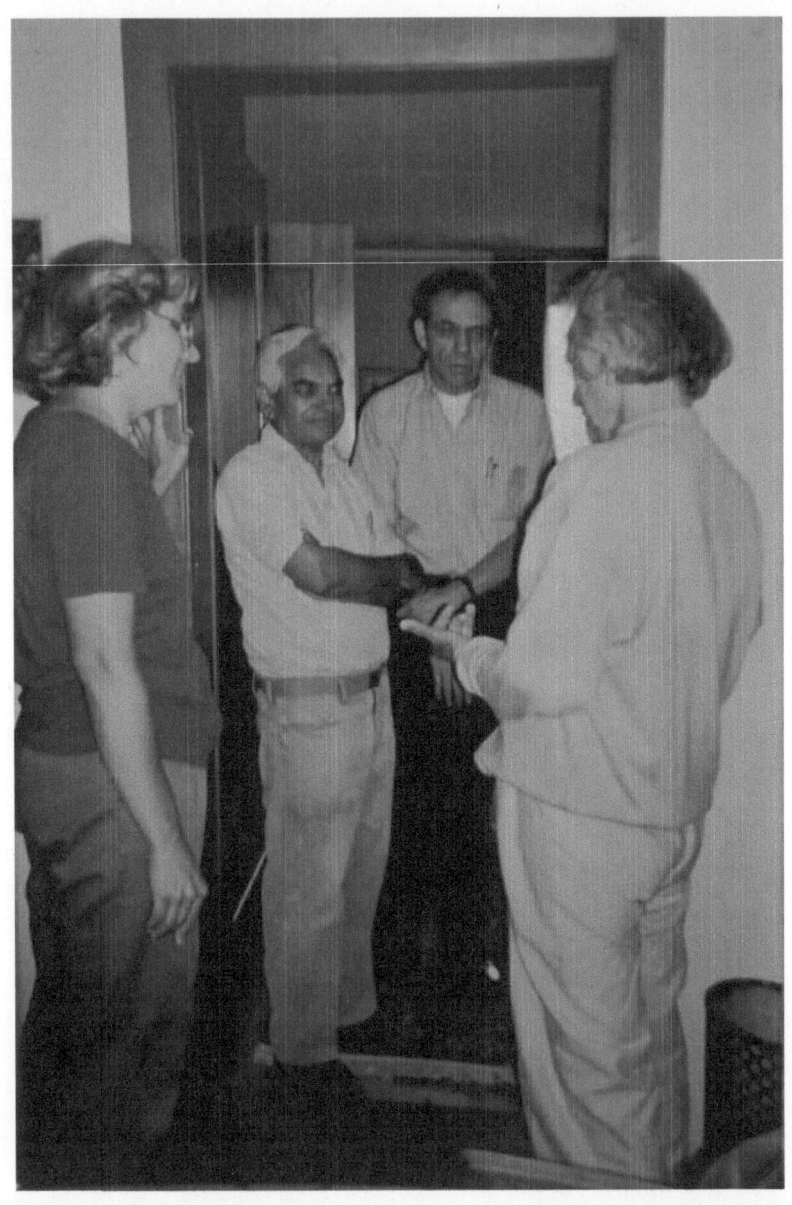

UG with Moorty, Wendy and Larry in Palm Springs

Part II

Gstaad Diary

1999

Switzerland – July 1999

"Since Shyamalamma has returned, you two can now proceed," so directs UG herding us to Switzerland. We haven't yet applied for the visas. Julie's letter of 'guarantee' hasn't arrived yet. UG says that we should leave for Bombay as soon as we receive the letter. What's UG's reason for asking us to go Gstaad? Narayana Moorty is there right now; also there are Guha and his family. UG has been working for quite a while at getting all of us together to foster a sense of belonging among us all. He got us to travel to Palm Springs the same way six months ago. Now he is bringing us to Switzerland at the expense of one lakh rupees. Why? What for? I can't figure it out. Sitting on the toilet seat I recalled the song:

> When a curly-horned ram
> Charges a mountain
> Does the mountain get hurt or will it be the ram?
> Tell me, O God, Samba Siva; open my eyes, Samba
Siva.

That's how it is trying to argue with UG. It's useless to contradict him. I tell myself, OK, we'll do as you wish.... I wonder how Bharati and Usha are doing. I don't know if Usha's daughter-in-law is still in the country or has gone to the US. I can only find out through Rajasekhar.

July 20, 1999 (Tuesday)

Preparations are under way to travel to Switzerland. Julie's letter has arrived yesterday at noon. By then I had already finished negotiating with Travel Air and booked the tickets. We leave for Bombay on the 25th morning. We leave at 12:30 am, and fly via Paris and arrive in Zurich at 9 am on the 27th morning. After that, we are in UG's hands. He says, "I am not spending all this money for you just to have fun. Moorty is leaving on August 10. There are things to be done before then." What needs to be done?

I can't think of what I should take with me. I have this book which I wrote long ago and which has never seen the light of day. It would be great to put all the videotapes on CD's but that requires selecting videos which are of good quality. It takes an estimated thousand rupees to transfer an hour's video onto a CD. After Raj Mehta transferred the photos onto a CD, I got the idea that it's best to preserve the videos too on CD's as well.

But I don't know for what purpose UG is asking us to come so urgently. If I go, the school business and finance business will take a back seat here. Before I go, I must see everyone I need to see. I must make the necessary purchases. I will stay in Bombay for a day. I may get to see Mahesh there.

July 21, 1999 (Wednesday)

Four days left for departure. I am worried that I have to leave home and travel so far. O God, why are you dragging me there rather than leaving me to my own devices in this corner here? What is it that I can do there? What am I going to gain? To visit Switzerland was my great goal 20 years ago. My idea then was to visit that country, sit on the bench on which UG had sat, and enjoy watching the seven hills of Saanen and the natural beauty of its seven valleys. I don't have any such ambition now. UG has taken us there three times before. The last time, we were there for 42 days. This time too UG insists that we must stay there for six weeks, but it doesn't seem feasible. We must return before the end of August. That's what Julie's letter states as well.

I worry thinking about the problems at the school, as if everything there depends on me. Why must I get entangled in every matter and get upset? It seems like an inborn trait of mine; just as UG says, "Misery is your lot." I am not able to stay in this moment, but rot in the worry about tomorrow. This seems inevitable, no matter how much I try otherwise. No matter how much I try to acquire the faith that whatever must happen will happen, that always fades into the background as my eyes are veiled once again by *maya*. That's what '*maya*' and '*moha*' mean. The mind knows what is real. It knows at an intellectual level that what I think and contemplate – all of it – is a concoction. But I don't see it. It doesn't come into the field of my experience. That's what I wail about: the things that I leave unfinished, the things I still have to do – they all clutter my mind like flies as soon as I wake up. Yet by the time I go to bed in the night, not even half of them will be accomplished. The brain keeps fabricating things to do... things to do... Why can't it stop just for a moment? It won't listen.

* * *

Major and I bought a jerkin for me in Jayanagar. Somehow, my enthusiasm is not kindled. On top of it, UG has been phoning and dampening my enthusiasm. What is this mess?

What do I want? What have I achieved through all this mingling with UG? What's left in life except moaning? When Nagamani says "You are lucky that you can get near UG," I smile to myself. What luck, to whom? What's all this? Am I lucky to be able to go to Switzerland? Am I not lucky to have the opportunity to spend a month in UG's presence? How many people have such luck? All right, what will I gain by that? What change has occurred in me? None. Will there be change when I die? In whom? Who will remain?

Why am I thinking now of death? I merely think that I am alive, but do I know that? If these words come out of me, they sound strange even to me. Why all this moroseness? Is it because of the weather outside? My mind does not rest even for the brief moment of my drinking coffee.

I guess I appear to be in a jolly mood to others. Watching Chalam, I used to think similarly of him. How I used to envy him sitting in a chair in front of Arunachala[4], with a jasmine garland around his neck, looking into himself with half-closed eyes! When I remarked, "How blissful you look, Dad!" he would answer, "What do you know about all the storms that are arising in me?" I didn't want to believe what he said. Now I understand somewhat.

Not all that appears on the outside is real. There is no rule that the agitation in the mind should be visible in one's facial expressions. One might show just the opposite expressions.

---

[4] The mountain in Tiruvannamalai.

Chalam might not have been sporting about in some heavenly region or might not have been in the midst of a rapturous state. The very idea of a rapturous state is a big lie in the first place. The remorse that trusting such a thing I have falsified my whole life haunts my miserable being. There are no states of ecstasy. What's here is nothing except this restlessness, the anxiety, the regret and the sadness. If I could remain with this realization, the next moment all these other feelings would vanish. In their place there would be quietness, restfulness and peace of mind. But then the struggle would begin to maintain these states.

*   *   *

July 22, 1999 (Thursday)

Writing for half an hour a day is not only a great pastime but is also a way to preserve my sanity. My mind would have gone crazy but for this writing and I would have been mad long ago.

A while ago Aruna called from California. She said that she and her husband are thinking of coming to India in the third week of August. He could only get leave from work at that time. She asked me to return [to India] from Switzerland by that time. "If you are not there, why should we go all the way to India?" UG asked us to get a visa for six weeks; he wants to keep us there for as long as possible. If we tell him that we will only be there for three or four weeks, what might he say? Aruna is worried: "No one seems to be excited about our visiting India," she says. She couldn't figure out why we have arranged this trip all of a sudden. She would like us to be here when she comes. When I suggested, "Why don't you wait till we come back; then you can come to India in the last week of August?" she became angry. Maybe they have already booked their tickets. I must talk to Venkat and find out the specifics.

*　　　　　　*
*

No one understands how much the school problems are bothering me. I must somehow straighten out Ranganadha Rao. I am worried about his ways. I must talk to him. I must talk to all the teachers. All these thoughts sting my mind but fly away before they are carried into action.

*　　　　　*　　　　　*

July 23, 1999 (Friday)

The Swiss visa I have been waiting for has arrived in time. They granted a 35-day visit. That means five weeks. We can stay till August 31. It's surprising that we could get a visa directly through the travel agent without Mahesh's intervention. When I called UG last evening to tell him that we have the Swiss visa, he said, "Suguna is rich, what more do they want?" I really think we got the visa only because we mentioned UG's name in the letter. Normally, they say we need police clearance papers. It's strange that they gave the visa easily without any such complications. We must now make the preparations to travel at once. Yesterday evening, I related the school problems to Venkata Chalapathi and asked him to visit the school in my absence. I asked Guravayya also to do the same.

*   *   *

July 24, 1999 (Saturday)

Tomorrow is the day of departure. All these days I haven't been considering the fact that we will be traveling that far. I won't be here, in these surroundings, for another month. I won't see these people. I'll be in a strange land among strange faces.

I am asking myself, "What will you be when you leave this world?" All of a sudden, I won't have any consciousness. All the things that these eyes are used to seeing, the sky, the trees, the glory of sunrise and sunset, the stars – none of them will be there. There will be no music or noises. Will it be an empty blissfulness? Will it be a state of nothing where there is everything? How can I imagine such a state? I won't even be there. "You can't preside over your own death," says UG. The 'I' must go first. The 'I' must go without a trace. Only then there is death.

If I myself am not there, who cares about this world? Who cares about the school problems, about these books, the tapes, giving hospitality, being nice to people, having affections, tears, spites and harassment? I won't be there, right? "How will it be on the first day when I am not around? How will the sun rise without me being around?" contemplated Papa Chalam. Even after Chalam has gone down, the sun continued to rise. No matter who dies or who is born, the rains keep raining, the sky will still shine, and the wind will still blow. There will be no change in the order of seasons. There won't be any change in the ways of nature in this vast universe. That's true even if I die tomorrow. So, what do I care when I am not going to be there? What do I care which party comes into power in what country? What do I care who becomes rich and who poor, what country is destroyed, or whether the whole world goes topsy-turvy? There won't be any of these things which I am thinking of now.

Would I know that I don't exist? How would I know? Would there be some way of knowing that I don't exist just as I know now that I do exist? I must first unravel this mystery. Is it really true that I exist? Do I truly exist? Where am I? I am thinking that I exist. As these letters are transferred to the paper, I read them and understand them. I know their meaning. I can feel the pain in my back and the pain in my ankle from sitting cross-legged. There is a ringing sound in my ears. The taste of the coffee made by Suguna is reaching my lips. Then it goes on the tongue for a moment. Then it's a mere memory. Isn't this true with any experience? It lasts only so long as we experience it; the next moment it's a mere memory. Recalling that experience and digging the memories, I keep fabricating the illusion that I am alive.

These fears, anxieties, emotions and passions – they all come from those memories. I don't understand how I remember. All these are basic, fundamental problems in my mind. I live writhing like a mouse in boiling gruel, not knowing about any of these, cloaking myself with the illusion that I am alive. How low to live like this, estranged from truth and reality! How long does this awareness last? Only for a moment, just as long as I write this. The next moment, I forget.

In Switzerland with UG

July 28 (Wednesday)

Exactly a day has passed in Gstaad. The Air France plane which had been scheduled to leave at 12:30 am left at 7:30 am instead and arrived an hour late in Paris, at Charles de Gaulle airport. The plane for Zurich had already left. Just as we got off the plane we were told that there was no other flight till 10:30 am. I sent a message to UG through the airline staff that we would be arriving late in Zurich, so that he won't be waiting for us there. They gave us free snacks at the Paris airport. It was 11:30 am when our plane landed in the Zurich airport. And by the time we got our baggage and got out of the airport it was 12:30 pm. The immigration check was easy. The police official asked, "What's your business in Switzerland?" "To spend time with UG Krishnamurti," I answered. "I see, to see UG," said the officer as if he was familiar with him. "When are you returning?" – the second question. "In four weeks," I said. Without another word he stamped the passport and said goodbye.

At the gate, Narayana Moorty, UG and Paul Sempé received us. UG looked like he had lost some weight. Paul Sempé brought his old Citroën car. In another 15 minutes we started on our journey to Gstaad. The car travel lasted about an hour and a half. It was 3 pm by the time we passed Gruyere and entered Berner Oberland. I remember the outskirts of Gstaad pretty well. At the beginning of the town, there is a big tent. It has been put up for a circus. Now they have completed the bypass road. They finished building the tunnel in 1996. It was exactly that year that we came here the last time. The city council got the tunnel built as part of the bypass road so that cars wouldn't have to go through the town. They created this facility because cars and buses on the main street were inconveniencing pedestrians. It's very nice now. There is no vehicle traffic on the main street. One can walk about freely. The place is busy with a variety of shops and restaurants. Yesterday afternoon, Moorty, Paul Sempé and I went for a walk for an hour and a half.

Paul Sempé

I got better acquainted with Sempé this time. Even the last time it was he who had driven us both to Gstaad from Zurich. He has known UG for 32 years. His place is near Gottfried's place in southern France near Sanary-sur-Mer. In those days UG used to go to the South of France every year and spend some time with Gottfried. Paul Sempé used to be a captain; he piloted tugboats. Now he is 77 years old. He looks pretty healthy. He still drives a cheap car. Whenever there is an occasion, UG makes fun of his driving. Even now, sitting in the front seat, he has to tell Sempé which way to turn and where to turn. UG has been giving him directions all the way from Zurich.

Sempé comes to Gstaad every summer to spend at least a week with UG. The rest of the time he is in his own world. He lives in a house in a desolate forest inhabited by wild animals. There is no electricity in the house. He uses a generator. He even has a computer. Books are his companions. He spends his time alone. His wife calls him when she needs him; then he goes to see her. He goes to his daughter's place if he feels like spending time with his granddaughter. Or else, he lives in the forest. I feel that he and Major have similar minds. Moorty told me that his wife is very beautiful. She too is older than 70 years. Sempé likes Moorty very much. He is thinking of visiting him in the US. He says a lot of good has happened to him thanks to his friendship with UG. For instance, he is freed from 'the madness of spirituality'. Once has realized that there is nothing permanent, worldly desires have lost their grip on him. He doesn't care if he doesn't realize the non-dual state that UG talks about.

It's now 9:30 am, which means 1:00 pm. in India. I'm getting very sleepy. That's enough. I'll continue tomorrow.

*   *   *

July 29, 1999 (Thursday)

Gstaad – Ludi Haus

Morning 6 am here; in India it's 9:30 am. There are no sounds around. Ours is a big room on the second floor. The houses here are all made of wood. Each of the beams in them would weigh some tons. The cornices on the roof reach out about 10 feet beyond the walls. Yesterday, I couldn't go for a walk because of the rain. Instead, Moorty and I went around the house about ten times. Not a drop of rain fell on us. The

cornice is so wide that it's like someone is holding a big
umbrella over our heads. That's what's special about these
roofs. These houses are called chalets. In this chalet, on the
first floor, there are shops and offices. UG's apartment is on
the second floor. There are other guest apartments. On the
third floor there are other guests besides us and Mrs. Lakshmi.
There are five or six apartments on each floor. Ludi Haus is a
house of four floors. It's very convenient. The living room in
UG's apartment is very big. There are many sofas, chairs and
tables. Everyone gathers there everyday. All day long, UG
doesn't move from where he sits; he sits there and keeps talking
from morning till evening. At the moment there are some
Germans in the room ~ Nataraj, Manju and his girlfriend and
others. Julie is living somewhere else. Tomorrow, Larry
Morris, Susan and Claire are leaving. Then Julie will move into
their apartment.

*   *

*

If we look outside from the window of the room, we see a high
mountain like Arunachala. There are clouds around its peak.
Trees cover the whole mountain like a blanket so that not a
single bare rock can be seen. From here you can see Chalet
Sunbeam where UG spent summers for 25 years. Across the
street, there are the tennis courts where the Swiss Open takes
place. When the tennis tournament begins, all the apartments
in this building are filled. In winter, the streets in Gstaad will
all be abuzz with ski offficianados. The local people's main
occupation here is business. No one excels more than the
Swiss in doing different sorts of business. There is a price for
every little thing. Tourists have to pay two francs a day to the

Swiss government to breathe the air here and roam about in these streets. The roads here are built with cobblestones laid in several designs – squares, semicircles and circles. In every city in Europe you can see this arrangement of cobblestones laid evenly with cement between them. How nice the roads look with these cobblestones! The roads remain intact for centuries; they are not broken even in rains or floods.

Behind the Ludi Haus there is a post office and a train station. You don't hear much noise from the trains. The trains run regularly. You hear their noise as if they are coming from a distance, not just from a few yards away. You don't hear the noise of vehicles honking or the busy sounds of men.

*   *   *

Suguna just handed me a hot cup of Swiss coffee made with cow's milk. It tastes great. Just a cup of it will do. The taste lingers on the tongue for hours. Yesterday afternoon, I had coffee with Chandrahas in Rialto.

July 30, 1999 (Friday)

5:30 am. Through the window you can see the silhouette of the mountain in the fog. Any time you look at it you have the illusion that it's about to walk into the room. Far away you hear the sound of a mountain train coming into town. Its whistle sounds like a bird's cry. But for that, it's silent everywhere. You can't believe that thousands of people live in this remote village in the valley of these mountains. Yesterday, while walking along the Saanen River, Moorty and I saw the place where JK used to give his talks. They used to erect a huge tent in which Krishnamurti gave talks every day. In those days you saw Krishnamurti people wherever you went. Now young people are playing soccer in that field. It was 3:00 pm in the afternoon when we took our walk and the sun felt very pleasant. All around you could see Christmas-tree-like pine trees. They grow tall, straight and in clusters on the mountains. Where you don't see trees, you notice green meadows spread out. But there is no dust or gravel. In winter, however, everything is covered with snow. All the paths on the mountains are filled with snow. Apparently, it's less cold when it snows. Moorty says that when it stops snowing it gets colder.

*   *   *

Chandrahas

What happened a couple of days ago concerns Chandrahas. When did I see him last? I saw him in Bangalore about five or six years ago. He was in Yercaud for a few days. Then he suddenly disappeared. A few months ago he phoned from Switzerland. How did he come here? To someone who observes his manner, he doesn't seem to be of a stable mind. But he is very intelligent. He comes from Bhopal in Madhya Pradesh. He had been spiritually inclined ever since he was a child. Sri Ramakrishna and Vivekananda were his idols. Mentally he is not fully developed and he has a mysterious interior. He is very emotional and passionate – having the same intense passions which possess every young person, creating havoc but then dissipating. He distanced himself from

RSS[5] for some time, escaping their hold, and landed in the South. He found shelter in Arunachala. He heard about UG while he was there and came to Yercaud in 1993. He was friends with a German girl. Chandrahas loves to drink. He is handsome. He looked quite attractive in those days. After he came here Swiss girls sucked him dry. He used to dream about going to Germany. I can't remember what happened after that. Once he came to see UG when he was staying in the Malladi's guest house in Madras. He didn't have a penny on him then. UG gave him a hundred rupees. From that moment on, his lifestyle has improved.

In 1996, he apparently tried to come to our place in Bangalore at the time of the housewarming. Major didn't allow it as he didn't want to bring a nuisance into our home at that time. Chandrahas was angry with Major for not taking him to our house in his car. Now, when tasting the pudding and the milk cake that Suguna and Lakshmi made, he said that he should have eaten these things at our housewarming time. He also said he came to Gstaad especially to see us.

His return trip is leaving from Geneva today. He is going back to Bombay. He has been in this country for seven months. His fortunes have changed. He guessed that UG might be in Gstaad and so he came here. He didn't know where UG lived. He didn't have his phone number. He is an absentminded fellow. He can't take care of his own personal belongings. He leaves them wherever he goes and forgets them. Two days ago, he left his purse containing his passport, ticket and money in a

---

[5] Rashtriya Swayam Sevak Sangh – a Hindu paramilitary organization.

shop and remembered them in the train station while chatting with me. After the train arrived, he looked for his purse, and then, not finding it, he ran to UG's house looking for it. It wasn't there. Then he went to the shop and asked for it there. They returned it to him. A little while later, he remembered his umbrella. He ran back again in the rain to UG's place and retrieved his lost umbrella from there. At last, he got on the train that day around 5 pm. Today he will first go to Montreau, and from there to Geneva.

How did he come to know that UG would be in this place? Something funny happened. While he was sitting in the train station wondering where UG might be and how he could meet him, another person came, sat on the bench and apparently started muttering to himself, "UG, UG." That man had just quarreled with UG and left in anger saying, "I'll never see your face again, I won't step in this place once more!" When Chandrahas asked him about UG, he relented and took Chandrahas over to UG's place. But for that man, Chandrahas wouldn't have been able to meet UG. He said, "Such things always happen to me coincidentally, without my will. I came to this town to meet UG. I was determined to see UG. It's all due to UG's kindness."

He took a 100 franc bill, placed it in front of UG, and said, "UG, you have given me the ability to return 100 francs to you for the 100 rupees you had given me before," laughing loudly. He then took several more hundred franc bills and piled them in front of UG. The day before yesterday it was Guru *Purnima* (full moon day). Chandrahas was overjoyed that just on the Guru *Purnima* day he had the opportunity to offer 'a gift to the

Guru' (*guru dakshina*). UG touched the money and said, "I don't need this; *you* do. Keep it," and gave the money back to him. Chandrahas replied, "I piled all that money in front of you with the hope that you would touch it. Now that you have, it will multiply a thousand-fold," and gladly stuffed the money back into his pocket.

Chandrahas encountered a lot of hardships in Switzerland. He made friends with some girls and got into trouble. He picked quarrels with his girlfriend's parents and doctors over their admitting her to a lunatic asylum. "None of you can do anything to me. There is nothing you can do to throw me out of this country," he challenged them. He keeps going on a tirade against the doctors in this country. He fights with the psychiatrists. Watching his behavior, they too got scared of him. I wondered how they could tolerate him for seven months in this country. I think the girls get romantically attracted to him. Apparently, he used to charge 150 francs per hour for his treatment. What treatment! They only want one thing. He enchanted them with his good looks and made a lot of money. But the man has gotten quite emaciated. He has grown a thick beard. He says, "The youth of this generation is becoming a bane to this country."

*   *   *

July 31, 1999 (Saturday)

It's only a quarter till six in the morning. It's all silent outside this house, and it's silent inside. However, the factories in my head have been working tirelessly, out of control. I can't stand their raucousness. I can't tell the difference between waking and sleeping. The wheels keep turning constantly. Hammer strokes. Incoherent thoughts. This pen is drying up; I mustn't buy this sort of pen again.

Is this Switzerland where I am? Am I in that Switzerland whose air rich people and people of status pine to breathe, the beauty of whose mountains people all over the world race with each other to worship, a country whose excellence is not equaled even by affluent countries – am I in that Switzerland? What a wonder! I am not worth a penny, yet how is it that I roam the earth? How is it that I could promenade in this most beautiful Gstaad? How has it become possible? You cannot appreciate too well these mountains, trees, valleys, flowers, the wooden mansions on hill slopes and the colorful flowers decorating them. These eyes are not adequate to see them. You can see so much variety only in the colors of flowers in this country. I can't describe how pleasurable and enjoyable life is here. When I look at the comforts here, I cannot but contrast them with the conditions in India.

By mistake Julie tossed Suguna's watch out the window along with some trash. It's forbidden here even to shake off a tablecloth from the window onto the street. But she did it. She went down looking for the watch after realizing her mistake and got the watch back. Someone carefully picked up the watch which had fallen from the third floor and turned it in to the shop downstairs. Such a thing would never happen in India. There, who would not pocket a watch found lying on the street?

* * *

Srinivas

On our first day here, on his walk, Moorty ran into a man called Srinivas. Srinivas is a Tamil who was born in Rajahmundry and grew up in Madras. When Moorty told him about UG, he was eager to see him. As he promised, he came the next morning. He is probably around 45 years of age. He may be older than that but he looks pretty healthy. He is tall and his body size fits his height. His complexion is light brown. He doesn't speak Telugu very well. Maybe he speaks Tamil well. He works as some sort of a history teacher in an American school in Holland. Apparently he worked in the diplomatic service for a while. As I was wondering why he quit such a good job, I learned in course of his conversation with UG that he had discarded many riches. The Krishnamurti Foundation has invited him here to teach yoga.

I am not sure if he had heard of UG before, but once he started talking to UG, he couldn't seem to stop and leave. And soon after he came, his self-confidence, his self-assurance and his pride that he 'knew it all' evaporated. He showed signs of agitation and confusion. I could see expressed on his face the feeling of being lost in what he was doing or looking at. In spite of UG warning him repeatedly that it was getting late for him, the gentleman was reluctant to move. I thought he was caught in a snare. He will surely come again. Such is the taste of UG. UG invited him for lunch and ate with him. His background and the things he talked about were quite interesting.

It will take a whole book to describe these things, especially what he said about Jiddu Krishnamurti. He was close to JK once upon a time. However, he didn't care for JK's style and found contradictions between what he had said and what he had done. So he moved away from him, probably in 1980. He worked as a teacher in the Rishi Valley School. He was surprised at the special attention JK gave him during his dialogues with the teachers that year. JK granted him, without even his asking for them, goodies such as eating meals with him, going for walks with him and having intimate conversations with him. It was all grand at first. When JK advised him to change his accent of English and acquire a British accent, he tried to cultivate it for some time. But he got tired of the task and decided to stick with his Madras Tamil accent. We were once again reminded, in the context of his eating meals with JK, how much of a glutton JK was. We found that Douglas hadn't exaggerated a bit.

Srinivas did not care for the method of teaching they practiced in the Rishi Valley School. He didn't quite understand what was so special about Krishnamurti choosing only wealthy children, creating all sorts of comforts for them and then educating them. The 'yes' men who had gathered around JK didn't let him breathe. Srinivas knew all of them – Pupul Jayakar, Achyut Patwardhan, Nandini, and others. Srinivas at last got out of that cage. As he felt he was obligated to JK for the special fondness and attention he received, he worked for such a long time at that Foundation.

Once during a public talk he had asked JK a very irksome question regarding the eradication of poverty: "How is it fair to live in such luxury in a country in which the poor suffer and are unable to afford a meal? What's your answer to this?" he had asked point-blank in front of the many people in the audience. He threatened those who then tried to stop him. "You are all his lackeys; you just shut up," he shouted at them. They calmed down. "Mr. Krishnamurti, please answer my question," he insisted. Although JK was startled at first, he composed himself slowly, said something in reply, closed the meeting, got up and left. After that he did not let Srinivas near him nor did he speak to him until Srinivas felt sorry that he might have pained JK, went to him and apologized. After that JK again showed fondness for him. But Srinivas did not like working in that school, so he quit. He is still fond of JK and respects him. But he admitted that like all holy men he too did not practice what he had preached and that he was a womanizer and had relations with some women.

* * *

Exactly one hour has passed. Outside, the sky is showering morning light. In this country they wash the roads with a detergent. Across the street the tennis courts look deserted. All day long children play in that wide space. They practice riding their bicycles; some also go around on their skate boards. It's not morning for any of them yet.

UG was reading aloud all yesterday from *The Letters of Gold* to everyone. He read the extempore lecture he gave on

Theosophy in Rendsberg. Then he read the letters Arundale and Jinarajadasa wrote to him as well as the letters he had written to Mahesh. Moorty, who had been listening to all this, thought that the letters should be included in a biography of UG. "These letters are quite useful. When Mahesh was writing your biography, I didn't know about these letters," he said addressing UG. I was surprised. Who stopped all these letters from getting into the book?

*   *   *

Time: 9:30 am. It's now 1 o'clock in India. I just returned from chatting with UG. The assembly started at 8:00 am. It will go on again from 3 o'clock in the afternoon till 7 pm. Now Nataraj, Mitra, his girlfriend, Nataraj's sister, Manju and his girlfriend are still here. Larry Morris, Susan and Claire left yesterday morning. Apparently, an engine from their plane fell off. The accident happened on their way from Atlanta to Albuquerque. The pilot brought the plane down carefully in Dallas. I never heard of such an accident of an engine dropping off before.

Larry Morris had a difficult time parting. I don't understand what the attraction is. "He is a real goner," says Claire. He sits in front of UG all day long. Those who have witnessed it say that when he stands on the pulpit in his church he is a completely different man. Once he sits in front of UG he forgets the whole world. Lakshmi says Guha is the same way. He forgets his own existence. I never felt that way. I used to be like that before when I sat in front of Shau. I never feel that way when I sit in front of UG. Sometimes I feel "That's enough, let's go;" but I never forget myself. Why?

Maybe that's the case with some people. A man thinks and feels the way he imagines. But it has nothing to do with who is in front of you. That's true even if God stands before you. It all depends on what we imagine. Devotees worship God only by imagining His presence. If God is omnipresent and omnipotent, then the very breath that moves in me is God. The pen that's writing and the thoughts that are spilled on the paper are all driven by God. What's there that could be called mine? Where is it? I just think that I exist, that I have a form, that I have a shape. If I don't think these things, then who am I? And who is there for me?

*   *   *

UG's words kindled memories of Valentine. Tears rolled in Suguna's eyes. Nine years have passed since her death. Tomorrow is the 1st of August, Valentine's birthday. It's the National Day, the day of the formation of the nation of Switzerland. They are decorating the whole town for the celebration. Flowers and colors everywhere – it's great! At night there will be fireworks, sounds of firecrackers, dances, songs and bands – there will be a big celebration.

When I think of living, I mean living in the past like this. Even thinking of tomorrow is living in the past. Where does the 'I' exist except in memories? This book is filled with shit. This writing is full of shit. Shit! Shit! Culture Shit! Shit! Shit! Stinking shit! Just as I feel relieved pooping out the shit from the guts in the mornings, I transfer the shit that has accumulated in my head to these pages. Then the head becomes a little lighter. Then once again shit gathers. As I empty the head, wash it out, the shit gathers again and again.

*   *   *

August 1, 1999 (Sunday)

5:30 am. It's still hazy outside. Today is Valentine's birthday. This is her last birthday in this century. It is the Swiss Independence Day. I wonder from whom they had gained independence. As a matter of fact, historically this county has always been independent. Although the country doesn't have an army, every citizen must undergo military training. The law here requires that every citizen must go through military training for a couple of weeks every year. But the Swiss are not warmongers; they are freedom lovers. They can't tolerate being subjugated by another nation. The country suffered seriously in both the world wars of this century. Apparently, they used to give a ration of 1½ egg per person per day. There was no electricity. In the winter time Valentine had collected twigs and branches to make fire for warmth. Although they had cars, they couldn't get petrol. For some reason Hitler did not attack this country. He did not touch this nation. It remained neutral and did not interfere in any other nation's affairs. England too did not attack Switzerland. After the end of WWII in 1945, this country has taken off. In 1950, the Indian rupee and Swiss franc had the same value. Now you can't buy a franc even with 30 rupees; it has gone up so much in value.

* * *

Just as I expected, Srinivas appeared again yesterday at 10:30 am along with two friends of his. This time UG spoke as rudely and abusively as he had spoken gently and respectfully the other day. Srinivas stayed for almost two hours. He was curious about the bodily changes that UG had gone through, the strange changes in his glands. But whatever UG said sounded to him like JK's words. "You are speaking exactly like JK. He too says the same thing," he claimed. It's clear that Srinivas was still deeply rooted in JK. No matter how much he tried to convince us by saying, "I don't believe in anyone. I don't worship JK," it was obvious how much his words imbibed JK's spirit. "If my words are similar to JK's words, it's only because there are no other words in the English language. We were both schooled by the same teachers. But you are not the same," answered UG.

"Perhaps I won't understand you unless I undergo the same kind of glandular changes that you have gone through," said Srinivas. No matter how harshly UG spoke and belittled him, Srinivas held to his manner of respect and humility. When I watched his behavior, it became clear to me that he was truly trying to understand UG. "I am barking like a dog here and you are creating meaning for those noises. You are trying to understand," said UG. When UG said, "I have no way of knowing that I'm alive. If you ask me, I will say, 'Yes, I'm alive,' but I really have no way of knowing that fact for myself," Srinivas admitted his inability to understand. "How can you understand? The existence of 'you' will not want to know your existence. It will safely continue through noticing similarities in words and deeds between JK and me; or else, you will 'die' right here and now. But you can't bear that."

"You can't be interested in this. How can you be interested?" UG asserted repeatedly. No matter how many ways Srinivas tried to argue with him, UG would nip his arguments in the bud. When UG said, "Man needs two 'F's – food and fuck. This body is not interested in anything more – just survival and reproduction," Srinivas asked, "Did you succeed in using the second 'F'?" UG replied, "I am 82 years old. What do I have to do with sex? I have become old." However, he didn't reveal that his sex urge was burnt out forty years ago. He explained that sex was not possible for him, citing his conversation with a Nobel laureate. "It's not just to know in words that there is no space or time. Where will your woman be if there is truly no space? How will sex be possible?" was UG's question.

Srinivas was flabbergasted. He said at last, "I don't understand you. But when I observe you, you look marvelous. Even though you are older than 80, you look so energetic. I won't be able to understand you unless those glandular changes happen to me too." UG showed him a video tape of Douglas's skit about JK. In the tape, Douglas acted out with words and gestures depicting how much of a glutton JK was and how much he appreciated things like sex.

Srinivas is leaving tomorrow. Maybe he won't see UG again. But the fire which has been kindled in him by UG will not die; it will continue to burn. It will consume him head to foot. I am wonderstruck when I think of how many thousands of people UG has helped like this. I am noticing all kinds of links on the Internet. Hundreds of people are anxiously seeking to know about UG. UG's command to us is not to let people know of his whereabouts. What I feel is that recently UG has been losing his patience. He knows that his end is nearing. He feels that he mustn't waste his time with groups. He cannot help everyone, especially groups. Maybe one or two individuals, those who have been burnt and consumed with intense yearning – for those one or two UG has been waiting patiently. Someone like me is thick-skinned. Not much has been ruffled in me in spite my thirty years of acquaintance with him. There has been no effect. I haven't lost my desire for these toys yet. I collect them and never think clearly, "What do I want?"

*   *   *

August 1 (Continuing):

I feel as if I am living to write this journal. There is nothing else. What I am living for? For myself? What must I do? What must I achieve? Am I truly alive? Or is my life living itself? I say 'my life' – what is my life? Just words. A lot of hot air. Meaningless, useless words. I just use them mechanically. I just think I understand them, but if I look into them, they are hollow.

*   *   *

After lunch and before dinner, Moorty and I were out for our routine walk. For about an hour and a half we went along the mountain paths, chatting. We pick a different route each day.

One day we leave from behind the Palace Hotel; another day from the front of it. When we walk along the paths we notice many wooden buildings. We saw a mansion built in 1650. The Palace Hotel has ten floors. I wonder how many hundreds of years old it is. It was world famous even in the beginning of this century. A Rolls Royce car was parked in front in the porch. People here are hard-working. They serve the leisure class of the world. From many countries people descend into these valleys, not seeking rest but tired of routine life. How many hundreds and thousands reside in this valley! Hundreds of wooden chalets. They are behind the trees, not visible from outside. Apparently, 'Gstaad' should be pronounced as 'Staat'. Moorty and I were remembering Chalam and the friendships of those old times.

Aruna and Venkat are planning to come here. We talked to them at length yesterday. They both will come on the 27th and we will all travel to India on the 30th. They will have to tour Switzerland in two days. I am not sure if Julie will still be here. Meanwhile Mr. Raju will arrive. Mittu and Guha will also come.

*   *   *

UG invited everyone to our room for lunch with the pretext of Valentine's birthday. Nataraj, Maria, Lisa, Lakshmi and her children, Julie and us two – we all had lunch together. UG and Moorty had their lunch in their apartment. There are many apartments in Ludi Haus. UG and Moorty are in 'E'. Lisa and Mario are put up in 'F', we two are in 'M' and Lakshmi's family is in 'P'.

I showed UG the dedication in my journal, which is to him. He merely said, "How can you write such a thing?" That's all. He read it all and returned it.

After lunch, Suguna and I went with Nataraj and Maria to see the place where Nataraj is living. It's near Saanen, near the tents where JK used to give his talks before. The rent is 600 francs a month.

*   *   *

There are mountains all around us. If you have to go anywhere from this valley, you must cross the mountains. The peak called Diablaret is very high. There is another mountain called Eggli. Each mountain has its own name. I don't know all the names. I must find out. Mont Blanc has the highest summit in the Alps. I am so surprised that Aruna and Venkat are coming. It's a strange coincidence that we come here and they come here too after planning to travel to India. I can't believe this.

*   *   *

John Piatras

UG used to be friends with a Polish youth called John Piatras when he lived in Chicago. Piatras used to talk to UG everyday. He attended UG's Philosophers' Corner to listen to his conversations and discussions. UG's wife Kusuma had a liking for him. UG lost touch with him after he left the US. But John kept himself informed of UG's news for some time - the hardships UG had experienced in London when he was penniless, his wife's death, the news of his children having to seek shelter in relatives' houses, UG's helpless state – he had learned of all of these events.

About the same time, he had developed an interest in JK and tried hard to meet him in person. He squatted in his car in front of JK's house and obtained an interview. When he talked to JK, in passing he mentioned UG. When he narrated UG's condition in London, JK was unable to contain his sorrow and cried out loud. John met UG again after almost 30 years and related this incident to him. After the web page was created for UG on the Internet in 1996, John chanced to see the website in 1997. He sent e-mails to Julie and Moorty enquiring about UG. At that time he was in some high-level position in the computer field. When he heard about him, UG gave him his address and phone number and invited him to Palm Springs.

One day, John came with his family to Palm Springs to see UG. Lisa and Mario were also present on the scene. UG was surprised that JK had cried aloud when he heard UG's sad story. Many years ago, when JK had asked him, "Have you ever shed tears, sir? Have you ever cried?" UG replied, "I never cried in all my conscious life. Maybe I cried when I was in the cradle or in my mother's arms. I can't remember." "But I feel like crying for you," said Krishnamurti. "Be my guest. Cry. Who stopped you?" said UG bluntly. But when we learn that JK had really cried for UG for fifteen minutes, sobbing, "Oh, that poor chap, oh, that poor chap!" we can understand how much JK was attached to UG. When John was relating this story to UG, Lisa, who was sitting there, couldn't restrain herself from crying. "I too was about to cry when I was listening to him describing that," said Lisa today when UG was recalling and relating that old incident. JK must have liked UG so much. Or else, why could he not let go of his friendship even when UG was so critical of him? UG says now, "I now understand that JK was using me as his mirror. He tried to look at himself in me and tried to correct himself. My thoughts and ideas were useful to him to shape himself." That was why JK was fond of UG's friendship and of arguing with UG.

*   *   *

August 2, 1999 (Monday)

Experiencing...

It has already been a week since I left home. It feels as if ages have passed. That's how it is when you visit new places; when you travel, you get feelings like that. How about when I exit this world? I just imagine time passing slowly, but is there any reality to those feelings? How do I know for sure that I am here? What's true and what's false? If something is true, how is it true? If it is false, how is it false? If you remove all measurements and beliefs then what will remain? How many millions of people have thought like this before me? What happened to them? Did they gather any wealth? Did they leave any mark? Are their names remembered on this earth? Why should their names remain? That's another absurd desire, the greed for fame. If I haven't hooked to this name while I am still alive, how happy would I have been! Valentine's name, fame and her possessions have all disappeared right in front of me.

But everyone is attached to life. A man becomes a zombie when his memories are burned up. The *'turiya'* state is nothing more than that, says UG, the state in which you remain without the self. There are no thoughts, no anxieties, no worries. There is not even a thought that one is alive. What greater fortune could I wish for than that?

But... but... if I don't experience that state, then of what use is it? If I don't know that I am happy, that I am content, then what good is contentment? I must clearly experience it. If I have to know it....I must stand apart from it and be able to experience it. Just as I watch and enjoy these mountains and beauties, I must relish my blissful state. Everyone must think "How lucky you are, how happy you are!" Then it means something. What will it mean? The next moment you will start worrying and then slide into an abysmal hell. That too you will experience. In this way, you will hop and jump from one thing to another as a monkey jumps from one branch to another. But the 'you', the permanent 'you,' that thing you will never experience. It's just not possible. However, you can't but long for it. If you do experience it, that means you are hanging onto another branch. To stand without any support, without any branches, is something beyond the monkey's imagination. I can imagine it, but it can never be a fact for me.

*   *   *

Swiss Independence Day

Last night, we all went out on the streets. It wasn't very cold. It was quite pleasant to go around with a jacket on. Children and adults, everyone, lighted firecrackers. All around on the mountain peaks they lighted big lights and bonfires. At 10:30 in the night there were fireworks by the Palace Hotel. The sky sparkled with the colorful lights for 15 minutes. Different sorts of firecrackers. Not so much bombastic noises as clusters of colored lights that were jetting around feasting the eyes – it's something that can only be seen and not described. We all wholeheartedly enjoyed the Swiss National Day along with Shilpa and Sumedha. UG, however, stayed in his apartment.

*   *   *

I discussed separately UG's behavior with Moorty and Julie. We can notice an increased energy in his speech and action. But his movements have diminished. From morning till night he sits on the sofa. Except for going into the kitchen or bathroom or onto the balcony, or climbing the stairs to come to our room or Lakshmi's room, he is not moving anywhere. Occasionally he goes around in a car. I wonder when he goes to the post office. He steps into it just for a second and gets out. Just to tease, two days ago, Moorty invited UG to go for a walk with us. But he was adamant and said no. Yesterday, we all went to Chalet Sunbeam along with Julie. UG, of course, didn't come.

*   *   *

Lisa and Mario

When we think of our past, we have old memories. Memories are themselves old. Why call them 'old memories'? Whatever stirs in the mind stinks of being old. Whatever moves in the stomach is old food. "UG is withdrawing from outdoor activities," said Moorty. Indeed, neither in his words nor in his actions and movements does he concern himself with anything.

But he seems to have a strong wish to get Lisa to have plastic surgery to make her face more attractive, with the hope that at least then a 'fat cat' might fall in love with her. He doesn't accept Mario as Lisa's partner. He rejects him saying, "You are a coolie. You are no match to her." Mario complains, saying that Lisa is his wife. UG denies that. Lisa is attached to Mario. It appears that UG is trying to separate the two. But it also appears that they two are getting closer to each other because of the influence of UG's words and actions. I think that as their suppressed desires are brought out into the open, their attraction to each other has become clearer and they have gotten closer to each other. There is a bond between the two. Lisa wants a child with Mario. Even UG says that her desire will be fulfilled soon.

UG doesn't care about our measurements and values. But he never subverts them. He may condemn them and ridicule them, but he will never violate them. We become conflicted by looking upon these values as great, on the one hand, and bewailing that we can't fit ourselves into their framework, on the other. That conflict is the main source of our restlessness. We might get interested in other women; our mind regards social values as false and prompts us to rebel against them. But our intellect tries to prevent rebellion; that's where our disguised warfare starts. At some level or other these conflicts occur in everyone at any moment. If we can prevent them as much as possible, then there is a possibility of harmony in life. The effect of UG's words and deeds seems to be such that they are preparations to lead us exactly to that state. We can't take them. They make us hop and jump around like a monkey whose tail has been stepped on. In the final analysis we may find that our conflicts have disappeared without our knowing it. Gradually, the organism will find ways of living without any interference from those values. That's the effect of UG.

*   *   *

This morning at 9:00 am, Moorty and I went out for a walk. There is a path leaving from the side of the Palace Hotel that goes alongside Saanen River. The river was flowing fast under the shadows of the tall pine trees on the slopes of the hill; on the other side, there was a cool breeze coming from the meadows on the slopes of the hill. If you follow the path, you can get to Launen; or you can go back to Gstaad. You can see the Hotel Parkview on the way; it's a big hotel.

On the walk, Moorty mentioned UG's letters again. He too thought that it would be nice to write a biography of UG inserting letters and photos in the middle. If anyone writes UG's biography, it must be Moorty. He told me that he set a condition with UG to write one. UG must live for a hundred years. He promised UG that for his 100th birthday he would write and publish a comprehensive and definitive biography.

He will include in it letters, accounts of meetings with UG and photos. The big book might amount to about 400 pages. Just like the effort of Rajasekhar. But if Moorty undertakes it, it will surely shape up into a biography which no one in the world has seen or heard. But how is his condition going to be realized? Can UG guarantee that he will live for a hundred years? Why should he give such a guarantee? A hundred years for the body? Why just a hundred years? He could live for even 500 years. But what about his form? Would he be in the same form? I can recognize him in this form for only a hundred years. That means that Moorty also must live so many years.

*   *   *

August 3, 1999 (Tuesday)

Leboyer

By the time I woke up it was 6:30. It's 7 am now. The town is still asleep. It doesn't get busy with people until 9 am. You don't see many people except on Saturdays and Sundays. When we went for a walk, we ran into a familiar face near the Rialto. He is a doctor. I couldn't recall his name readily. He is a famous doctor who has done research and written many books on natural childbirth. Suguna prompted me with his name. Dr. Leboyer. He has been a friend of UG for almost 25 years. He has taken many photos of UG. Although he saw us, he didn't show any sign of recognition. He looked at us as strangers and shook us off like insects and passed us. Moorty said a couple of words of "hello" and remarked after he had passed, "He is one of those pompous ...." It's not just Leboyer;

few have that broadmindedness to treat other men, especially those who don't measure up to their status, at least as fellow human beings if not as their equals. You see this trait in some of the people who visit UG. They can't be inclusive of people. It's rare to see noble persons who can take people in without any prejudice or question about their race, religion or caste and respect them. Chalam was such a man. I see UG the same way. There are many who cannot live on that level and mingle with common folks; they are blinded by their power or their money. Moorty and I talked about many such people.

* * *

UG was playing dice with Sumedha yesterday. In one game, he cheated. Sumedha detected it and complained, "You cheated!" UG didn't agree; he said, "I played straight." Sumedha couldn't contain her anger and said, "You may be a very great man, but you are the greatest cheater in the world." She got up and lay down on a sofa. We all laughed. UG pleaded with her to come and play, but she wouldn't.

* * *

Lisa brought a picture postcard with the caption "What's on a Man's Mind" and gave it to UG. It had the picture of Freud with a naked woman's body on his face. If you look closely you find the picture quite significant. I thought it was quite interesting and wanted to get it copied; but instead, UG gave the card to me.

* * *

I spent the whole day looking into the UG sites on the internet. You can find hundreds of links connected with UG's name. Lisa is cataloging all of them. It's a pretty complex task. Yesterday, Nataraj's sister, Maria, has left for the US. I too went with Nataraj and Mario up to Zweisimmen in Mario's car. From there Maria had to go on to Zurich by train.

Today Leboyer came. Denise also came and ate lunch with us. She stays in the Christiania Hotel. She will be here for a month, as long as UG stays. She brought a couple of cashmere sweaters for UG.

* * *

August 4, 1999 (Wednesday)

About 6 am. Today Guha and Krim are arriving from the US. Lakshmi, UG and the children are going in Julie's car to receive them. The car is big enough to hold all of them. It may be late afternoon by the time they all come back. Lakshmi's mother is ill. These must be her last days. Lakshmi wanted to take her whole family to India, but UG insisted that the children shouldn't step on Indian soil. So Lakshmi is leaving for India by herself on the 6th and will return on the 20th from Delhi. Both her children were born in the US and they grew up in that environment. UG forbade taking them to India, thinking that if Guha and Lakshmi expose them to two different cultures and traditions, the children wouldn't know which one to choose and would be confused; as a consequence, they will not belong to either culture. There is a lot of wisdom in what he says. At first, we didn't quite understand why he was forbidding them from going to India. Now I feel he is right. "They become neurotic when exposed to two different cultures and traditions," he says. Shilpa and Sumedha will stay here with their father. They won't have any problem as UG is with them. Lisa is also here to help.

*   *   *

Leboyer at Dinner

It feels like the days are picking up speed. I have the illusion that time is flying. UG invited Leboyer for dinner last night. He asked that the foods made by Suguna and Lakshmi to be brought downstairs. Leboyer is French. UG asked Moorty to eat with Leboyer alone. Leboyer was hoping to eat with UG. Later, Moorty related what happened at dinner.

UG didn't even sit with them at the dinner table. He left Moorty and Leboyer at the table and came upstairs with the pretext of finding out what we were all eating. "Julie made a salad again?" he asked. He doesn't like salads. He had prohibited her from making salads. For that reason Julie has not been making salads, but Suguna, Lakshmi, and I made a salad of carrots and cucumbers. We cut them up into small circles and sprinkled a little salt on them without pouring any olive oil. I was filling myself up with them. UG came upstairs and saw pieces of *papads*. He put two or three pieces in his mouth in spite of our warning that they were hot. He said, "I don't know that it is hot unless you tell me it's hot. If you don't say they're hot, they're not hot." He took a few more into his hand. Back downstairs, when UG was about to hand one or two pieces to Moorty, Moorty snatched them all. He was worried UG wouldn't be able to tolerate all that hot stuff and would vomit again. UG said, "I already ate six of them upstairs," and then went into the bathroom and threw up. Once he finished with that process, he stayed in the kitchen washing dishes. Moorty had to keep Leboyer company alone.

The French don't like to eat their dinners at the table silently. It's customary for the host to converse with the guests while serving food. Moorty had to pick up some conversation and entertain Leboyer. But UG didn't bother about his guest. Moorty said Leboyer seemed to like the Indian dishes. Soon after dinner, Leboyer got up and left.

I remarked to Moorty that this looked like some Zen dinner. Leboyer likes the style of Zen. Once, when he came to India in 1973, he had stayed with me in Sastri Sadan. I can't remember if UG was there with us or not. He used to practice Tai Chi in the mornings. He is now 81 years of age, exactly the same age as UG. As he was born in November he is younger than UG. I told him, "In another three months, you will have your thousand moons completed." He didn't quite understand what that meant; UG explained to him.

All yesterday they read to UG the numerology and astrology written by Satyanarayana. After hearing everything UG said, "*Saku, saku*[6]." The seven-year stage of Kuja is going to be fantastic, according to Satyanarayana. "The mission for which UG has come down into this world will be fulfilled in these

---

[6] 'Enough', 'enough' – in Kannada.

seven years. The climate for that has already begun in the *Chandra*[7] stage." If we watch the links on the internet, it is evident how many thousands of people are influenced by UG in so many ways.

*   *   *

Moorty said while we were walking, "Leboyer is terrified of dying." The fear of death is at the root of all fears. The 'I' that I have known of ever since I have been conscious suddenly won't be there one fine morning! Will the world still be the same? For whom will it be there? Who cares what happens to this world when I am not there? Chalam thought of this a lot. He used to say, "I detest death." In his last days, he was unable to bear the possibility of his own non-existence and shrunk with fear like a little bird. "I too am afraid of death sometimes. But I surrender to the fear completely whenever it arises. Then it goes away," Moorty says.

You must give yourself over to death. UG is not a person. He stands for our ending. UG is a compassionate being who can help us taste death by ending things then and there.

Moorty was playing a card game alone on the computer. When I asked him what he was doing, he said, "I am playing a game just to spend time." I quoted a Sanskrit verse from Bhagavatar to the effect, "One must not indulge in a pastime; each moment, your span of life will be shortened and Yama won't

---

[7] The Moon.

take pity on you. It's better to sing the praises of the Lord."
"That's nice, I understand," said Moorty smiling.

I feel that sitting in UG's presence is the same as singing the praise of the Lord. We don't need to do anything. It's enough if we just sit there and take in the words he speaks. Sometimes they pierce into our bones like thorns. At every opportunity UG presents death to us. In his presence, the fear of death itself gets terrified!

*   *   *

August 5, 1999 (Thursday)

Today it's already 6:30 am. As I went to bed late last night, I got up late in the morning. Suguna has not woken up yet. Last night I talked to Aruna before I went to bed. They have booked their tickets for the travel. Apparently the airlines staff told them that there is no problem with the baggage as they can carry up to 35 kilos each. I asked her to make sure by enquiring again. Before, when I asked a travel agent here she told me you can't carry more than 20 kgs. I must ask Julie to find out for sure. I guess we could just look up in the Swiss Air schedule. They would mention all that information there. Will that apply to us too? How much luggage can we carry? I guess I must ask Air France people because we have Air France tickets.

As soon as I got up this morning I have had no other thoughts but these. Why do I think them? Outside, there is a truck going on the street with a roaring sound. Normally you don't hear such sounds in this country. Even trains run quietly. The sounds don't last very long. They stop pretty soon after that start. Maybe because of the thick growth of trees on the mountains, the whole valley is quiet. When I went for a walk yesterday morning, I felt like dissolving into that silence. I didn't feel like moving my lips. Today Moorty and I talked about my relationship with Baba[8] when I was little. We also chatted about Chalam. Walking along the mountain paths, we went almost as far as Schonried and returned to Gstaad.

*   *   *

Francis

Guha arrived yesterday; also Krim. A Swiss friend of Chandrahas called Francis came. After he sat around UG for a couple of hours, we invited him for lunch at UG's suggestion. UG sometimes asks us to invite people, especially those who are here the first time. Francis spent his time from 12:30 to 3 pm with me. We talked a lot. When he told me he was only 48 years old I couldn't believe. You can't estimate his age. Apparently his sister had introduced Chandrahas to him. Everyone in his household was fascinated by Chandrahas. They thought he was a yogi. Francis asked me, "How do you regard Chandrahas in India? Don't you consider him a yogi?" I explained to him "that true yogis don't publicize themselves. As much as possible they don't let things about themselves be known to others." Poor folks! They are easily deceived by appearances. Chandrahas is taking advantage of them. He

---

[8] *Satya Sai Baba*

has exploited them all. Now they are trying to be cautious about him. They seem to be prepared to help him with money, but are not ready to sponsor him by inviting him to Switzerland.

Francis has two sons. They are still studying in school. Francis used to work in the Swiss government as an officer investigating refugee problems. He lost that job. He said he has an interview for another job today in Bern. He worries that there may be situations in his work in which he may have to act contrary to his conscience. In contexts where he had to be harsh with the refugees, his superiors found fault with him even when he carried out his duties. This hurt him.

The troubles began in Berlin in 1984: when the Wall was brought down and West and East Germany were united, he was given the responsibility of examining refugees coming to Switzerland. In that situation, no matter how reliably and responsibly he conducted himself, in the end his superiors blamed him and found faults with him. That discouraged him. He felt humiliated when the Swiss police admitted their defeat before some arrogant refugees and admitted them into Switzerland as if they couldn't do anything else. But what could *he* do? He suffered silently.

He says that there is no problem with the refugees from Sri Lanka. Only the refugees from Yugoslavia are creating havoc; still the government is lenient with them. It hesitates to take action against them. So this is his problem. The Swiss nationals are caught in the middle. He says, "I wouldn't be surprised if there is a civil war in this country soon." Some condemn the government severely and some others support it. I told him that such a situation exists in every country. I reassured him saying "it will take a long time for a civil war to develop." Francis is a sensitive person. I feel that police work doesn't suit him. I don't know what he will do today. But after all these years this Swiss man got caught in the 'snares' of UG.

*   *   *

Krim

Last night, I chatted with Krim for an hour and a half. His whole life is a tale of sorrow. He got caught in mire when he was only 25. Now he is 41 years old. He saw UG for the first time in Switzerland when he was 16. That means 25 years ago. Later, when UG was in Mill Valley and Krim was about to go for a walk with a Russian girl named Elena, UG warned him, "Make it a short walk." Not heeding that warning turned into a curse for him. Becoming close friends with Elena, spurning the help of friends who tried to extract him from that mire when he was struggling to get out of it, and foiling all UG's efforts to get him out – all these events prove the influence of planets on him.

Next year, starting from this coming September, there must be a change in his fortunes. His life must take a turn for the better. He now has a daughter with Elena. That crazy lady has tried to keep their child away from him. Krim's father is Russian, and Krim visits Russia now and then. I looked at his palm and told him that there are indications that his life will change completely in the future. If he has the grace of UG, everything will be set right. Coming here after so many years is indicative of his good fortune. If he leaves everything to UG at least now, his life will get better. Am *I* leaving everything to UG? He is bending my back and kicking me on my butt, pinching my ears and hitting me on my head. If he didn't, would my stubbornness go away?

*   *   *

It's 4 o'clock in the afternoon. I have a little time to write in the diary. Everyone has gone downstairs. Today Leboyer gave UG a ride in his car. Denise went with them. Leboyer has had open-heart surgery; so he is still scared of climbing mountains and heights. "I have confidence if you are by my side," he said and drove UG up to Les Diablettes. UG complimented him for his driving, saying, "I give five 'A's for your driving." Pleased, Leboyer bowed his head. Later, everyone dined in our apartment. When Denise was about to sit at the table, Leboyer forbade her, saying, "Women can't sit at this table; this is just for men." Denise felt humiliated and sat down on a sofa away from the table. UG didn't know about this.

A little while later, UG came upstairs into our apartment after finishing his meal. Krim, Guha, Leboyer and I were eating and chatting. Guha said, "UG, we are eating without you." "It's uncivilized to eat food at a table. I never do that," UG said and started attacking Freud. He condemned psychologists and doctors. It was all aimed at dealing a blow to Leboyer. The great doctor didn't raise his head. He worships Freud as a god. That's why UG tears Freud apart. Fed up with UG's scolding served with the dinner, Leboyer got up and left. That's how UG invites some people and serves them.

* * *

UG is talking about a lot of things. I note them down with the idea that my notes may be of use for the definitive biography Moorty may be writing. Shall we write it together?

* * *

January 26, 1950, the first Republic Day, was an important day for India. On that day UG gave a lecture in Andhra University. In it he criticized Gandhi on occasion. Apparently he had said that Hitler was instrumental in bringing independence to our country. He quoted Shakespeare in that talk and said, "Some are born great, some achieve greatness, and on some greatness is thrust. Tagore was born great, Gandhi achieved greatness through his effort, and greatness was thrust on J. Krishnamurti."

* * *

He met Tagore twice in the period between 1939 and 1941 in Santi Niketan. Tagore presented UG with a volume of his complete works and inscribed a special poem in it:

> The shy little pomegranate bud
> Blushing today behind the veils
> Will burst forth as a passionate flower
> When I am gone tomorrow....

I think this poem is from Tagore's *First Gathering*. I should look it up. UG has a great respect for Tagore.

*   *   *

August 6, 1999 (Friday)

The alarm rang at 5:15 am. I decided to get up then.

Some days, the pen writes on its own without my involvement. Chalam used to say that he used to feel a great joy when what he wrote was printed. Perhaps that was true. But how could printing this writing be of use to anyone? What's there in it to learn from or to change oneself? How is it different from writing the same thing over and over as in 'imposition'? In olden times they wrote 'Rama' thousands of times in rote. There was no meaning in it. If I were to write it so many times, I guess the sound 'Rama' would be imbedded in my thoughts like a drone sound. Maybe the sound of 'Rama', like the sound of 'Om', would resound in my background behind whatever I did or whatever I looked at. If the way to escape from this world is to write 'Rama' thousands of times, what I am doing now is just that.

There is noise inside me. Outside there is silence. I make the effort is to bring the internal noise out. Do thoughts exist only in my head? How do they get there? How do I get the thoughts such as "I am" and "I am thinking?" Do I exist apart from them? UG was saying yesterday, "Whatever I have learned in life, I have learned on my own; I didn't learn anything from others. No teacher or professor had ever taught me the things which my son had taught me when he was a baby. I did learn a lot about life from him by raising him." These words of UG are pearls of wisdom. The things he had learned and known shine as lights of wisdom, shedding light for so many people. Everything he says is contrary to the things we believe in and act upon. Why is there such a contrast? This is true not just in spiritual matters but also in matters of everyday life.

Yesterday evening, Anthony Nahas came. He has three sons and a daughter. Each of the boys' names starts with 'A' and the daughter's name, Zoe, ends with 'Z'. He said to UG, "My baby is close to your Natural State." "How old is she?" UG asked. "Eleven months." "No use; she has fallen away from the Natural State long ago. When she was just born she was in it perhaps for a few hours, till her mother gave her a kiss. That means that as soon as the baby felt her mother's touch the world has entered the baby."

Does UG live from moment to moment in that fresh, childlike state? How is he able to shine like that gathering all that innocence in the midst of all this horror, evil, cruelty, injustice, disorder and crookedness? No matter what you say to him, how much you abuse him, how much you harass him, how much you are mad at him, it doesn't touch him. Such a man has never existed before nor will exist again. Is it possible really to shine like that through our own effort? "I am ready to die any moment. Every action of mine reveals that readiness of mine for death. I act as if I may die the next moment. I don't put off anything," he says. It's the same for him with any experience or thought. You will find 'tomorrow' only in his vocabulary; he does not experience it.

Only when we have the ideas of space and time is the world present to us. Where is the world, if space and time don't exist? Last night we were all sitting in front of UG and talking. The clock struck 10 o'clock. "If you don't count those rings of the bell, there is no time. Counting 'one...two...three...' is the continuation of 'you'. It's the same with everything else; that's true every moment," says UG. The mind is imagining things, saying that this is what constitutes living from moment to moment. No matter how much it imagines, I cannot realize it. "The sound of the toilet flushing upstairs breaks the midnight silence and fills me. At that moment there is nothing else except that sound. I don't have a separate existence." How can I understand if UG talks like that? I must think like Srinivas, "Unless there are changes in our glands similar to yours we cannot understand you."

This summer it's a full 25 years since Krim has met UG. Henk arrived last evening. For him too it's the 25th anniversary. "Although we have been coming here for so many years, there's not much change in us," Henk bemoaned. Overhearing this UG retorted, "Even if you spend another 25 years with me or hear me that long, there won't be any change."

*   *   *

August 7, 1999 (Saturday)

The last day of the second week. Time 6 am. Silence everywhere. As I woke up I could hear the rhythmic sound of blood circulating in the artery under my neck. This small heart, many glands, different organs – they all work ceaselessly without any involvement on my part. They are never tired. I for myself am occupied with seeking pleasure. They don't worry about all that. They don't care if my God exists or not, whether what I am experiencing is joy or sorrow. They go on carrying out their functions. They don't think of tomorrow. They have no fear of the future. They don't worry that the body may not act as a unit. The organs are only concerned with carrying out their duties without a flaw. Unless you observe it, you don't know that the lungs are breathing in air and letting it out. I don't know how the couscous, the lentils curry, the salad and the yogurt that I ate last night are digested in the stomach. I have no way of knowing.

Moorty gave me a multivitamin pill for the sore in my mouth. There is riboflavin in the pill, a chemical which can help heal the sore. How are such chemicals manufactured in the body? If not only the essential chemicals, but also metals and alloys are produced in this vast factory, is it a wonder or what? Where are all these substances transported? To the organs that need them. The insulin manufactured by the pancreas controls the level of sugar in the blood. It makes sure that the glucose in the blood which gives energy does not put a lot of pressure on the kidneys or exceed a limited level. If it exceeds that level, doesn't the body have the wisdom to bring it back under control? Do I need to stuff medicines in it from outside? Isn't that what we do in fact? Or would the organs be in ruins and give up helplessly?

The organs keep working on their own. If there is any problem anywhere, all the organs in the body collectively work together and make an effort as a machine and cooperate with each other unstintingly. If the effort is fruitful the body will continue for some more time. If it is not successful, the organs will collapse. The body will become lifeless. The mechanisms let go of their functions just as easily. Does this heart which has been beating for so many years have any attachment to the 'I'? Does it have any vanity that it has been running this body? Does the brain have such vanity? If the blood stops flowing and the heart stops beating, what happens to the chemical processes which cause the electric transmissions that buzz in every corner of my brain?

Isn't all this knowledge based on the knowledge which knows that I exist? How can I forget such an important existence? Why can't I keep my mind on it? And why am I again standing apart from my mind and expecting it to focus? What is the nature of my existence? Is there any way that I can know myself? Why did I get the sense of separating myself from that existence, dividing myself into two, and trying to know it? How did I get such a sense? Why am I creating this division without being united with that existence?

Who told me that I am creating this division? Am I not separate from my body? But if I am, how am I separate? How do I know that I am separate? If I can't solve this problem, what good is it to have many other things? The consciousness of 'I', the feeling that I exist – are all these mere words? Or do I truly know that I exist? I am just saying that I exist; but that 'existence' is just a sound. Do I know what it really means? But [when I ask that], that [asking] too is noise. I need knowledge to know that [I exist]. Based on that knowledge, I think I feel that I exist. The brain formulates these sounds into words and transfers them through the fingers of this hand to this paper. Then what truly is my existence? How do I know that I experience my existence?

Whatever I know are only words. These are all internal noises. I have learned to formulate these sounds as words and I give meaning to them. But the meanings too are indeed sounds. Everything is sound. All my questions are sounds. My thoughts are all sounds. My ideas are all sounds. Is my whole existence a mere sound? Is the 'I' a mere vibration? Here, just now I am using a new word, the English word 'vibration'. What is the meaning of that word? Who knows? I think I understand that I know the meaning of all these sounds. Even that thinking is a sound. My whole existence is all a big sound wave. It constantly rings, whether I hear or not. It remains constant and without any support. If it does, then what is this form? How does the vibration change its forms? Am I thinking? Or is it just a verb in grammar? Do I really know what it is to think?

*　　　　　*　　　　　*

What I have written above, is it philosophy? Why do I start making such a hubbub from the time I wake up in the morning? My nostrils sensed the aroma of coffee. The taste buds in me have been getting anxious that I haven't graced them with coffee yet. How long will the taste last on the tongue? If the very 'existence' which knows it is a mere sound, what else could coffee be other than sound? Even this debate is sound. What could knowing the taste, then, be? I believe they are all one.

I forget that the mountain top visible through the window is also sound. The peak attracts clouds. There are trees on the mountains behind the cover of clouds. The fog is getting less dense. After a while, the morning sun's rays will lift the fog. Along with the peak, they also embrace all the living things. Although so much is happening, my existence, however, remains a mere vibration. Where is space and where is time for this vibration? Where is its location? There are vibrations being generated by the vibrations – 'I' 'know' wherever they spread. That's what's happening.

The yellow stand in the tennis courts across the street is drawing my attention. Doesn't my consciousness change into that shape as soon as I look at it? The next moment [*my attention goes on to*] these letters on the paper, this book, and the next moment, to the very clear presence of coffee in the stomach. The coffee tastes good. I am spreading this way everywhere like a sound wave. If Suguna is also me, then my intercourse is also with myself? I am going crazy. Who is going crazy? 'I'?

*   *   *

It's 3 pm in the afternoon. It's quite sunny outside. It rained all night last night. There was lightning and thunder shook the valley. By the morning you could see the clear skies. I could feel the cool breeze while I walked with Moorty. The sun was mild. All around, you could see thick green. Krim said it was a 'picture postcard beauty'. Beauty just like the sharp print on the Swiss postcards spread out right before our eyes. The whole valley looked as though green carpets had been laid over the mountain slopes. Here the trees and bushes look so healthy and shiny. Not a single wilted leaf. The bushes are quite full. The trees and leaves look healthy and alive with vitality. Moorty observes that perhaps the magic is in the soil. You don't even have to mention the flowers. Bunches and bunches of flowers everywhere, flowers of many colors. In the plants there are more flowers than leaves. They give you the illusion that the beams of the buildings are blossoming. And there are trees on the tops of the houses.

The men here look like milky-white dolls. They always look smiling and happy. Moorty says, "But no one is as rule-minded as these people. Normally, Germans are reputed to be rule-minded. The Swiss are more rule-minded than them." According to the Swiss way, everything has to be done by rules. If they have formed a method or a rule, they will never break it. It's in their blood. They will forgive anything but the breaking of a rule. Here we must act with the understanding that there are rules and regulations everywhere in this country. For example, everyone has to stand in line. If by mistake you move ahead of the person in front of you, they will frown at you.

On the whole, however, people here are friendly and business-minded. If they have too many rooms in their houses, they rent some of them. They look at everything through business eyes. They make a lot of money but they don't necessarily enjoy it. It's the law that every Swiss citizen undergoes army training for a couple of weeks every year. Some train here. There are training grounds on the banks of the Saanen River. You hear gunshots there. Every Swiss house has weapons and guns. But no one is more peace-loving and independence-loving than these people. There are separate laws for each individual canton. If two thousand people in any canton do not agree to a particular law, then the law has to be repealed; then they have to call for a referendum. On the issue of whether women should have the right to vote, women in Switzerland voted against the proposition. Laws of marriage and divorce differ from canton to canton. Parliament members in this country don't have any powers. The president has only a two-year term.

Now I must end my writing in this book and start writing in a second one. From tomorrow I will start writing in the diary that Raja gave me in Hyderabad.

          *   *   *

August 8, 1999 (Sunday)

Time 6 am. I finished one diary this year. Raja has given me this diary. He knows that I have a habit of keeping a journal. Guha has given me this pen the other day – a Pilot gel pen. It writes like a fountain pen.

There is a tiny hope somewhere in my interior that perhaps this writing might be of use to someone. "There is no such thing as a motiveless act," says UG. He says that his own actions and behavior are not motiveless and that he acts at least temporarily with some intention. Is that true? If what he says is true then I must have a motive in writing this journal. If there is a question of its use – I feel alive when I am writing this; and I feel the satisfaction that my life is meaningful. As time passes, the things I have written surprise me and make me happy. I learn how many turns my mind has taken and how many guises it has put on. It's hard to say if it is of any use to someone else. How could someone else care for the chatter I make?

I have another hope: perhaps the things I write about UG in this might be of interest to others. I have that motive too in writing this. Sometimes I think that no one else should read my writing. I attempt to bare myself in this writing. I feel shy and ashamed of revealing the ugly and base parts in myself. But once they spill out of my pen, I can't take them back. How much dirt is there in my head! The more I clean it, the more it gathers. I am not sure that my mind is clean even for the time that I write. Yet I take up this writing because I can't help it, because it calms my mind, and because when I turn these pages later on some old memories are revived and I am tickled by them. By the time this book is finished, a new age, a new century will surely dawn. Will my cherished desires be fulfilled before that time?

*   *   *

Hymn to Annapurna

Yesterday, I felt like reciting the 'Eight-verse Hymn to Annapurna' in UG's presence. Guha who was sitting by me evoked the idea of the Goddess Annapurna in me by uttering unintentionally the words *"bhikshan dehi"*[9]. "I feel like singing a hymn. Can I?" I asked UG. "Go ahead, as long as you are not singing about UG," he replied. When I finished two verses and was about to start the third, I got very emotional. The Goddess Annapurna appeared before my closed eyes. My voice choked. Due to the intensity of emotion tears rolled down my eyes. I sobbed and cried. It took me ten minutes to calm down. I was happy that I was able to complete the recitation. I had such an experience two or three times before in UG's presence. Normally I don't cry. No matter how many hardships I go through I don't shed tears. But when such emotions overwhelm me, crying aloud is not uncommon for me. Such things happened to me sometimes when I was alone.

Yesterday, referring to my crying UG said, "Emotions are the effects of strange chemical reactions in the body. There's nothing more to them. In those moments, there is a danger of the eyes becoming too dry and going blind. There is nothing spiritual about those tears. There is no connection between those tears and the 'Natural State' I talk about." I think that's true. After I shed so many tears, I feel light as if a burden has been lifted off me. I too, like many others, used to consider that crying is a sign of weakness of mind. Even now I can't stand people crying. I always wondered, "Why do these people

---

[9] "Please give me alms...."

cry?" But if on some occasions I can't help crying, I can understand how helpless they are. Anyone can become emotional. I didn't expect yesterday that emotion would overwhelm me; if I'd had any warning of it, I would have been careful. How suddenly it surged forth and inundated me like an ocean wave! That's right, they were internal waves. I am not worried or concerned about them.

* * *

Auto-writing – Rajyalakshmi's Story

Yesterday, in conversation with UG, there was a mention of automatic writing. I heard that someone, I can't remember her name, came to see UG. She was an auto writer. That means that some force makes her write things and the writing is not under her control. What she writes depends on others and their desires. As usual UG had asked about his travels and money. Then the pen in her hand wrote some lines. Long lines were going upward on the paper and some short lines were going downward. They answered UG's questions: his travels will increase. He will have enough money to spend but none to save. That's how it has always been with UG.

In this context, I remembered UG's cousin (his mother's elder sister's daughter) Rajyalakshmi. She is a couple of years older than UG. I think she and her family live in Machilipatnam now. In 1994, when UG went to Hyderabad, we all went to visit her in Maredpalli in Mr. K.G. Krishnamurti's house. She was quite famous as an auto writer thirty years ago. Apparently, *rishis* and sages spoke through her writing. She answered people's questions instantaneously. Rajyalakshmi didn't know anything about those sages. Some wonderful things were revealed in that writing. All those great things rolled out onto the paper, she acting as a medium, without any volition on her part.

In the course of time, she acquired a coterie of disciples and her house became like an *ashram*. Her husband was a lawyer. But she became more famous than him. Once, when she prayed for guidance and the writing said, "You have now reached a certain stage. We can't help you any more. Your cousin Gopala Krishnamurti has attained a great state. Go to him. No one else can help you." She was stunned.

Later, when UG started visiting India, she came to Bangalore in 1973 to meet him. He was then in West Anjaneya Street. She bowed to him and said, "Krishna, I don't know if I should address you as 'cousin' or as 'my teacher.'" She had tears in her eyes. She was lean like a creeper and shone with a golden complexion. "She resembles my grandmother," UG said. Then she told him about her auto writing. "I don't know how I go into it, or why it comes to me; it's as if some force is making me write. When I feel like writing, if I can't find any paper readily, I fill the empty spaces in newspapers. I can't help it. I have accumulated bundles of books of this writing. You probably know what makes me write, who those teachers are and why they are making me write. These teachers don't let me live my family life quietly; instead they drag me into the public arena. When I begged them, 'Please show me a path to spiritual realization,' they asked me to go to you. You're the only one to save me. I'll do as you say. You're my guru," she said.

UG smiled faintly. We all anxiously awaited his reply. UG did not initiate her with any *mantra*. He didn't give her any advice. He just heard whatever she had to say. "Why are you concerned with the writing? Don't stop it. Don't think about it. You just mind your own business. When you feel like writing, go ahead and write. But you are not involved. One day the writing will go away. Don't get into starting an *ashram*. And don't bother about *sadhana*," he said. She stayed for a couple of hours, reminisced about their childhood and left. She didn't start an *ashram*. After some time, her auto-writing stopped.

* * *

Afternoon 2:15 pm. After snoozing for ten minutes, I feel fresher. This morning Moorty, Krim and I went for our usual walk along the Saanen River from behind the Park Hotel. I like that path very much. On the one side of it are the pine trees which have grown tall and the sound of the river flowing on the other. While I was walking in the shade, I felt like I was in another world. The rain that had started last night had still been going on this morning, but at 8 am it cleared up. Now it's quite warm. If I stay inside, it's quite pleasant.

On our way back we saw an exhibition of paintings by a Tibetan artist. We ran into Anthony Nahas on the way. "How is UG?" he asked Moorty. "This morning he looked so fresh and bright, like a jasmine," Moorty replied. Later, Robert Geismann came. He has been coming to see UG in Switzerland for the last 35 years. In the JK days, he used to record on tapes JK's talks in the mornings and UG's talks and conversations in the evenings. He gave some of those recordings to Paul Sempé, who re-recorded them on audio cassettes and sent me a copy. Among those tapes is also an interview with David Bohm. Apparently there are many other tapes.

*   *   *

August 8, 1999 (Monday)
UG Website

Yesterday afternoon, while I was writing, Julie came upstairs and said UG was asking to see me. I closed the book and hurried downstairs into the living room. UG had some papers in his hands. Moorty, Guha, Krim and Julie were there. As soon as he saw me, he said, "Hey, Chandrasekhar, please come here; come and stand here," as if I were a criminal being asked to stand before a judge. I was worried that perhaps I had committed a big crime of some sort. In his hand there were some pages from the photos site which Raj Mehta has just created. It looks like Julie has copied them from the Internet. "He has mentioned here all those who have helped him. Listen, I'll read," he started reading one name after another, laughed aloud after he read my name and smiled at me. Raj Mehta had made albums of UG's photos, added the quotations I had sent him and set up a website. Everyone liked the site. Yesterday Moorty linked it to the main website. That means those who want to can go to Raj's website directly from UG's website and look at the photo albums. "I didn't know till now that you were the one who selected those quotes. All these days

I have been criticizing Raj for not picking the right quotes," said UG.

*   *   *

UG's Consoling People

Robert Geissmann's wife died recently. Her name was Michelle. I can't remember her face. I can't tell unless I look at her photo. Sometime ago, Eddy called from London and asked me to tell UG that her condition was serious. I think UG was in Bangalore at that time. Later, she died of cancer. Eddy said that Robert was devastated and he would be comforted if he spent sometime with UG. UG is not accustomed to consoling people who lost their loved ones. As a matter of fact, consoling is not in UG's dictionary.

Everyone knows that we can't die along with people who have died. Everyone also knows that anyone who is born must die. However, when someone close to us passes away, it's hard to bear the shock. No matter how experienced one is, how adept in worldly affairs one is, and how philosophical one is, it's still natural to be upset. It's sheer good fortune to be able to come to UG in those times. Without doing anything specific, he can create a wonderfully consoling atmosphere. He doesn't have to say a word. It's enough if he sits next to you. Whether he says something or not, waves of consolation rise high from his body and inundate us and comfort us. Such compassion! It's not pity, it's not sympathy and it's not palliation. It's merging with the sorrow that's afflicting the other person. There is no separation in the merging. He has no thought that he is there separately. But the afflicted will feel that UG is sharing their sorrow without their knowing it. There is no need to talk to him. Usually he remains silent on such occasions.

Twenty years ago, in 1972, Mr. Thakur, the director of *Deccan Herald*, brought to see UG a lady who was a relative of his and who, having lost her husband suddenly, was upset with utter grief. She talked to UG about death. I don't remember the details of the conversation. But I remember the mild smile on her face when she left. I don't know how he was able to erase her pain. I mentioned this before [*in my journals*] when Pramila died. Now Robert is another instance. UG didn't raise the subject [*of the death of Robert's wife*] until Robert mentioned it. As he felt that UG was giving him support, Robert stayed there for an hour and a half.

Moorty mentioned Susan's story on our walk. She is Larry's lady friend. She had a handicapped son. He was an invalid and fought seizure for three years and finally died one day. She was shattered. Friends thought that she would never recover. UG was in Hemet, near Palm Springs, at that time. Susan spent a week with UG there. UG didn't raise the topic of her son even once. He talked about everything else. Susan is an intelligent woman in her own right. She is a psychiatrist. But she didn't realize the gravity of the situation until she had to face it. She said that because UG acted like that she felt a great relief. Did she know how the sorrow of the loss of her son was allayed?

*   *   *

Last night around 8 pm, UG came and sat in our apartment. Everyone else joined us – Julie, Lisa, Guha and Krim. The children were watching some video downstairs in UG's living room. UG didn't want to disturb them, so he came upstairs and sat with us. Moorty also came a little later. Denise had invited him last night for dinner. You can see Chalet Sunbeam from our apartment window. Julie told UG about this and was about to show him. "I don't want to look at that. I am finished with that chalet," said UG.

This house, Ludi Haus, is really more convenient in every way than Sunbeam. Mrs. Miedler Ludi is the owner of the house. She told UG that if he comes every summer, she wouldn't bother to rent it to anyone else. It would be nice if he rents this house from now on. Besides, UG's apartment is spacious. There is a big balcony. There is enough space for any number of visitors in the living room. Besides, they built conveniently four or five apartments and studio rooms in this building. We are on the third floor. There are also rooms on this floor.

The children came upstairs around 10 pm after finishing watching their video. UG closed the meeting and went downstairs.

Guha and Lakshmi are not yet American citizens. They have a 'green card'. UG insists that as the children were born in the US they must grow up there. Both the children are very intelligent. UG says, "They are my only hope. They alone can save the US from going to hell." He says that the US must be leveled and China must thrive. "Who gave America the right to boss over the rest of the world? That bossiness must go," says UG.

The mountain peak is covered with a blanket of thick clouds. Maybe we are not going to see the sun today. Last night it rained for a long time. Tomorrow Moorty is leaving. It's his last day here. If he leaves, I won't have a walking companion anymore. He and I have gone around a lot and have talked about many things. We became closer to each other. He gave me B_{12} pills for my mouth sores. In a couple of days they were significantly better, although they didn't go away completely.

*   *   *

The four of us were talking about UG, sitting in the front of the Rialto Restaurant. Anthony and Krim were sipping coffee and I was drinking milk. Moorty was drinking beer. We were debating about if there are any easy ways of understanding UG's teaching. Moorty was trying to show us how you could break the vicious circle by using the principle that "Conditioning is a pleasure movement and there is no end to conditioning," and thus find the trick; and he told us how he could extract this principle from UG. "UG does not make things easy for you. He doesn't explain things. You must do your homework. You must think and investigate; you must break your head," says Moorty. "But, if you think you understood, and if you break the logic in his words and feel like you have opened a door, you will notice a hundred other closed doors mocking at you. It's useless to think. Arguments and intellectual feats are of no use. All those attempts must stop instantly. Not that *you* must stop. Stopping itself is an effort.

They must stop by themselves. That's total surrender. That the state of 'Only you are the refuge and nothing else.' UG is in such a state constantly. It's not surrendering to a force outside of you. It's a state of surrender," he says.

"You stop at every moment. In the stopping the search for pleasure disappears, stopping at every moment." Then how could you continue? "You turn in any direction; there won't be any shadows of the past. I feel that stopping, staying in any moment without expecting or desiring anything is what UG is teaching. You cannot achieve this through effort. It's not in our hands. But you can't just sit there twiddling your thumbs either. There must be effort. There must be yearning in the heart. The yearning must stifle you without letting you rest even for a moment. Then it must dry up."

I am writing all this down, not that I have really understood what Moorty has said. I feel as if Moorty is hopping and jumping in front of UG. In his essays he had given many clues to help understand UG. But how helpful are they? They just lead to an illusion that one has understood UG. Finally we must go beyond all those. It's not good enough to write commentaries on UG's statements. We will be in a state like the one described in the Telugu proverb: "Words go far beyond the castle, but the foot doesn't step out of the door." We can only roam about in the castles of air, floating in the worlds of imagination. The truth in UG's words is right in front of the threshold mixed with the dust. We can never understand it.

*   *   *

August 12, 1999 (Thursday)

Zurich – Hitl Restaurant

It's strange even to my mind that I haven't kept the journal for two days (10th and 11th) in this week. We went to Zurich on Tuesday (10th). We started out early in the morning in Julie's car. She rented a big Volkswagen station wagon this time. In the trunk in the back she placed some soft cushions for the children. Five adults can sit in the seats. The day before yesterday, Guha did all the driving. The rain didn't stop even when we were about to leave. UG says that it has been raining all over Europe. "Nature is angry because Moorty is leaving," Guha said poetically. The rain cleared by the time we arrived in Zurich at 10 am. By the time we helped Moorty with the baggage checking in, said goodbye to him and got out into the town, the sun had pulled aside the cloud blankets and peeked out. We ate our lunch at the Hitl Restaurant at 11:30 am. UG and Suguna ate just tomato soup and bread. We two ate vegetable pilaf. This restaurant opened in 1898; last year, they celebrated their centenary. From there we walked around in the town for a little while and browsed in the shops.

Everything is expensive. Even a calendar costs 25 francs. That means 750 rupees. It's a shocker. The amount may seem small. But it's 30 times more in rupees. 'You must go to America if you want to shop,' says UG. He says it's cheaper to travel to New York, shop and return than buying things in Europe. Apparently, even the rich go to the US for shopping. Then I don't know who buys all these expensive things here. The supermarkets here are not like in the US. You won't find goods manufactured in Asia or China. Everything is Swiss made. That's why things are so expensive.

We left Zurich for Berne at 1:00 pm in the afternoon. I felt that Berne has grown much bigger in all these years. It has been 10 years since I was in Berne before. We didn't see the Parliament House but went on the main streets. We saw the Bahnhof. They are building some new structures in front of it.

We were taken to an Indian market. There we bought all the supplies we needed – rice, legumes, oil etc. We left at 3 pm. It was 4:30 p.m. by the time we arrived in Gstaad by way of Zweisimmen. It's a mountainous route. The road is curved. But you can't describe in words the natural beauty: wherever you look you see green meadows, mountain slopes decorated by wooden buildings, mountains, streams and green trees – endless beauty.

*   *   *

About Krim Again

Our returning to Gstaad synchronized with and Mittu and Prasant getting off the train in Gstaad. We brought them home from the station. Their plan is to leave tomorrow after spending the night in Gstaad. Prasant is working as a programmer in Stuttgart in the Mico Bosch Company. I was glad to see Mittu. In the afternoon, we took them both in Julie's car and showed them UG's 'bench', Chalet Pfynegg and Chalet Sunbeam and returned to the main street. They were very happy to see Gstaad. Prasant is a nice young man. We chatted with Anthony for an hour at the Rialto. After dinner, we arranged our room for them and we both slept in UG's living room on the bed on which Moorty had been sleeping before. The living room looks bare after Moorty has left. Julie, Lisa, Guha, the children and UG remain.

Krim has been eating with us everyday, twice a day. While poking at him by saying, "He eats like a pig, a hog and a swine put together," UG stuffs him with more food. "He came to see me when he was 16 years old. I have known him for 25 years. I used to call him a 'walking garbage can'. In Mill Valley I used to make him clean up all the leftovers. Valentine would come to his defense when I scolded him using words like 'garbage'."

UG must have someone around to tease and make fun of. He has Krim – Karimulla – for a week. He teases him: "Confess that you are a CIA agent. I know. Yours is a family of agents. If not, why did you go to Russia twice? What business do you have there?" Krim is not offended by UG's teasing. However, he hasn't yet recovered from the confusion of whether UG is just teasing him or is serious when he accuses him of being a CIA agent. Apparently, his uncle is a well-known spy and escaped from Russia with some important secret information. His father was a US government official.

Krim's background is interesting. He was born in Germany. He spent some time in Switzerland. He went to school in England. And he worked in the US. Before that he apparently worked at a small job in Zurich, in the chain store called 'Migros'. He lived in Turkey for a little while. Currently he lives with his parents in Virginia. His relationship has turned into a noose around his neck. He is hoping that he will have better luck in the future. In his palm there is a big 'island' in his fate line. Fourteen years of his life were trapped in it. However, Krim performed a great deed: he took pictures of UG and Valentine from the year 1981. There is no count of how many hundreds of dollars he threw away doing that. He took some great pictures of UG in those days. Raj Mehta put them up now on the Internet along with the excerpts of UG's sayings that I had picked for that purpose. Krim is the best among UG's photographers; Arhat is next. I don't know how Arhat is in Bombay or what he is doing there. Besides these, Leboyer and Scott also have taken some nice pictures.

* * *

Yesterday it was Wednesday, the 11th – there was an eclipse of the sun. There was a big hubbub in Europe, especially in Stuttgart. For the last ten days, newspapers and TV have been announcing in a big way that it would be possible to see the total eclipse of the sun in Stuttgart. Many different sorts of beliefs and fears have been surfacing such as that this is the last solar eclipse of the century; that Nostradamus predicted in his almanac that the world will be destroyed because of this eclipse; and that that day will bring harm to everyone in the world. It's a big celebration for everyone. Some hundreds of thousands of people gathered in all the cities where the eclipse could be observed. There was a lot of noise on TV all day yesterday.

After all this, by the time the eclipse happened the sky had become overcast and there was rain. All those who stood with their umbrellas in the rain expecting that something would happen or that the skies would fall apart were disappointed. The eclipse occurred at 12:30 pm. At that moment, there was no show to see on except what was on TV. "What's the big deal? Why have they been fussing all these days about the eclipse? What will you know about what happens there thousands of miles away?" asks UG. In India they would be performing fasting, worships in temples, propitiations, and so on, without end.

Never mind the sun eclipse; UG for his part created a big havoc last night in our room. We all gathered for our supper around 8:30. Mittu and Prasant were present. All the food dishes were placed on the table. UG doesn't like people eating in groups like that. He has been warning us since the day before yesterday that we should all eat in our own apartments and not eat communally. Since Moorty has left, there is no one to cook for UG. UG said he would join us. He got furious when he saw a crowd there. All that anger flowed like lava from a volcano eruption on to Julie. He drove Julie away saying, "Get out of this place; go and eat somewhere else." He banged on everyone saying, "How many times did I tell you that there must be no eating like in an *ashram*? If you eat so many kinds of foods, your poop and urine will become more expensive! You will gain nothing more than that!" Julie left without saying a word. Sumedha went after her to console her. We all stood still like statues for a little while. No one was able to move for some time. Then we somehow finished our meal.

*   *   *

August 13, 1999 (Friday)

Morning 6 am. Although I got up late, I still feel very drowsy.

From the window I could see the fog, and appearing in it, the tennis court, the wooden houses behind it, the train track above them, and a thick growth of pine trees behind the track. Above all this, a whole section of the mountain was drowned in white clouds.

Almost all yesterday it rained. In the evening, around 8 pm., Suguna and I went out to phone Archana. It was very cold outside. Inside it is warm. They insert thick insulation between the wooden walls in these houses. That prevents the cold from outside being felt inside the houses. There is heating in every individual room. It gets to below zero degrees here in the winter. And it snows. I must come here once in wintertime. Unless we wear thick clothing, we wouldn't be able to bear the cold outside. An insect is hovering around the lamp and making a bee-like drone sound.

Yesterday, Krim and I went on foot for the first time to see UG's old house and bench in Saanen. It may be a bit more than two or three kilometers from here. All these times I have gone there by car, but not by myself. The bench is in ruins. Chips of wood have fallen off of it onto the ground. We saved all those chips in Krim's bag. It's on that bench 32 years ago that the 'Earthquake' had happened to UG. If we sit on it, a vast expanse of nature spreading its beauty is unveiled before us. According to the Telugu calendar, UG's 49th birthday occurred that year, in 1967, on August 13, the first day of the month of Ashadha. Today's date is that date.

I narrated to Karimulla, like a story, all the details of the events surrounding the 'Calamity' that had happened that day. I was surprised to learn that he didn't know about UG and the details surrounding the Calamity, although he has been seeing UG for 25 years. The name of the chalet UG had lived in before is 'Pfynegg'. That is the chalet behind the bench. I showed it to Krim. From there we walked along the trail on the mountain back to Gstaad. UG didn't know that we had brought back chips of wood from the bench.

*   *

*

Everyone is coming for UG's talks in the afternoon. About ten people came including Nataraj, Mitra, three Italians and a Mexican woman called Prabha. Henk and his friend come every day. UG asked Henk to postpone his journey for some days. He gave him 700 francs yesterday. He can stay here for three more weeks with that money. Karimulla is also postponing his journey till the 20th. We have less than three weeks time left here. I am beginning to feel that the days are rolling fast. Lakshmi is returning in exactly one week. Then, on the 24th, their whole family will leave. It will be pretty quiet here when the children leave. They both have gotten close to Suguna. Sumedha doesn't eat unless Suguna prepares and gives her food. Suguna takes good care of them. I thought what she cooked yesterday was quite tasty. She cooked the spaghetti well. She also makes good lentils soup and yogurt rice.

Karimulla ate with us last night; he ate with Julie in the afternoon. Lisa and Julie are cooking separately. After UG's banging the other day, people have stopped eating together. UG's word is our command.

*   *
    *

There was a discussion last night as to whether the link to Raj Mehta's website "Essential UG" should be on the top of the webpage created by Moorty. Each may express his or her opinion, but UG has the final say. Only in name Moorty's decision is above UG's, but he will never oppose UG's decision. Raj Mehta was upset that the link for his website was put in at the bottom of the main website's homepage. UG made sure that even that link was removed completely. I read Raj's e-mail to Julie. I too didn't like it. I felt like that he was forming a misunderstanding of Moorty. What say does he have in this matter? That's why UG took such drastic action against Raj.

*   *   *

UG's Euphoria – Internet Links

August 14, 1999 (Saturday)

Morning 6:10 am. I had a disturbed sleep just before I woke up. Some dreams! I was woken up at 3:30 am. Again at 5 am I heard the sound of the alarm. But I still lay there lazily. For some reason my enthusiasm is down. I don't have the same enthusiasm in writing this journal as I had before. Some fear has been creeping in from some corner.

What terrific energy there is in UG! What a flood of enthusiasm! Yesterday he held the files of the Internet links prepared by Lisa in his lap and read each page aloud. "There are 21,023 links to my home page. They are including me in so many fields. They have listed 'UG Krishnamurti' on the California tourist page! In the middle of the writing about Indian dances, women's ornaments, and beauty shops they mention 'UG Krishnamurti'! Speaking of the greatest scientists, intellectuals and thinkers of the 20th century, they mention UG Krishnamurti's name! You won't find a single place where Jiddu Krishnamurti is mentioned. They forgot about him completely. Good thing! I am very proud. J. Krishnamurti's name is obliterated after so many years. They included my name in so many thousands of links without any advertisement or institutions. They don't know in what mold or framework they should fit UG in. That's why they are including me in all the branches of knowledge from philosophy to science. Something very good is happening. Lisa, you have done a great service in preparing all this patiently. I don't know how to thank you." With such jubilance of a child, he has been holding all those files sitting in the sofa and going on for a whole week.

It's funny when he announces to everyone who comes, "There is not even a mention of J. Krishnamurti; there's no mention of him in thousands of pages; he deserves it!" Sometimes you wonder: Why such jubilance in an 80 year-old man that his name is spreading all over the world? What does he care about what the world thinks about him? Where does he get such enthusiasm? Then, the next moment, he sits back as if he doesn't care and it doesn't concern him. Why such jubilance in a man who lives as if he is ready to exit this world the next moment? Where does he get such enthusiasm and joy? Do I wonder about that because such enthusiasm and joy are getting scarce in me day by day?

*   *   *

UG and Julie

Then he starts cursing Julie. He constantly points to her that she hasn't prepared the files as Lisa has done, pulling all those pages of links from the computer. "You are useless; you can't do anything. You are dull-headed and mean. You head is full of clay. How did you get work for *Time* Magazine? How could they hire you? Tell me the truth: how many people did you sleep with to get that job?"

She is able to bear all these insults, curses, scolding, and ridicule. No matter how much he scolds her, how much he insults her by calling her a 'bitch', by sending her away in rage, she endures it all like the mother earth. Why? Is she so much attached to UG? How has she become so attached to him? Someone else wouldn't have tolerated even one percent of the foul language UG uses on her. Even the greatest devotee would have run away. On top of it, he makes her spend a lot of money. He makes her give money to whomever he likes. If by mistake she leaves her purse with people and forgets it, he hides the purse and collects a penalty from her for forgetting it. The money he collects that way he gives away right in front of everyone to some children or someone else. He is as generous in giving money away as he is tough in collecting it.

But why does he frown on Julie so much? What sin has she committed? He can't stand it if she sits in front of him on a sofa. He says, "Don't sit in front of me. Get up and leave," and spurns her. But Julie bears all this spurning with a smile. UG's mistreatment of her has been getting worse all these ten years. On the other hand, her sense of service and her devotion to him have been increasing hour by hour. Day and night there is nothing else in her world except UG. She doesn't care about her children or their future; she doesn't care about her mother who is close to death. She doesn't care about the affairs of the world or about friends. I only read this verse from Bhagavatam which says, "This son of the enemy of the gods[10] was so constantly devoted to the pair of lotus-like feet of Sri Hari[11] that he forgot this world." But in reality it's only in Julie that I could see such total devotion and dedication. No one else has them.

But you don't see in UG that filial affection for the devotee or compassionate regard of Narayana.[12] He shows compassion to everyone else. He entertains all those who come to him, answers their questions, satisfies their needs and sends them

---

[10] Prahlada.
[11] Vishnu.
[12] Vishnu.

away. But with Julie, he says, "If I am tolerating you, if I am letting you stay here without driving you out, it's only for the children and this couple. If this couple (pointing to us both) were not here, I wouldn't have the slightest need for you or your computer. You think that I will miss him and suffer if I don't see Moorty again in my life? You think I need all these things he does for me on the computer? I don't need anyone. I don't lose a thing if all those links to the homepage are destroyed," banging her. That's how it is, the true attitude of this merciful man toward Julie.

*   *   *

Time: 3:15 in the afternoon. There is still 45 minutes time before everyone assembles in the living room downstairs. For some reason, I'm a little depressed today. It's foggy in my head. I feel that I am my own enemy. I detest this body of mine. I don't feel like sitting in UG's presence. I feel as if I've lost something, as if I am wasting my time. What can I do? I can't sleep; and I can't sit idle. I must do something; but what? Everything seems meaningless and empty. Living itself seems unbearable. Who are all these people? What do I have to do with them? Why am I here? Who is this UG? Who is Julie? Who is Guha? Who am I? Why am I here? Why did I get trapped here?

... I pick up something to read; but I am not interested. The weather is pleasant outside, but the miserable polenta which Mario has cooked yesterday mixing it with cheese is upsetting my stomach. How did UG like it? I ate a piece even though I didn't like it. I have never eaten worse food before.

To add to this, all kinds of thoughts have been cooking in my mind. Who is the root cause of all this? UG. I am very angry at UG. Why? I am furious that all these people are praising UG and his dress. Why? What did UG do? Is it that he caused such a confusion in me? Is it that he is turning me into a crazy man? Who is responsible? Am I? Where am I? Am I in this writing? In this thought?

I read the paper Henk gave me. It felt like someone put a chili up my ass. If that 'gentleman' is in front of me, I would knock his teeth out! Why does he talk like that? As a matter of fact, it's those who listen to such things that don't have sense. Does the writer have it? Mario's miserable food is upsetting my stomach. Do I need to calm down? I can't stay alone. And I can't mix with people.

What do I want? Last evening, UG asked everyone the same question: "What do you want?" ... Knowledge? Calmness? Peace of mind? Happiness? What do you want? How do I know what I want? If I haven't known about it beforehand, how do I know that I don't have it? Do I want to be like UG? How do I know how UG is? Can I see inside myself? How about this body?

Who is this person called Chandrasekhar? Am I the husband of Suguna? Do I have children? What was I before that? I am the son of so and so? Who was I before then? A baby in the cradle? Before that? I was an embryo in a womb. What was I before I was that embryo? Whence did I come? If I don't have this memory, the memory that I am such and such or that I am this way; if I don't have the memory that my mind is unhappy; if I don't have any of these, then who am I?

I am writing and I am thinking. There is memory behind my thought. Who? What's the connection? If the memory that got trapped in this body is the 'me', then how would I know that memory? The awareness that I am, the awareness that I am breathing, sitting, writing – whence this awareness? Whence is the awareness which reads this writing and understands it? Whose awareness is it? How about the memory that thinks of events that will happen in future and worries about them?

I can't let it go. I can't stop. I can't throw it all into the wind. The memory of UG is [like a] hearth on my heart. My memory. Can I ever forget myself? My memories are my burden. I can't breathe. Old memories and the things that were supposed to happen (but didn't) – all get mixed together and become my burden.

Everyone will gather downstairs in a crowd. UG's meeting. And they talk. I will listen? *I* will listen? Who am I?

* * *

August 15, 1999 (Sunday)

Morning 6 am. It's three weeks since I have left home to travel to this land. We will have a new apartment starting tomorrow. UG decided that Julie should vacate her room and move to this room. He doesn't want her to stay close to him. Lisa and Mario are leaving for Germany today. They are returning on the 24th. We two will put up in the apartment of Julie and Lisa. There is a separate room for Aruna and Venkat in that apartment. On the 24th, Julie and Guha and his family will all go back to the US. Then Lisa and Mario will stay in Julie's room; and if Mr. Raju comes he will stay in Guha's room. That's the arrangement.

The landlady Meddler Ludi is not only arrogant but also thirsty for money. Everyday she brings a complaint. She raised a big complaint the other day that someone was drying clothes on the balcony. Because of dampness from the rain the clothes hanging indoors didn't dry. The electric drier was not working. So, Lisa and Suguna tied a wire across the balcony and hung some clothes on it. The landlady was upset. "This is Switzerland. No one dries their clothes on the balcony. Those who see it will object," she told Julie.

Then came another big complaint, namely, that we are not closing the apartment doors but are leaving them open. "In this country everyone must close the doors. We must close the doors whether we stay in the apartment or go out. It's bad manners to keep the doors open," she instructed Julie to tell us. The day before yesterday, when we were returning in the evening from our walk, she unlocked the front door for us and repeatedly asked us, "You weren't the ones who left without locking the door, were you? Were you?" "From now on, if anyone leaves without locking the door, I will call the police," she said arrogantly. I got so angry that I thought of knocking her teeth out.

UG, who has been watching her behavior off and on, is also angry with her. He asked Nataraj to talk to her in German and tell her that if she continues to behave in this manner we will have to look for another place for the next year. Julie pays the rent for the rooms promptly. But these white folks here look down upon Indians. They are proud of their wealth. They think that India is a poor country and that Indians are poor. Even UG refers to himself as a 'poor Indian', but who can compare with him? If a billionaire like Bill Gates comes to see him, then the judgments of these stupid people would turn topsy-turvy. It all has to do with the magic of money.

* * *

Gottfried and Bodil

Gottfried and Bodil were teacher and pupil. The teacher fell in love with the pupil while his wife was sick. Their friendship turned into love and they came close to marrying. His wife was bedridden with cancer. Because she was his wife, the government was paying for her medical expenses. Gottfried decided against marrying Bodil, because if he divorced his wife, the wife would have lost that benefit. He thought that his wife should spend her last days comfortably. She died after some time. He took her ashes to the top of a mountain and scattered them in the waters there.

It's strange that Bodil didn't want to marry him after that. UG said that she had a passing relationship with a Christian priest. She would have had to become a German citizen if she had married Gottfried. She objected to that. She hated Hitler. She is Swedish. She doesn't want to be considered a German citizen.

UG advises her to marry him because she would get a good pension after Gottfried dies, and then she could live securely till the end of her life. "How are you going to get any money after Gottfried dies? Marry him. What do you care if he is German or French? Money is more important," he has been putting pressure on her for many years.

Lisa and Mario – II

Lisa and Mario is another unmarried young couple. They have been eager to get married and stay together. But UG has not been allowing it to happen. "He is a coolie; he works as a handyman. He is no match to you. You must find a rich man, a fat cat," he tells Lisa. She works in the Givenchy Spa and Hotel in Palm Springs, California, as a masseuse. He has given her much encouragement in Palm Springs and straightened out her life there. These two once belonged to the coterie of Rajneesh's disciples.

After Rajneesh died, all his disciples had no one to look up to; they were unable to find livelihoods and their lives went on a decline. UG had the burden of reforming many of them and helping them stand on their own legs. Nataraj makes his money by doing astrological readings. He deposited money in our finance company through UG.

UG has been preventing Lisa and Mario from marrying. They didn't want to go against his decision. "Why are you so attached to him? How good a fuck is he?" UG asks her rather crudely. Apparently she replied that once she had spent the night with a boy from a gas station and no one had ever matched him in fucking.

*   *   *

Sabyasachi Guha's Life

August 16, 1999 (Monday)

Yesterday morning, after eating my oatmeal, we vacated our room and moved our things to the 'F' apartment next to UG's room. It took an hour and a half. Suguna and I moved to the room where Lisa and Mario had been. Every day, Guha and I eat oatmeal in my room for breakfast in the morning. At those times, Guha talks about the lives of Sri Ramakrishna, Vivekananda and Tagore. The day before yesterday, he and I went for a walk under the shade of the trees along the Saanen River. Guha related his story.

He has been going through a lot of bodily changes. I don't normally hear of such things happening. Even in UG's case, I only have *heard* him talk about those things. I don't remember everything, as I am becoming increasingly forgetful. Sometimes I am forgetting my own affairs. I feel like recording here what Guha has told me. I feel like writing concisely whatever I have heard from Guha in different ways, not just in one day or on one occasion, but in all these ten days, starting from that morning of our oatmeal breakfast time to the time when we got back to our rooms in the nights after seeing UG.

Guha comes from Calcutta. His father was a well-known doctor who was reputed to be a good healer. Guha had a huge family. When his father died suddenly, the responsibility of his family fell on him. I think he still has four younger brothers and three sisters; I can't remember clearly. Ever since his childhood, he has been spiritually inclined. I don't know how. Just like in my case, it must have been in his blood, or it's the influence of the planets. Such a disposition is surely not the result of one's own effort. It's not something that one tries and learns through effort. Guha used to go to Dakshineshwar. He is thoroughly familiar with all the places where Sri Ramakrishna spent his time. "I used to be so sorry that I didn't have the opportunity to meet such a great man."

While talking to Guha, I recalled the days when I used to cry that I wasn't born when Sri Ramakrishna was still alive. It's not clear how Guha got involved with the Naxalites. In those days many students came under the influence of that movement. Guha's life took an important turn in 1981 when he joined the Indian Institute of Science in Bangalore. By then he finished his B.Sc. He was selected to do research for an M.Sc. He got acquainted with Lakshmi when he was in college. Love landed him in marriage. Everything was fine until then. I can't remember whether the marriage took place after he came to Bangalore or before – probably while he was doing his research or when he was working after he finished his research.

Lakshmi apparently taught in St. Joseph's College for some time. She came first to America to Rutgers University. Then she helped Guha come to the US and become a research scholar in Rutgers. It has been more than 15 years since they have settled down in New Jersey. Both their children were born there. Later, Lakshmi quit her job to take care of their children. How did they get acquainted with the Ramachandra Mission? It happened soon after they started living in the US. I can't remember clearly. There was some pressure building from inside. Maybe it was the spiritual disposition that lay hidden in him unbeknown to him. After some days, he experienced a great promise when he started *sadhana* and meditation according to their instructions. He got immersed in intense *sadhana*. Meanwhile, there was the influence of J. Krishnamurti. I can't remember which came first and which later. It's all mixed up in my head.

Whatever it was, in 1995, Guha read UG's webpage on the Internet, and that was another important encounter that shook his life and made it turn a corner. UG's book *Mind is a Myth* blasted his mind. He started an e-mail correspondence with Moorty. Later he saw UG in Julie's apartment in New York. Ever since then, whenever he is with UG, Guha is in another world. Later, he went to Palm Springs and spent two weeks with him.

Recently, that is, a couple of years ago, strange changes occurred in Guha's body. Apparently he felt that his skin was burning on the right side of his heart, exactly above the navel, at the alimentary canal. He suffered for 21 days after the burning had started. Before it happened, his guru

Parthasaradhi came to New York and called him on the phone from the hotel. By that time, Guha had severed his connections completely with the Ramachandra Mission. Before, his friends with the Mission thought that Guha was attaining a high state spiritually. His guru was giving him confidence and support. After he became acquainted with UG all these lies burned away.

(The narrative about Guha is not coming through freely. Something is obstructing its flow. The things he has told me are not coming in a connected way. I laugh at my own state. I wanted to write it down so I wouldn't forget; but even in these four or five days I have forgotten the details. I can see through the window the rays of the dawn behind the mountain. Today too the sky appears to be clear. Still there is rain.)

Why do I feel like writing this great story? I know that UG knows what's happening to him. Guha told UG about it. UG is constantly watching over him with a thousand eyes. He doesn't let him go for a walk. He tells him what to eat and with whom he should eat. I feel that UG will certainly go from here to New York and I think he will spend a lot of time with Guha. Guha needs him very much right now. It's hard to figure out what's happening in him.

Yesterday evening, Denise invited us two, Sugana and me, and the children for dinner. I think UG asked Guha not to go. I ate falafel. It's causing some disturbance in my stomach.

I can't remember whether the date yesterday was the *Naga Caviti*[13] or *Naga Pancami*.[14] Last evening, I narrated to everyone the manner in which the yoga called 'Brahmanaspati' yoga had happened to UG. I told them of the experience UG had about the cobra on the Maha Sivaratri day and my dream about it. I felt very happy. Everyone who heard it enjoyed it. While we were dining in the Christiania Restaurant, I met Volker with his friends. He said, "I had a feeling that I would certainly meet you this time. When I asked him to go see UG, he said, "If he wants to see me, invite him to come to my home. I'll be happy." His outlook has not yet changed. Has mine changed? Except in regard to worldly affairs, has anything changed in me?

*   *   *

About Volker – My meeting with him

Afternoon 3:30 pm. It's been raining without a break since morning. Mitra took me in his car around 10 am to Volker's place. Earlier, as I had sat in UG's presence and was wondering about how I should go to see Volker, Mitra offered to take me to his place. I asked UG if I should bring Volker back if he wanted to come. "I have no hostility toward him; even if you invite him to your apartment for dinner I have no objection," he said laughing. I knew that. Things went wrong between them ten years ago in Bangalore. Since then Volker has never stepped in UG's place. After I talked to Volker I learned that he also has no hostility toward UG. "UG is always

---

[13] 'Cobra Fourth' – the day of cobra worship.
[14] *'Cobra Fifth'*.

welcome whenever he wants to come to our home." "He came here before many times. I used to celebrate Valentine's birthday every year in this house. They both used to come," he said. He was very happy to hear that I have been running a school in Valentine's name.

The wooden building he lives in is 400 years old. He has been living there for twenty years. A German lady called Anusati and another German young lady called Nutan are living with him. He says they are 'bursts of energy'. When Mitra and I got there, he was making an omelet-like pancake. He served me coffee, cookies, pieces of bread and butter mixed with honey. There was nice music in the background. We talked for a long time. They both heard with interest the details of Aruna's wedding. He will come to 'Ludi Haus' again on the 27th. If possible, he will see both Aruna and Venkat. But they both must be free to see Volker.

Meanwhile, Henk came in. Volker brought me back here around 12:30 pm in his car. I wanted to talk to him about a lot more things – about what he is doing and how he is making his living. I don't know anything about it. But the earlier mischief and excitability in him are gone. He has calmed down, maybe due to his aging. I notice a certain peacefulness in him. I don't see his earlier aggressiveness. But he has the same beard and same long hair. He spends four or five months a year in Gstaad. The rest of the year he spends in Germany. I sang "*Bhavani...dayani...*". Then we sat silently without talking. There is some strange attraction between him and Anusati. She is his companion in every way. I see the characteristics of a housewife in her. I notice certain contentment in both of them. What is he expecting from his life? Has he been able to get what he wanted? How far has he traveled in these 25 years?

*   *   *

Guha's Life – II

The teacher of Sahaja Marg, Ramachandraji, put Guha on the spiritual path. Guha used to read JK before then. He read all his books and heard his tapes. Once JK appeared in his dream and said with his hand under the cheek, "I haven't been able to help you. There is nothing I can do for you." Since then Guha started searching for another living guru. He got involved in the Sahaja Marg of Parthasaradhi Rajagopal, a disciple of Ramachandra. That institution was everything for Guha till he met UG. He roamed all over India visiting all the branches of that institution. After UG came into his life through the Internet, the people in the Marg attempted to stop him. Its followers and his old gurus tried to entice him in various ways and turn him back to their side. They threatened him saying, "If you leave, then we will have to explain to the Chief Guru. Many others who have left before have tried to come back, repenting. The doors will be closed to you." Guhaji adamantly refused. He wiped it all out of his mind. Now he is totally under UG's spell.

UG's Initial Meetings with Others:

A disciple of Ramachandra, a Frenchman named Anthra Poray, met UG in 1967 and invited him to his house in Marseilles.

He also invited Gottfried at the same time. That's how UG and Gottfried had met.

In Bombay Maurice Friedman invited UG to his house. He also invited Nisargadatta. That's how those two had met. Friedman said that his wife or daughter was sick and she was eager to see him. When UG actually arrived there he ran into Nisargadatta. That day Dr. Leboyer was also there. Leboyer then got hooked to UG. He took many different kinds of photos of UG.

Punjaji came to see UG the first time in Bombay. Apparently Subba Rao, the manager of a coffee estate, told him to meet UG. Punjaji asked UG to introduce him to some of his friends in the US. UG replied saying that he had severed his connections with that country long ago. Punjaji met UG again in Gstaad. Later on, when he was circulating as a guru, he started telling people that UG had come to him asking if he, Poonja, had any connections in America!! That's how things are!

August 17, 1999 (Tuesday)

I woke up late. My early morning dreams were heavier than daydreams. There were noises of me talking to myself incessantly. "Even though you don't talk, your vocal chords are still active because you are talking to yourself. Your existence is nothing but sound," UG said yesterday. I am writing thinking it is silent all around. But I can't write this without telling myself so. "If you can sign your name without telling yourself your name, I will take that check," UG challenged a Chinese man and opened his eyes. I can't sign my name without telling myself my name. Then what can I do? It's my delusion to think that my hand is writing without my involvement and that this writing is taking shape without any connection to me. Only when I spell out each word in myself can this hand write it. Where is this 'speaking stone'? Whatever I am writing, someone is spelling out each word of it within myself. "That is you," says UG.

It's the same in dreams. There is no difference between waking and dreaming. When a person is awake, that 'I' is shouting out loud. He recognizes everything he sees and makes loud noises within himself whether or not he says words aloud. He listens to the sound of the train on the rails and recognizes: "it's a train." Those train sounds can only be heard from outside. I don't have the idea that the train is running in my chest. When I write, I can hear the sounds of these words as if spoken aloud. Is the 'I' nothing but these sounds?

This whole sentence is echoing, just as I can hear the same words that I speak into a telephone echoed back to me. All the thoughts that I think – every word of them – are sounding aloud within me. They are appearing on this paper. How is my hand able to write them? The sounds in my head are taking the shape of letters and making my pen move by jumping through the collection of nerves at the tip of my fingers. What a strange thing! How is this happening? My visual perception is also the same. Am I seeing everything that I think I see first only within myself? That's because all the images that fall on the retina the brain translates as things existing outside. Do they really exist outside?

Is my body 'outside'? Is the face I look at in the mirror mine? Where is the outside? How can the reflection in the mirror be myself? Is my essence inside me? This graying hair, this wrinkled face - are these mine? What am I? In all these things - the hand, the leg, the chest, and the head - which one is 'I'? If all of them together constitute a single form, how come I can't see all of them at once? When I focus on something and stop looking around, only then I can see that thing.

This is all confusing. The things that I thought I had known all these years are confusing to me now. What is it that I can know now? This is all a lie. It's a lie that I am silent. It's a pure lie that I am alive. That I was born one day and that I will die some day are both stark lies. I am deluded in thinking that I believe all these things.

I go around remembering in myself all the things that are dinned into my ears by others, talking to myself, making noises within myself and telling myself that I am experiencing things and that I am awake. I have no relationship with any of these. All these are shadows - echoes. Where does light come from? Where does sound come from in the first place? Where does it sound? I am watching in myself the sound of taking a long breath in and letting it out. Where does that breath come from? Who breathes? If I don't watch it, I am not even aware that I am breathing. Now I can see both.

This breath, these words echoing, these two words - they are sounds ringing in my ears. It's some kind of noise. I can't say why I hear it. I feel that this sound will pierce my ear drums.

Who is this 'I' who is experiencing all this? Do I know all of these at once or one after another? I experience as if I know them all at once.

The noise the door is making doesn't mix with the sound made by these words. It's heard separately at a distance through my ears. The brain knows what they are. It recognizes them, changes them into words and spells them out. I hear the sound of a car going in the distance. All these sounds get known in the brain. When I write here the vocal chords in my throat vibrate. The ears are able to hear all the words that I say within myself even though the words do not make a sound outside.

It's past 7 am. Suguna is setting the table for breakfast. The coffee is not ready yet. I must drink my coffee and wash. These tasks are all things I impose on myself. I think that UG lacks all this. I look into myself and listen. I experience. I think that such a process doesn't go on in UG. I believe what he says.

*   *   *

August 18, 1999 (Wednesday)

Last night, I watched Mahesh Bhatt's movie "*Dastaq*" on the video till 10:30 pm and went to bed. Yet I was able to get up from bed this morning at 5:10 am. Much of yesterday it was raining. We went to Zweisimmen in a car. We went to the Migros there. UG bought the stuff we needed. Suguna bought a vanity bag. It looks pretty good. I bought four flashlights.

The process of purchasing things has begun. I went again with Guha to the Co-Op and bought batteries.

When we were about to go for a walk, UG stopped Guha. All yesterday morning Guha was talking about the changes that were occurring in his body. He says that they are more intense in UG's presence, particularly the changes in his pineal gland. In the place where there is the *Ajna Chakra* he has different sorts of experiences. He says that he has profuse saliva in his mouth. His appetite has slowed down. He can't eat much. He always stays close to UG. UG also constantly watches him as well as Nataraj. UG calls Nataraj '*Mahamuni*'.[15] Every now and then he shakes his hand. He asks him about his future. "Believing in you and your astrological reading I have spent thousands of dollars and become poor. Money hasn't rained yet. It's almost the end of August. When is the money going to rain?" he asks him. Nataraj laughs boisterously about everything. I don't know with whom his astrological predictions work.

Mr. Raju from Machilipatnam is arriving. He will be here for four days. Lakshmi is coming on the 20th. The kids are happy. UG has already started his travel preparations. On the phone Julie has reserved a room for him in the Southgate Apartment Hotel. The rent is $300 per day. UG will be New York for three days starting on September 1. Perhaps he will be on the East Coast for another week or ten days. Because Kittu, Kamesh and Kumar are all there, I think he will see them. He may go to Palm Springs from there. He talks about Brazil, but

---

[15] 'The great sage'.

there is no sign that he would go there. "Mr. Narayana Moorty, you must come too. We both can drink the *soma* juice there and will talk above love and bliss of Brahman," he says. Moorty says, "OK, let's do it." It's exactly a week since Moorty has left. Moorty has moved the link to Raj Mehta's website to a more prominent place on the UG homepage. That's better.

I am losing my interest in all those things. I am not even thinking much of preserving UG's tapes and books and making them accessible to all. Even though a couple of people have written letters to my Internet e-mail address, I don't feel like replying to them. The tapes I have brought I am taking back because UG has asked me to. The question arises in my mind: how long will this go on? My time here is coming to an end. But before I leave I must give some kind of shape to the tapes I have with me. Everyone will be leaving. Moorty too sings the same song. He is not giving any suggestions as to how to preserve the tapes. What does UG care about all these things? What does a man who lives from moment to moment care about what happens to his 'teaching' after him? His only concern is that all this stuff should not be in any one person's possession. He says they will be preserved in the Davidson Library archives. Then who will undertake that task? But why should I care who will? I am completely losing my interest in such activities, particularly in organizing the materials relating to UG.

I am wondering about what I have gained from all these activities and how they have helped me. Have I truly attained any higher state? When I look into myself, I realize how horrible my state is. Economically and in terms of family pleasures, my life has gotten a lot better. No one is more fortunate than me in those areas. My health is also good. It's quite remarkable that I have been able to manage to this extent for twenty years even though I have diabetes. Besides that, there isn't much to be proud of. I am of no use to anyone. It's all finished. I have no further role to play in this universal drama. It's enough if that book of mine is published. I don't know if I'll be able to bring it out in Telugu. Unless some publisher comes forward, such things won't happen. Be that as it may. But what have I gained personally?

To be sure, I have had the opportunity of being around UG so closely for 30 years. But what kind of change has happened in me? What higher states have I attained? Who would have a better opportunity than me? Has my mind become any broader? There is no light anywhere, in any corner. Life is as it has always been – living in narrow alleys, in sewers, in dirt, in dust, like a leaf-platter torn by street dogs. Is it because of my disappointment that I am like this that my interest has been dwindling? Or is my disappointment getting worse because my interest is diminishing? Or is my dullness due to my thinking that UG has been trying from time to time to keep me away from all these things? Or am I imagining that UG has been trying to keep me away from all these things because he has been noticing me becoming lazier and duller. This matter is not clear to me.

One thing is becoming clear: I won't have any role to play in future affairs. Those are all things that involve high-tech and computer technology. They're beyond me. Whatever I have in my hands I must hand over to capable people. I haven't met such a person yet. Especially UG's letters. They must be put on the Internet. For that, they must be given some shape. Moorty can do that. I don't have such ideas. Moorty says that he will write UG's biography. But he has a condition: UG must assure him that he will live to be a hundred years. Moorty says he will start it when UG is 95 and finish it by the time he completes 100 years.

* * *

I am getting sadder as my time of leaving is getting closer. I still don't know when exactly we are leaving. It could be any moment. Preparations have been underway all these years to die at any moment. Who can teach me how to prepare? That's what needs to happen. When we feel things are heavy, we drop them without anyone telling us. Everything must happen like that. No use to prepare. The time to part ways is nearing. UG will suddenly disappear. I have a longing to get closer and closer to him. But each day I am moving away from myself. The true 'I' is going away to far off places beyond where I can see. The colorful 'I', created by my imagination, is far removed from the true 'I'; but my true form is completely masked. I can't even remember what it is like. Only this false image appears as true. I have the illusion that only the things it does are real.

Sometimes, at some moment, there is a flash in this darkness. Then I forget again. In that moment I feel that I am walking in some abyss and my whole body trembles. The next moment the usual layers of clouds and thorny bushes press around on the way; it is a utter darkness in which I can't see even with my eyes open. I distrust those who offer light. Even if I see any light, my ego prevents me from going on that lighted path. "Why should someone else show me the way? Can't I find it myself?" says my ego. I feel as if I should let everything go and surrender myself. My mind asks, "What should I do to surrender?" But it doesn't stop with that question. There would be no problem if it does.

This is all useless. This is all going in circles which won't lead me anywhere. "You must first let go of that hope. Then you will stop. You must stop everywhere, at any place, without making one step forward, without looking back; you must stop wherever you are forgetting yourself" – if you even think that sort of thought, then you are moving. There is nothing to be done. There is no path to walk on. There is no direction to turn to. It's not even possible to breathe. I must stand. I must stop. I must stop all this running and stand quietly. Even if heavens collapse on me, even if the earth under my feet cracks, I must not move a foot. "If you move, your mind moves. If your mind moves, worlds move."[16] Beware. Stop. Stop wherever you are.

*   *   *

August 19, 1999 (Wednesday)

Days are passing by at lightning speed. As we get older we often feel that time is moving faster than when we were young. I can't believe that I have already completed 54 years. How

---

[16] From Chalam's *Sudha*.

many illusions I have!. To begin with, that I am living is itself an illusion.

Last night, I saw another Hindi movie, *Raja Hindustani*. The songs in it are popular. Archana used to sing the song "*Pardesi, pardesi, jana nahin.*" In the '*Dastaq*' movie I saw yesterday, there were scenes from Gstaad and Saanen. The Miss Universe of India, Susmita Sen, acted her role very well. Both the heroes were new actors. I don't remember their names.

Yesterday afternoon at 2 pm, Francis, his wife, his son Alexander and his sister Evelyn came. After spending an hour with UG, they came to my room, had coffee and cookies, and chatted with me and Suguna. I tried to explain UG to them as much as I could. I don't know how much I succeeded. Alexander sat quietly when he was with UG, but asked some interesting questions in our room. I felt that some conflict was raging in him. I noticed that the more he heard about UG the more curious he became. Francis's wife is beautiful. She also seems pretty intelligent.

Francis was translating whatever I was saying into French for them. They spent plenty of time with me, almost three hours. Denise took them out to her hotel for coffee. Evelyn talked about her problem. Chandrahas had gotten her into some trouble. Apparently he claimed that he had helped her daughter a lot and that he had prevented her from committing suicide. It seems that Chandrahas is now involved with a girl named Lisa.

I didn't care to hear their stories about him. Their current problem is whether they should or should not sponsor Chandrahas in this country. They seem to fear him more than they like him; I can't understand why. Perhaps they are afraid because they considered him their guru. I guess that's how gurus hold their disciples in their grip and squeeze the life out of them. I understand why they are afraid of contradicting him even though they don't care about him.

"What do you want from him? What are you expecting?" I asked. They don't know. Apparently she has given a lot of money to Chandrahas. Lisa too gave him money. He spent all that money lavishly. They don't seem to think that he is crazy. They didn't even have that suspicion of that until Guha raised the question. They said they would come again this weekend. Francis can't find work. But he doesn't seem to be worried about it.

*   *   *

Bharati's Predictions – *My Guru Daśa*

The writing is not flowing smoothly. I feel as if something is blocking it. When I put the pen on paper the flow must go on till I lift the pen. That hasn't been happening recently.

UG came to our apartment after they had left. Talking about them, he congratulated us for involving them in conversation for so long. "Bharati's prediction is coming true. You are excelling me. You can take my place. Instead of me talking you talk from now on," he said making fun of me. Bharati made some predictions ten years ago while she was in an inspired state. "In the coming Guru *daśa*, Chandrasekhar will presume that he knows everything and even a bit more than UG. Sixteen years after that, as soon as the Saturn *daśa* sets in, his delusions will cease, and he will repent, realizing that he doesn't know anything and that he hasn't moved one step beyond the first square," she said. Two days ago, UG read all that to everyone.

"Then, has the Guru *daśa* arrived yet or not?" he asked. I answered that the Guru *daśa* has been going on since 1995. That's a great stage for both Suguna and me. Maybe that's why, although he is making us roam different countries, he is keeping us close to our guru. This year we both have already spent four months with UG. We have the good fortune of spending one month in America, two months in India and these five weeks in Switzerland with UG. To enable us to do all this UG had to spend four lakhs of rupees on us. It's not cheap to come to a country like this and spend such a long time. It is thanks to these aspects of my horoscope that I have the grace of my guru. That is the first good fortune stemming from my horoscope.

The second one is Saturn being in the 7th house. That means money and income will come through the wife. I must not analyze my own horoscope. But sometimes I wonder what would have become of my life if I didn't have these two good fortunes. We want to think everything happens as a result of our own efforts, but my faith that nothing is in our hands and that we are all being played like puppets by some force is being reinforced. "If you have such faith, why do you have so much conflict? Why do you try to change or shape yourself?" asks UG. That is the main source of sorrow in life. Everyone worries that things don't happen according to one's expectations, while things which one wants not to happen do happen.

If we get what we wanted and achieve what we plan for, what else could we want? But that's not the way things happen. "As long as you are succeeding, there is no problem at all," UG says. The key is in that one sentence. It's impossible to keep succeeding continually. So, problems must come up. But if this truth takes root in the mind strongly, and the truth that "success and failure are not in one's own hands, they are ordained by God," keeps shining, then most, if not all, of our worries will be gone. No problems will remain if we can gain the confidence that we can accept anything that happens. But that's not so easy. We must experience many vicissitudes in life. Still, we won't have this wisdom. If any wisdom dawns, it will only last for a little while. Then the pride will come sprouting, saying that "this blessing is due to my greatness; it happened because of my effort." This is the nature of delusion. Did Chalam get out of that web of delusion? Did he attain any higher states? Are there really such things as higher states? Are there other lives and worlds which don't depend on my believing in them? Isn't it also a belief that the 'I' who asks such questions is real? Where is the proof that 'I' exist? Tell me.

* * *

Yesterday I talked to Bob, Eddie and Lulu. There was an earthquake in San Francisco last night for a few moments. It was mild and there was no extensive damage. "People complain about earthquakes, volcanoes, floods, cyclones, meteor showers, etc., calling them disasters, but all these are necessary in creation," says UG.

Raj Mehta wrote an e-mail telling that every day there are two thousand hits on the UG photos website. Many people are writing e-mails to him asking about UG.

August 20, 1999 (Friday)

Morning 5:30 am. It's all quiet. It's noisy only in my head. The sound is ringing at a high pitch in my ears. It has gotten worse recently. I thought there might something wrong with my ears; so I went to a doctor a year ago. He said there was nothing wrong with them. But then there is no satisfactory answer if I ask why I hear this constant noise, day in and day out. After I learned that the doctors don't know really what it is, I gave up on it, thinking that I shouldn't worry about what it is from. Major and Chalapati say that it's the sound of *Om*. If that's true, I'm happy. And I am even proud in some way. It's OK. I am getting somewhere spiritually. Don't I believe that all these sounds and visions are all steps toward living liberation? Then I'm proud of myself.

Occasionally I get swellings around my neck. Early every morning I check in the mirror to see if I have a swelling on my neck. When I saw a big swelling on my throat on the left side, I was reminded of what Guha said the other day. Apparently, his left chest becomes larger. He gets bumps on his forehead and also bumps on his head. He has swellings under his navel, on the abdomen. In the middle of his chest, he has a two-inch round patch on the skin. He has some burning sensation internally, as if it's being burned by fire. He experiences these things more intensely in UG's presence. His appetite has diminished. He would like to be in UG's presence all the time. These burnings, he says, become quite intense sometimes. It seems that last May he suffered a lot due to them. He thought of quitting his job at the University and leaving for India. UG scolded him and prevented him from doing that. Meanwhile his bosses gave him a bonus of $2,500. He must be doing good work. This year he has taken 40 days off. They granted him leave for these 21 days again. When UG goes to the US, he will apply for at least a week's leave. It looks like he keeps a record of the physical changes that happen to him.

He reports everything to UG. UG knows of what he speaks; so he apparently told him, "Under these circumstances it's essential to be with the guru." Even Guha was surprised at those words. He thought, "What difference do time and space make? Wouldn't a guru's influence be felt no matter how far away he is?" "Not true; it's important to be physically near him," UG replied. Sometimes, Guha apparently has profuse saliva. Sometimes he feels that there are huge lights in his chest and he feels profound peace. He feels that this peace can pass on to someone around him without any involvement on his part. When I talk to him and watch his behavior, I don't see any craziness in him. He seems normal in all his affairs. But internally something is happening to him physically. Lakshmi knows about it, as also does UG.

It seems like Guha hasn't discussed these things with anyone else. What's the meaning of all these? Is there a possibility of something like a 'Calamity' happening to him? As for himself, he is not worried about those changes. He used to be worried about them before. But that's all in the past now. He is content that he has attained the high state he has desired in life. He doesn't want anything more. UG and UG's presence is all that he wants. He is happy if he just listens to UG and watches him. This is his present condition. UG says to Guha's daughters, "Your father is a total goner."

*   *   *

Julie's Punishment (Training)

UG was scolding Julie yesterday for buying some creams and oils for Guha's two daughters. "Their skin will be damaged; these things won't help. Doctors say that they may even cause cancer," UG warns the kids. "These kids are my hope. I am hoping for so much from them. America's future is in their hands. You think I would give them so much money otherwise?" he asks. "Julie, you can use those creams and die, but don't get the kids addicted to all that stuff," he warns. He watches what they eat and how they look. Whatever they want, Julie must get for them. Only they shouldn't go to India.

Shilpa says that she definitely will go. And UG replies, "Want to bet on it? I can stop you from going." "I won't bet. I don't like to. But I will go to India," says Shilpa. She has her cousins there; she would like to see them. She watches a lot of Hindi movies. As there were indications that she might want to become a dancer, she has been learning *Bharatanatyam*. She has a lively face. UG says, "If you want to become a movie actress, I'll take you right now to India. I will come to India if you want me to." He sees a glorious future for her. "Your parents' bad influence is enough to spoil you; you don't need to go to India. Your mother is OK. But your father must have no influence over you," he says looking at her father and mother. "Will you get married and stay home and cook?" he asks Shilpa. "I'll never marry. I'll become a movie star," answers Shilpa.

And UG is very fond of Sumedha. I never saw him being so nice to kids and spending so much time with them before. How lucky they are! They are growing up under the supervision of UG. He keeps a watch on them every moment. He allows them a lot of freedom. "Julie, if I am tolerating you, it's only for their sake. That's why I let you come here – because they need a car, and because they need your money. Remember this well. If you try to be clever and act out of line, I'll kick you out that very moment!" he was banging on Julie yesterday. That's quite normal. Yet, Julie does go out of line. Every now and then UG lashes at her just like a circus man snaps a whip at a cheetah in a circus. She calms down somewhat when she hears UG's sounds. She is quite friendly. When he notices that cheetah trait coming back up in her, he snaps the whip again. She then yields like a cat. UG has been taming Julie like this for the last ten years. What's funny is that Julie voluntarily submits herself to such treatment in order to stay near UG.

Julie is ready to take any amount of abuse from UG or to be insulted by him in front of everyone.

*   *   *

I have been writing for an hour. There is no more hope of any letup in the sky today. It has been raining incessantly since last night. Today Julie and Guha went to Zurich to receive Lakshmi. She is returning from India. The children also got up early in the morning and went with them to Zurich. Julie left in this rain at 4 am driving her van. They will return with Lakshmi by about 10 am.

*   *   *

Trip to Neuchatel and La Chaux-de-Fonds

Yesterday around noon, UG suggested that we should go somewhere. Where? We have already seen Geneva and Zurich. I suggested Neuchatel and La Chaux-de-Fonds. He thought that was a good idea, since we hadn't yet seen Neuchatel, and La Chaux-de-Fonds, on the French border, is Valentine's place of birth. Mitra came ready with his Volvo. Yesterday after lunch we started out around 12:30 p.m. – UG, Mitra, Suguna, Krim and I. Krim is leaving today for the US at 2 pm. After 12 years, this is the first time that he has spent so much time with UG. UG asked Mitra to take us on a route to Lausanne via Gruyere and Bulle. UG is thoroughly familiar with all these highways. From Lausanne we would then go to Neuchatel. Neuchatel is on the shores of a lake, a big lake near Lausanne. We read the sign as Lake Geneva, but it has a different name,

Lac Lémon. This is the biggest lake in Europe. It's a fresh water lake which looks like an ocean. On the opposite shore you can see France. It's about a 100 miles in circumference. We parked the car in Neuchatel and the five of us had coffee in a lakeside restaurant. UG also drank coffee. Krim paid the bill.

I liked the city very much. It felt as if I was going around in the US. We also went into supermarkets like EBA and Globus for a couple of hours. Suguna bought a few purses. From there we went to La Chaux-de-Fonds. They have dug a big 20 km-long tunnel and laid roads for cars to travel. All along the way, we saw beautiful nature. The beauty here is something different from the beauty of Berner Oberland. Apparently, UG first went to La Chaux-de-Fonds in 1964. Valentine, when she became acquainted with UG, drove UG there to show him her place of birth and the house in which she was born. The town has changed a lot since then, UG says. It has turned into a city in these past 35 years.

How to find Valentine's house? Krim, Mitra and I went into a tourist office. It was almost 5:30. I told the lady there Valentine's father's name and said also, "He was a famous doctor here about a hundred years ago. We would like to find his house." She asked us to go the nearby library that had computer access to such information. The library was less than a kilometer from there. Unexpectedly we found great help from the librarian. Valentine's father was Frederick de Kerven. The librarian remembered the name and searched for it in the library cards. "There is a road with his name near the hospital. It's hard to know exactly where he lived; but we can try to find the details of his life," thus saying, he searched the cards and brought us an essay on him written in a magazine called *Optima*. The article included his photo. We made a copy and hurried back to UG who had been patiently waiting for us for three-quarters-of-an-hour. From there our return trip via Fribourg took two hours. On the way it started to rain from Bulle onwards. By the time we got home it was 9 pm. UG cooked his oatmeal and ate it and we two ate couscous with *dahl* and yogurt. UG asked Julie to make couscous for Mitra and Krim. Julie cooked it right away and fed them.

* * *

Morning 8 am. After eating our oatmeal, we both went to UG and sat with him. There was no one else in the living room except UG. No one will come till 9 am. Guha, Julie and others won't come till after 10 o'clock; maybe even 11. It's still raining outside. At 9 am Tanuja called from Bombay. Her movie has not yet been released. She directed it herself. "You are very intelligent. You're the first Indian female director. You will shine. Why do you care about the planets? You will have a brilliant future. I am telling you. From now on demand 50 lakh rupees per movie, not a mere 30 lakhs," he was advising Tanuja.

Censorship

It seems that Mahesh will be giving a talk in some seminar about censorship and he wants some tips from UG. Whenever he has to speak from a platform, or give a press interview, or talk to an important person, he becomes UG's mouthpiece.

UG is experimenting extensively with publicizing his ideas about world affairs through Mahesh. "Why do you need censorship? Why should a government or other agency stand in the way of anyone watching, hearing or enjoying anything?" questions UG. Parents too forbid their children from watching x-rated movies. What would happen if they watched? Do the adults fear that their children will be corrupt?

This issue has been debated for a long time, at least since the time of Chalam. Who can say that the movies are pornographic? Our generation acquired some of its culture and traditions from watching movies. Does that make those movies great? Whether it is music or literature or some other art, they are all dependent on our upbringing and environment which determine our tastes. Who gave me the authority to impose my tastes on my children? Who gave me the authority and power to put restrictions on them as I please, just because they are helpless and dependent on me? I am afraid that they will become corrupt. I am afraid that such music or literature will make them morally degraded. We have so little faith in the intelligence of our children! In spite of the censorship, they still try to rebel against us and live as they please.

The present generation does not realize the bitter truth that what the society considers now as decent had been considered obscene some time ago. "If censorship is gone, then adults and children will have total freedom. If they have complete freedom to watch, hear or read anything, then moral values will be better," UG says. He criticizes J. Krishnamurti on just that issue. "Why do you drag children onto a hilltop to watch a sunset? It's just as much a craving for pleasure to enjoy watching sunsets as it is sensual to watch the nipples of girls' breasts. If one goes, they all go. These two are not separate things," UG says. "What's the difference between varieties of foods and varieties of girls? They practice *brahmacharya* saying that it's sinful to sleep with a girl. Isn't it sensual pleasure to eat to one's fill all varieties of foods?" UG asks.

People never listened when Chalam declared: "Where do you find obscenity and immorality? Only in one's mind." So much later, UG couples spiritual talk with much more foul language and feeds that mix to the traditionalists. The sages blink their eyes – they can't swallow it and they can't spit it out. Holy men, you carry on about morality and obscenity! Your lives are nothing but obscene stories. How can they all go? Morality, immorality, virtue and vice, knowledge and ignorance, these pairs are each entwined with the other. Unless one of each pair goes, the other doesn't. If you hold on to one of them, and try to throw away the other, it will bounce right back and hit you. Is it possible to throw both of them away? Can both of them go? Can both of them be erased from men's minds and their habits? Is that possible? The 'I' wields the authority of censorship. "A moral person, a truly moral person will never preach morality to others," says UG. All those who condemn immorality are those who secretly worship it. People hated Chalam because he exposed the lives of such people in public and condemned them. Since they can't do that to UG in any way, they attribute divinity to him and [*mentally*] shroud him with sacred clothes.

* * *

August 21, 1999 (Saturday)

Morning 5:20 am. It seems like the rain stopped last night. Yesterday morning an American tourist group was going around the tennis courts. Their guide was talking to them about this town in English. Last night for sometime I heard sounds of firecrackers. In the afternoon around 3:00, Suguna and I went in Julie's car to Volker's place. It was still raining a bit then. The pavement was full of water, yet you can't walk on the grass. If the grass appears to have been trod upon, then the landlords fine the renters to the extent of 50 Swiss francs. The laws here are strange. If you go off of the pavement onto the grass, they will jail you. People here have never heard of burglaries. You can leave your suitcase on the railway station platform, go around the town the whole day, come back and still find your suitcase there. They don't touch another's property.

How did these people acquire the trait of not coveting what doesn't belong to them? Isn't stealing part of human nature? Yet there are small burglaries sometimes. Recently, when Moorty and I went on our walk, we saw on the way broken glass in front of a car and the car doors seemed dented. It seemed like someone had broken into the car and taken the stuff in it. It was clearly a robbery. It's rare to see such incidents in Switzerland. But as there are different kinds of people coming into this country, there seem to be a change even in the people here. Here people normally don't lock the doors of their houses. We too don't lock our room door here. Our landlady keeps insisting that we should.

Volker and Anusati made a great pear cake. They call it a pie. To make it, they make a dough with wheat flour, spread it in a pan and arrange pieces of pears or apricots or apples on it. They cover the fruit with more dough, and bake it in an oven for ten minutes. Then they apply some butter on it and eat it while it is still warm. How tasty that pie was! The fruit combined with the wheat tasted great. Then Volker gave us bread with gooseberry jam that he had made. He makes things of that sort. Cooking is his hobby. They spent three and a half hours with us and we all had a very good time.

"Since we have visited you here, you both must come and visit us in India," said Suguna. Volker was happy at the invitation. I told them that this year is our 25th wedding anniversary. Twenty five years ago, Volker had given us a gift of a big brass pot at our wedding. Today too, Anusati gave us a gift of a beautiful towel with pictures on it. We walked around their garden. Volker took many pictures, indoors and outdoors. By that time, it had stopped raining. He played the music of Mandolin Srinivas on his music system. Suguna felt very good in their place. We talked about Ed and Lulu and Ruth. Volker knew Ruth very well. He made some herbal tea for us. He took some leaves from his garden and put them in hot water and filtered the tea. It was very good. He gave us some more leaves to take with us and make tea.

*   *   *

"The day you introduce thinking into computers, their usefulness will be completely gone," says UG, "Thinking means selectivity and censorship. As long as man has in his mind the idea that 'You must have this and you must not have that,' he will not be happy. That's the cause of all his troubles and sorrows. If that's gone then he will become like an animal. Animals don't eat everything they find. But their selectivity does not come from thought."

Yesterday Julie printed out an item from the Internet. They are doing some research in Emery University in Atlanta on rats in the fields. It was written in the article that attempts to enhance love and cooperation in the rats by modifying the genes in them were successful. The article said that some monogamous rats started making friends with other female rats after their genes were modified.

Gradually, they will apply the results of such research to humans. "The brainwashing process is very laborious and takes a long time. As a result of genetic research they can bring about the desired changes in people in one moment with the help of some chemicals," says UG. When that is accomplished, man will become a puppet in the hands of government. A government will be able to mold a man into any kind of person it wants. The only hope that man has will be gone. "If there is truly such a thing as perfect justice, mankind should have been wiped out by now from the face of this earth," UG says. Where is perfect justice? If God is truly merciful, he should have exterminated man by now for the horrible injustices he has done and the terrible atrocities he has committed against nature.

*   *   *

Mahesh has sent the video tape of the ten-minute program *Real Time Travel India* produced by BBC World. It is a documentary made in Bangalore with Mahesh, myself and Dakshinamurti in it. BBC was successful in showing the huge city of Bangalore through Mahesh's eyes in ten minutes. In it, Mahesh also mentions UG. He doesn't say or do anything without alluding to UG. He never forgets that the center of his existence is UG

*   *   *

The sky has acquired a red tinge. The clouds have moved away. Today, the sun is about to shine bright and clear in these mountain valleys. Krim is leaving for America. Lakshmi returned yesterday from India. She doesn't appear to have recovered from her travel fatigue. She is traveling back to America in three days. Both her children have become attached to me. They listen to my stories. The house will feel deserted after they leave. Julie will also go with them.

Sometimes a question arises in my mind: "What was UG's intention in calling Suguna and me here? What was his intention in calling us here the time before?" Only UG would know. I can't. Why did UG spend so many lakhs of rupees and make us come here? What have we accomplished here? At least Moorty and Guha have been working on making UG's stuff presentable and putting it up on the Internet. Julie has been helping in every way. Only I am useless. I can't do anything except eat and roam about. I don't know anything about computers. I can't even learn about them. Lisa has learned a lot. She learned some tricks from Moorty. I should try and see if I can learn some tricks while Aruna is with me, especially about web browsing. Lisa has prepared a huge file about UG. When you look into the files you will know how many UG links there are. UG keeps pointing to Julie that she couldn't do that kind of work. Is Julie truly so fond of UG? Is she bearing all this because she needs him? There is no one like Julie and there never will be.

*   *   *

Mr. Raju is arriving in three days, bring with him the nice 'perfume' of astrology. He will be here for four days. People here have invited him to lecture on astrology and give lessons. I think this is the second time he is coming to Switzerland. There was a huge earthquake in Turkey the other day. The news mentioned that there were ten-thousand deaths. Bob said that there had also been mild tremors in San Francisco. I talked to Aruna. Yesterday it was Venkat's birthday. He has completed thirty years. I talked to him last night on the phone. Henk will perhaps leave tomorrow. Nataraj will stay here. In a week this house will all be vacated. UG will also leave. We too must get ready.

*   *   *

August 22, 1999 (Sunday)

Morning 6:30 am. It was strange that I didn't wake up early this morning as usual. First, I woke up at 1:30. I went to the bathroom and went back to bed. I didn't wake up again until Suguna got me up at 6:10 am. Just at that moment I was having a dream. There was some kind of feast. It looked like an RSS (Raastriya Swayam Sevak Sangh) feast They were serving food to everyone. When I finished my meal and was about to leave, a volunteer came to the gate and brought me back. When he was serving, I asked him for some rice. Before he brought the rice, I got up from my seat and was about to leave; but he followed me, pleaded with me and brought me back. I didn't know why I tried to leave; I apologized and started eating my meal again. He served me so much rice that could be eaten by twenty people and then poured *rasam* over it. I was worrying so much about how I could eat all that rice. At that point Suguna woke me up.

They say you mustn't have such dreams. Our elders say that dreaming about rice is a sign of bad health. Whatever be the reason, why did I sleep so long? The alarm had gone off at 5 am. Still I slept. Why did I sleep like a log? We had gone to bed early. We watched a movie called *Sabut* for a while; we didn't like it; so we got up and left. I wondered who would watch a movie like that. What horrible trash! The actors are famous: Akshay Kumar, Karishma Kapur, Sunil Sethi and others. Shilpa likes Hindi movies. She likes the stories in the movies. She has memorized the names of all the heroes and heroines. How they watch the movies with such interest, without even blinking their eyes! The girls don't usually watch Telugu movies. I guess they don't follow them. Maybe they understand Hindi. They learn the language by watching the movies. Guha and I recalled bits of a song of 'Surdas'...."*mayyamoni makhan khayo.*" Anup Jhalota sang that song well. I used have that album.

*   *   *

Francis – II

Yesterday, Francis and his son Francois came at 10 am. I spent time with both of them till 6 pm. All three of us ate lunch in the afternoon at the Christiania Restaurant. I ate *rösti* with soup. The dream I had last night must have affected my choice. Francois says his grandmother makes *rösti* much better than the one I had. He told us he got very drowsy sitting in UG's presence. After lunch he went to bed and slept like a log for three hours. He works in the Nestlé factory in Vivey as an apprentice. He is also taking a small course in business administration. He has two more years to finish it. He will get a diploma then. Then he can find another job elsewhere if he wants it. These people have all kinds of fringe benefits. There are opportunities to go to school. But this boy has no drive. He is 18 years old. He is very tall and looks healthy. But he is not a hardworking type. "If I want an easy way to make money, I must rob a bank. If I steal a million francs then I can live happily for the rest of my life" – he thinks in such lines. Good! But what if he gets caught? Or else, he would like to work hard for some years, save money and enjoy his life. People here have no big ambitions like doing something in life or achieving something. "No, such a big job, it's beyond my level," he says. He knows English a little. But he speaks mostly French. If I stay with them for ten days, I could learn French well.

Francis is unhappy that he can't find work. That's what worries him day and night. When he was short of breath and was holding his chest, UG asked him, "What happened?" UG must have known of his bodily pain. The government gives him unemployment compensation till he finds a job.

Apparently they give 75% of the pay he earned in his previous job. In India, if people are given such a benefit, people would take it easy, thinking "That's great!" Here Francis is working hard to find employment. That's his only worry, poor fellow, that he doesn't have a proper job. He worked for twenty years in the police department. It's hard for him to look for another job. The man appears to be soft and gentle.

Apparently, he left his job in June. That means, he has been unemployed for just two months. Even that he can't accept. He says he doesn't have enough money and has to sell his house. He wants to sell it and live in an apartment. He is worried about what will happen to his life. He becomes paralyzed with those fears. "So, what's the worst that could happen to you?" I asked. "Death," his son answered. I was amazed at his intelligence. "I'm not afraid of death," he said. I couldn't but congratulate him in my mind.

*   *   *

August 23, 1999 (Monday)

Morning 5:30 am. It looks like it rained last night. Saturday and Sunday the valley was clear and bright with sunshine. Everyone came out into the streets looking around as if they might never see sunshine again. All yesterday none of us had stepped out of the house. After lunch, the children insisted that I should tell stories. Then Lily, a friend of Julie, came to see UG. Apparently, she had lost her mother recently. She took good care of her till the end. Julie and she have been friends for 25 years. During the conversation, Nataraj looked into her palm.

I too followed suit. I made my own readings as they came to my mind. Later I regretted trying to show myself off. This trait of mine will never go away, this miserable quality of showing myself off. What do I know in the first place? Who asked me? I could have nicely shut my mouth and sat in a corner. What have I learned about palmistry and astrology? What's the extent of my knowledge? Why should I talk about what I don't know? When will this miserable urge to poke into everything go? When his guru roared, "Hey, Sadasiva, when will your mouth shut up?" Sadasiva Brahmendra Saraswati said, "If that's your order, it will shut up right now," and he became silent for the rest of his life, never again speaking a single word. All the debates, the logic sports, the scholarly persecutions which had gone on up to that moment ceased at once. Sadasiva Brahmendra was a great sage and a scholar in all the scriptures. If he paraded his knowledge, that meant something. Why should an ignoramus like me, a fellow who doesn't understand anything, do cartwheels in front of UG? Who cares for my advice? What am I and what's my intelligence?

This ego never dies. UG reminds me of Bharati's reading again and again. I loathe remembering the warning of Bharati that in my Guru *daśa* my pride will peak and that it will pull me down. UG never misses an opportunity to remind me of that item and bang me on my head. I must show the way to someone! I am such a fool.

I have been groping in the dark without any direction. My Guru must save me, from all these boastings and foolish showing off. That's all I want. In the little time that remains, I must make all the effort I can to find light for myself. I understand my mental condition. I started crying again. I can't leave this foolish mind alone. Why should I wish that I should always have pleasure, happiness and gladness? Happiness for whom? I will never learn no matter how many times UG bangs on my head saying, "Everything you do is a pleasure movement. Why do you hanker after walks on the mountains?" Why this nuisance? Will I be healthier by doing it? Will the glucose level in my blood go down? Don't I eat again when I am hungry? "If you walk, your appetite will go up. If you are hungry you will eat more. With that the glucose in your blood will go up again," says UG.

Let it all go to hell. For how long should I be so careful? And who cares if I am gone? What is there that I must accomplish? These dry philosophies are of no use. UG says that there is no such thing as willing your own death. Suicide is the only way. How is my will involved either in my living or in my dying? Was I born because of my will, so that I can will to die? "If I had a choice, I would never have been born in India. There is no question about someplace else. But I would never have chosen India. I was born without my will and I will go the same way," he says. Will I be able to stand the shock of his being gone for one day? Why not? I am trying to escape.

When Henk wanted to leave, UG stopped him for some days.

* * *

Errietta is a Greek lady. She is tiny and thin and looks very young. She has a small face. She has been seeing UG for 20 years. She undertook the care of her father and is living in Schonried near here. Recently she wrote UG a letter blaming him and condemning what he says. UG says we must put it up on the Internet. She later regretted writing it. She came three or four times at night and held UG's hands indicating that she was asking his forgiveness. She came yesterday evening and sat with UG. UG asked someone to give her a copy of the book *No Way Out*. "I really don't know what there is in it," he says. She threw kisses at him in the air. She didn't care if everyone was laughing at her. She kept throwing kisses at him looking at him as if she was going to gobble him up. That 'old figure' [*of UG*] has such attraction for people. How can they help it?

A young woman called **Sagar** is coming. She says she is a Polish Hungarian and lives in Germany. She too loses herself in watching UG.

*   *   *

UG's Field of Attraction

It's amazing how many people UG has enchanted like this! What an attraction! Guha can't remain at any distance from him. Every now and then he makes an attempt to touch UG. UG doesn't let Nataraj sit away from him. Once every hour or so, he stretches out his arm and shakes his hand. Last night, while Eva Sagar was shaking UG's hand to say goodbye before she left, she lost her bearings and did a dance. Such self-forgetfulness happens not only to women but also to men. The first time they come they sit at a distance out of respect. UG somehow pulls them near him. Why do they sit there for so many hours in the first place?

Yesterday in the evening, the talk was about JK. UG was saying the same things which he had said a thousand times before. Why don't they get bored hearing all that? How could he repeat all those things without getting tired? He tells the same things using the same words in the same order. He never gets tired of it. How is it possible? Giovanni, an Italian man, is coming with his wife. He translated UG's books into Italian some time ago. There will be another lady, her sister, with him. Her daughter, of the same age as Shilpa, is in the hospital with stomach pain.

All these people have come to visit UG. What an attraction! I could understand if he invited them and gave them some hope. But he does no such thing. He doesn't let some people stay even if they want to. He pushes them out forcibly. What's he stirring up in them? Why is he drawing them toward him? Why do these people go to him? I understand none of that.

It's no different in my case. Why did he call me from such a long distance? Looking into Suguna's palm, UG says, addressing me, "He's the only lucky fellow." "Are you already a millionaire?" he asked me yesterday morning. "Because you've ordered me to be one, I might become one," I answered. What desires are there except worldly desires? What's the purpose, otherwise, of striving so much for God's grace? *Pujas*, worships, *homas* – they are all "for longevity, health, wealth, prosperity and other fruits one desires." We all know that. There is no doubt that UG is like a *kamadhenu*[17] or a *kalpataru*[18]. How he graces and whom he graces only he would know. Whether he himself knows or not is difficult to tell.

But Julie gets special treatment. She is special.

*   *   *

"To live with me is like, 'Each day there is danger, yet you live for a hundred years,'" said UG to Julie yesterday. "This body lives like that. It survives from moment to moment. It's not eager to live forever. It's only 'you' that is concerned about that. That's why you are in misery, sorrow, and you are so worried," he says. "Why do you hoard all those tapes and photos? What will you do with them? Give them to someone. Or do something else with them," he said addressing Suguna and me.

Soon, all of UG's astrology readings will be on the Internet. Raj Mehta is going to put them up on his website.

*   *   *

August 24, 1999 (Tuesday)

Morning 5 am. Today Guha and his family are leaving. We are leaving next Monday. The countdown has begun. Mr. Raju is arriving today. UG, Suguna and I, will go to Berne,

---

[17] The Giving Cow.
[18] The Giving Tree.

meet him at the train station and bring him from there. Aruna and Venkat will arrive in a couple of days. By tonight Lisa and Mario will be here. Some arrive and some bid goodbye. The day you have been waiting for will come.

Yesterday, UG was furious with Julie. All day he was reading out the astrology stories that Raj Mehta is going to put up on the Internet. By today, an introduction to that page has been prepared. We put in there whatever UG might want to say about *nadi*, astrology and palmistry. Yesterday, Julie would write down what UG dictated and then she would read back what he said, while UG would scold her and correct the sentences – that's how it went on. Finally, some five or six sentences were made ready. It was easy to get some of it from the book of readings itself. Julie e-mailed the text of the letter to Moorty. He will edit it and send it back.

In 1995, a Hungarian lady in San Rafael did a reading of UG's horoscope. It's quite interesting. So are all the astrology stories I have collected in India. UG praised T. Prakash's reading. But all yesterday he has been showering fire on Julie. He has been scolding her all the time. Mitra brought a friend with him. The friend has been watching this spectacle without saying a word. In the night, after dinner, I was watching UG joking around with the kids, playing with them; I couldn't believe it was the same UG that had been venting fury on Julie that morning.

I saw Errietta at the stationery store yesterday. She asked me why UG calls some women 'bitches'. "It would be nicer if he calls not just some but all the women bitches. According to

UG, all men are bastards and all women are bitches," I replied. "The real meaning of the nickname 'bitch' in India is 'Beautiful Indian Teenager Causing Heartbreaks;'" I amplified as if it were an acronym. Errieta was amused. She comes from Athens. "Why does he abuse JK? Did you ever meet JK?" she asked. I told her about my meeting with JK. "Why would UG be so personally hostile about JK except to root out the JK that has been buried in us?" I said. JK became a huge obstacle in UG's life. He constantly talks to us about how he freed himself from JK's corrupting influence. He explains that whatever had happened to him did not happen because of JK's help, but happened in spite of his influence. Errieta is still regretting writing that letter to UG the other day and hurting him. That's why two days ago she came and showered him with kisses before she left.

If UG wants to come to Switzerland next summer, he must make reservations now. UG asked Nataraj to talk to Miedler Ludi. She says she will look into the situation in April and let him know. But UG insists that she must tell him now. She hopes to extract more money from UG, nothing more. UG always has problems with landlords.

It looks like it rained outside last night. I can tell from the wet surface of the tennis courts. Will I ever come to this country again? I feel that this maybe the beginning of my visits. After staying here for so long, this time I have developed an attachment with the surroundings here. But you need a lot of money to stay here. If I think in terms of Indian rupees, it's not possible to survive here unless one is prepared to spend at least Rs. 3,000 or 4,000 per day. I am beginning to understand the laws and customs here. You must follow a special procedure to throw away trash: you can't just toss it here or there. You must have special plastic bags. You must attach the city council labels on them. You must neatly put your trash in those bags, tie up the bags and deposit them in big metal containers. If you can't find the designated plastic bags, then you must put the trash in regular plastic bags and deposit them in another container far away. If we put the bags in the container near the house, they are cleared everyday by the workers of the City. You can't park cars anywhere you like on the streets.

*   *   *

Rukmini Arundale

Apparently Rukmini Devi Arundale came to Gudiwada with the purpose of contesting her brother in the election for the President of the Theosophical Society. You can see UG's grandmother Durgamma in a photo taken at that time. Apparently, Rukmini had asked UG to help her with the canvassing. She is credited with earning respectability for Bharatanatyam as an authentic fine art and not just as an art of the *devadasis*[19]. It's strange that such a woman wanted to become the President of the Society. We also heard that, perhaps 20 years ago, she was contesting in the country's Presidential elections in which V. V. Giri was elected. Giri's

---

[19] Female temple attendants.

becoming a President at that time was shameful not only to the Andhra State, but to the whole country.

The time is now past 6 o'clock. Now I must get ready for the car trip. Guha, Julie etc. will leave at the same time in their car. I must leave for Berne with Mitra in his Volvo.

*   *   *

"You are talking even when you're silent...."

August 25 (Wednesday)

The alarm went off at 4:30 am. I wasn't deeply asleep; I was half asleep. But after getting ready, it's now 6 am.

I am writing this because if I talk to myself like this, time will pass more easily. Although my lips are closed tight, sounds are raging in my throat. Words are trying to spill from my throat. Even my teeth are grinding. I guess no one from outside can hear that. Must these sounds go on like this day in and day out?

Yesterday morning we were going to Berne with UG. Mitra was driving. We were near Bulle. Beautiful natural scenery on the way. The valleys near Rougemont were resplendent with the morning sun. Green meadows. In the meadows there were clusters of pine trees looking as if they were arranged artfully by someone. You couldn't see any bare rocks or dirt anywhere on the mountains. It was all green as far as you could see.

Suddenly, as I was immersed in this nature worship, UG said, "Chandrasekhar, this is something you have to experiment with and learn from your own experience. The external sound comes out only from the lungs and the throat. Those two are the only causes of our words, nothing else. The brain is not the cause at all. If you want, you try and find out. You observe. Even if the sounds are not heard outside, you are talking to yourself. The vocal chords in the throat keep moving. Then the lips also move. Or else, you must be involved with something totally disconnected with the present. Your vocal chords keep moving even when you are silently talking. You can observe it if you want," he said.

"One more thing, when I look at the horizon, the eyes do not see it. It doesn't exist for them. The trees, mountains and all look like in a picture. The eyes do not see beyond the two dimensions. Just these two dimensions like in a picture. The eyes cannot see the third dimension of distance or depth. 'You' are noticing it. 'UG' is the third dimension. As soon as 'UG' comes, he knows. I don't tell myself that 'this is the distance,'" says UG.

Although I have been listening to UG for so many years, I don't understand his words; I can't experience them. He says so emphatically, "that the eyes only see two dimensions, but not the third one." UG says he will shut Einstein's mouth if he speaks of the fourth dimension.

How do I know that I am writing if there is no space between this book and me who is writing in it? How can we conduct our affairs if there is no space between the seer and what is seen? This is a challenge that my logical thought poses. But why is it not possible? UG says that in his case it happens all the time. He pounds on the table and says, "I have no idea that this is hard. I don't know that this table is hard no matter how many times I pound on it. They tell us, 'this is lifeless; this is inert.' And they say that this is all energy vibrations. They talk as if they have experienced it." When UG says, "there is no such thing as a solid thing. It's our knowledge that teaches us that that some things are solid and that there are animate and inanimate things. In reality there are no such things," that is something he experiences. "I don't feel pain when I hit the table. Later, I may feel pain, but at that moment I don't know that it is pain, that the table is solid or that it is hard,'" says UG.

I can't understand it a bit. No matter how many years I have closely observed him, I don't understand the manner in which UG lives or talks. I can't experience it no matter how much I try. How can I experience the vocal chords in the throat vibrating even when I am not saying anything, as he says? UG challenges, "You can't sign your name on a piece of paper unless you tell yourself your name." It's the same with everything else. We can't do anything without first telling ourselves to do it. We can't write. It's a lie that we can think silently. We talk to ourselves. "The navel, heart, throat and the tip of the nose are essential to sound; they are its places of origin," says Tyagaraja. Is that an expression of his experience of *Sabda* Brahman[20]?

---

[20] The Absolute regarded as sound or speech.

According to UG, only the lungs and the vocal chords are the cause of sounds and nothing else is. The cause is not thoughts and it's not the brain. "If I want, I can keep talking like this all 24 hours of the day. My throat may be stuffed after sometime, but there's no such thing as being tired for me. I can go on endlessly," says UG. I have seen it myself many times. He can talk for hours at a time. Sometimes his voice vibrates with such energy and intensity. You wonder where his words get so much energy. It's not anger. It's not fury. Just intensity! The roar of Narasimha[21]. Resounding in our ears with such force, like firecrackers, like cannon shots, his words explode. Just listening to them makes your heart palpitate. The next moment all that subsides. UG then calms down like a volcano after the lava has flowed out. And you notice a smile on his lips. The same eyes which have been showering fire shine innocently like the stars in a clear sky and confuse us.

No use. No one can ever understand UG. No one can figure out the force hidden in this form. Why is it here? Why does it gather all these people like this? It doesn't need anything. Does it care about this world? It doesn't care about these men, humanity, the ways of this world – any of them. These are all like dust for it. Yet, it has no quarrel with this society or this world. It never thinks, "Why should I live in this world? What business do I have in this world?" It asks, "I didn't want to be born here. Am I born, in the first place? Am I living?" How can you know it? That tremendous force pretends like it exists, pretends like we are all around it and plays with us.

---

[21] The Lion Man; an incarnation of Vishnu.

What could we call such a divine force? How is it possible to know it? Sometimes it seems to try to open our eyes, to make us realize, without our knowing, that we are not different from it. But that's just for a moment. Instantly it abandons its attempt. As I wrote before "The wise find it is foolish to try to explain the unknown and so remain silent," but the urge to explain does not subside.

There aren't a million answers to the question, "What do I want?" There is just one. If I can stand on one leg [i.e. meditate] thinking I want just one thing, there is still no guarantee that I will get it. What is there to get? When the one who tries to get realizes that he is not different from what he is trying to get, where is the question of getting it? If I try to grasp through thought and words, then it's all empty philosophy. That's why UG never lets us indulge in such discussions. "When you go to bed with your wife, when you put your thing in the hole, if you don't know your wife, if that awareness is suddenly gone, can you still make love?" UG roars. Unless he speaks in those crude terms people don't understand him. That's why he freely uses vocabulary which we consider foul, cleaning up the obscene cobwebs of our minds.

'Obscenities, foul language' – these are all just ideas, fabrications. When I was young, I even heard some adults using such obscenities in their homes. Apparently Suguna's father used obscenities in front of everyone to abuse his land-tenants and servants. Yet, no one was offended by them. They say that whenever Sri Ramakrishna opened his mouth, foul language flowed out of it. Does the obscenity lie in the minds of the 'gentlemen' who listen to those words and picture them as scenes or in those who listen to them yet brush them aside without imagining any pictures before their eyes?

*   *   *

Mr. Raju, the Astrologer

Mr. Raju will come at 7:30 am for breakfast. I must get ready. I haven't had my coffee yet. Last night, we picked up him at the Berne train station and brought him home. Lisa, Mario and Simon came with us. Mario brought a big van which could seat seven people. Coffee is rather late today. I must drink it and finish washing.

Afternoon 2:45 pm. After lunch, at 1:00 pm, we went with UG in Mario's new car to Launen. We came back at 2:30 pm. It must be about 10 km from here. On the way we passed a peak. On the peak there is a glacier shining like silver. Snow melts and flows like a river from that glacier. On the same Saanen Mountains you can see waterfalls. Mario says it would take three hours to get there. We wet our feet in the mountain streams. The water is cold like snow. Mr. Raju came with us.

*   *   *

Raju with UG – UG's Past life

August 26, (Thursday)

Morning 5 am. What does it mean? (I am talking to myself.) How do I know it's 5 am? What's the difference between 12 noon and 5 am? Is it to notice the light rays outside and think that it's dawning? If there is no cause-effect link, what is night and what is day?

Last night UG was talking to Raju and me, recalling all the highlights of his past life. "I never believed anything that the world has taught me. It never got into me. I have no quarrel with the world. I always knew that the world is what it is. It cannot be otherwise. I never had the intention, as you do, to change the world or shape it in any other way," UG said. It's not that he agreed with the world either. His individuality is different from what the culture had intended to cultivate in him. People's opinions, their faiths, the beliefs that most everyone adheres to and the truths that people accept without question had no effect on UG. Ever since he was a child he always had questions. "Why should I accept the logical cause-effect relationship imposed by the world?" he thought. He had questions like that in every field. To accept something faithfully because our elders have dictated it is something that hasn't worked with UG. UG questioned even trivial rules like "one must not eat at the time of dusk; one must not drink water before one eats; one must respect the elders."

It's an innate trait of UG to learn the truth of everything by investigating and experimenting with it. I feel that it would be nice if astrologers would try to find out what influences of the planets might be responsible for such a trait. It's common for men to accept the ancient beliefs handed down to them at least to some degree, if not exactly verbatim. If the trait of not accepting anything without first questioning it, investigating it and researching it deeply is so inborn in UG, it only means that his life is special and not like everyone else's. However, UG doesn't go about like a revolutionary trying to overthrow the established structures of the world or revolt against them. He only likes to know things for himself and puts them into practice. There is no question of imposing his theories on others. He didn't even force his views on his own wife or children.

If UG sat in a Manhattan hotel room and wondered "How do I know I am in New York?", then we can understand how his way of thinking is different from others'. It's not an ordinary thing to argue with a great intellectual like Bertrand Russell as UG did, saying, "Can you do away with the policeman? The nuclear bomb is an extension of the policeman. One cannot condemn one without condemning the other." It's not an ordinary thing that UG grasped clearly the truth that "Whatever I know is only because of the knowledge I already have; if I don't have any information, I have no way of knowing anything."

How did he get to have such a nature? If all the knowledge that man has gathered from the time he has been a brute till the time he has become a city dweller and the essence of all experience that man has thought, imagined and experienced have been washed away in UG, have been emptied without a trace, there is nothing more wonderful than that. UG never condemns the world nor does he question it. He hasn't run away from it saying "what do I have to do with this world?" He has lived in this world, completely digesting life's experiences like everyone else. UG has outlandish opinions about raising children, principles of health, methods of education, beliefs of elders, and all such subjects. Clearly such an investigative mind is deeply rooted in UG.

How UG has acquired such a trait, by the influence of what divine planets such a trait found place in him, is an important matter that astrologers must investigate. Such research has not yet been done. I strongly believe that after UG's horoscope and details of his life are catalogued on his website on the Internet, such great projects and activities will begin. I believe that there are great benefits in investigating UG's life extensively and deeply. That's why recently UG has been repeatedly relating to everyone all the events of his life. A definitive biography must be written. It should show UG not from a single angle but from all perspectives.

* * *

"Everything that man has thought, felt and experienced was flushed out of my system," becomes the 'key' needed to enter the mansion of 'understanding UG'.

* * *

The personal secretary of the famous palmist Cheiro was UG's neighbor when he was living in Chicago. Apparently, after looking at UG's wife Kusuma's palm, she told UG privately that until Kusuma exited from his life, his real life wouldn't begin. "She must move away from you. Her life must come to an end," she asserted. Many years later the lady's daughter came to see UG in Bangalore. UG says she came in 1971, when he was living in Jagannadh's house.

Last night he talked about things from 60 years ago. In 1939, as soon as his Saturn *daśa* had ended and his Budha *daśa* had begun, a new chapter commenced in UG's life. He did his foreign travel with the ten thousand rupees his grandfather had given him. To undertake traveling alone in foreign lands and the elders not to object to it were unique events. I don't know if people at UG's home knew if he was going to England. Precisely when, in 1956, his Budha *daśa* had ended and Ketu *daśa* had begun, UG's life in foreign lands – settling in America and moving away from his native country – occurred. He was separated from his children. All the properties he inherited had evaporated. One must look for such things in the horoscope.

If we can arrange UG's life according to *daśas*, there will be an opportunity to render UG's biography uniquely valuable. By 1963, his Ketu *daśa* was completed. Exactly on the day on which his Śukra *daśa* had started, in July 1963, UG had the thought that he should go to the Ramakrishna Vedanta Center in London. Later, the day on which UG met Valentine in the Indian Embassy office in Geneva was a very important day in UG's life. I must ask UG precisely what day it was and make a note of it. Similarly, May 15, 1943 was UG's day of marriage, and Kusuma's death occurred in 1962.

Today, I must ask UG about the important events of his life and their dates and prepare a list of them. Tomorrow Aruna and Venkat will come. She is traveling to her native land after a year. She is also visiting Switzerland. The travels must be overwhelming her. It is so interesting that UG creates the opportunity for both of them to come here!

*   *   *

Mrs. Saraswati and Mr. Raju:

Mr. Raju put UG's horoscope on the computer and brought it over here. There are differences in the number of months between the calculations which Mr. Raju has made and those Satyanaraya had done regarding the periods of the *daśas*. Raju said he had counted 360 days per year. If he takes 365 days as a year instead, the calculations will probably tally. Apparently, he needs the exact time of birth. Last night, even UG said that the *daśas* did not tally exactly with the events of his life.

Yesterday, during conversation Raju mentioned how powerful UG's influence has been on Mrs. Saraswati. About a year or two ago she had decided to leave Raju. She had a bus ticket reserved. She was about to travel in a couple of hours. Raju didn't want to come in her way; instead, he waited in the school and phoned UG. UG was then in Bangalore. "Saraswati is about to leave in another hour," said Raju. "I see," said UG and kept quiet. In another half hour Saraswati changed her mind. She apparently cancelled her ticket and her travel. Later, talking to her from Palm Springs, UG apparently warned her three times, "Don't leave Raju!" With that Saraswati ceased her attempts to leave Raju. It's surprising how many lives UG affects in this fashion.

*   *   *

"In 1974, a very important event must have taken place in your life. A home or a family must have gotten better," said Sitara, a German young lady, looking into UG's horoscope. Apparently, in UG's 27th year and 56th year such things had happened. I said, "If it is 1974, that's when I started my family life." "What do I have to do with your family life?" said UG. As a matter of fact, he had everything to do with it. I became acquainted with UG at the same time as Suguna entered my life. That one event helped create a lot of changes in both our lives. Did we ever dream that 25 years later we would be in UG's presence in Switzerland like this? "The events that had occurred 60 years ago seem as if they have only happened yesterday," said UG recalling incidents from his past.

*   *   *

Programming the Body

August 27, (Friday)

I don't know when the rain had stopped last night. Now, at 6 am, the whole tennis court grounds are wet and are reflecting the lights. Yesterday, UG took us all with him to Geneva. The drive took an hour and 45 minutes for an expert driver like Mario. After we got into the city, we lost our bearings and didn't know where we were going. But UG is thoroughly familiar with that city. First, we went to Lake Geneva. There you can see a fountain 100 feet high. There is a huge hotel on the other side of the lake. UG said that he stayed in that hotel in 1953 when he came with Kusuma, his wife. The rent then was 11 Swiss francs a night. Kusuma thought that was expensive and wanted them to move to a cheaper hotel. From that you can imagine the cost of living in those days. In the city, UG showed us Valentine's own old house where she used to live in those days. The house is still completely intact. Someone bought the house from Valentine about thirty years ago. With the proceeds from the sale of that house, 'Hridaya Vihar' has come into being in Bangalore in her memory.

Then we went around shopping in the important shops in the city. UG had his last dream in another hotel in Geneva in 1967, before his 'Calamity'. He showed us that hotel as well. Lisa took some pictures. I used to be keen on preserving all the things connected with UG for posterior generations to remember. Now I have lost my interest in collecting photos and tapes. My own time is nearing. I don't have the time. There is no worry because there is the Internet. Without much expense, you can put up whatever you want on the Internet with the help of a computer and present it to the world. UG is getting to know some experts in that field. They will help. That'll be good enough.

*   *   *

I must mention another thing here. Yesterday UG has demonstrated to us how he keeps his body under control. Just as we were about to leave in the car around 9:30 am, while going into the bathroom UG said, "I am going to program this body such that it won't need to use the bathroom for another eight hours." Lisa, who was standing close by, said, "It would be great if you could program my body like that too!" We all laughed.

As soon as we arrived in Geneva and parked our car, right away all six of us started looking for the toilet, as we had been traveling for a couple of hours. Then we roamed around the city for another two hours. UG took us for a good lunch in an Indian-Pakistani restaurant called 'Shahi'. One of the people there is a Bengali. Her native place is Calcutta. We started our return trip around 2 pm. It was 4 pm by the time we got home.

UG didn't need to go to the bathroom for seven hours, that is, since 9:30 am. If his body is carrying out his orders even at this age we can imagine how much more control he had before. Normally, people over 80 have prostate problems. They can't travel in cars. But UG is a wonder to watch. Even though he has traveled in the car for so many hours, walked with all of us in the city and made the return trip back home in the car, he hasn't shown any fatigue.

In the afternoon around 4 pm, Nataraj, Mitra and others gathered in the living room. Dr. Leboyer came again. Because he was there, UG spoke energetically for two and a half hours. Where does he get all this energy from? It's amazing. Raju complained of a headache and went to sleep in his room upstairs. Suguna too rested for half an hour.

I had been watching UG. He never got out of his seat. How could he control his body so much that he didn't need to go to the bathroom for so many hours? Sometimes, he can wait for 12 hours. Once he traveled for 12 hours in a car from Albuquerque to San Francisco. It was in Douglas's Infinity. Everyone else got out and went to the bathroom four or five times on the way, but UG never moved out of the seat. It's a wonder how he could be that way. It's not surprising that a person who could control his body to such an extent could achieve anything. Yet UG says, "That's all the intelligence of the body." How come, then, other bodies don't have such intelligence? Unless the 'you' in there moves out, it's not possible.

It would be nice if I could at least learn tricks of this sort from UG. UG has one formula for everything. "First 'you' must go. The monopoly of 'you' on this body must go," he says. That means 'thought' must not only loosen its grip on the body, it must completely step out of the way. Then how can thought control the body again? "Unless it's released from the tight grip of this thought, the body cannot function with its own intelligence," says UG. Is the body in such a helpless state? No. The body keeps trying to expel this squatter called 'I' from time to time, as much as it is able to. It's the nature of thought to hang on to the cornices of the house even after it is expelled. It's this battle between 'me' and my body that causes this anxiety. All the feelings and suffering I experience in myself are a result of this battle. At the end it's the body that wins. It pushes the 'me' over into death. Until then this restlessness is inevitable. This is UG's teaching.

All my attempts to escape this restlessness and try to gain some calm, peace and happiness are virtual poison for the body. By itself the body sails in an ocean of peace. 'I', on the other hand, hassle with this writing for hours and hours, struggling in this restlessness. There is an end. But it is really not an end. It's a start, not an end: my body functioning all by itself, freed from the monopoly of the 'I'.

But actually the body is not in my control. If it is, why should I still worry? It doesn't obey 'me'. It doesn't do my bidding. It acts independently. As for myself, I am struggling like a bird with broken wings. The body is free from worry. But then how is UG able to control his body? When he has no awareness of the body, how could he issue orders to the body? Does 'UG' appear then? He is not there at other times? Is 'UG' not there when he kicks the table so hard and when he yells at people so passionately? Where does he go? Does he appear when UG wishes to control the body? I don't understand this.

    *   *   *

UG Talks About...

Krishna:

"He was a blackie. He belonged to the Dravida race. He became a traitor to his own race because he handed over to the Aryans his ten-thousand-strong army. All of them were killed in the war. He had eight wives and 16,000 concubines. He was a clever bastard."

Earthquakes:

"Earthquakes are essential to the planet. No matter what they say, the planet has to realign itself from time to time and earthquakes are essential [*toward that end*]. A few thousands may die and many people may be wounded. In the recent quake in Turkey 40 thousand people died. It doesn't mean anything to the planet.... There was a tremor recently in San Rafael. One day, the whole of California will go under the sea. The Himalayas are the youngest mountains. When they start growing India is finished. Why should India remain? It must go."

The human race:

"The human species are the worst on this planet. There were so many species on this planet. What exists today is not even 0.5% of what existed millions of years ago. But for medical technology the human race would have been wiped out long ago. Why should the human race survive? The planet is not interested in keeping the human race going. They are the worst species on this earth. If there is any perfect justice ruling this universe, the human species should have been wiped out by now for all the crimes it has been perpetrating on nature. Nature never rewards. It only punishes."

Rama:

"He killed Vali hiding behind a tree. He had no guts to face and fight him. He was such a coward. People gave lots of explanations, as, for example, that Vali had obtained the boon of taking away the power of anyone facing him in the battlefield. Rama had no decency. He made his wife Sita leap into fire. He deserted his pregnant wife and left her in a jungle. I was better. I put my wife on a jumbo jet and sent her back to her place in comfort. Yet people worship such a fellow as a hero in this country."

August 28, 1999 (Saturday)

Morning 6 am. I have already finished my bath before sitting down. Yesterday, Raju has left for a town called Rosegg. A friend of his from a town called Wil near Basel came to see UG. His name is something like Domtak. He is part of Raju's group. I don't know what he thought after hearing UG. He seems to be devoted to Ganapati Satchidananda. When I observe these people, I can't but feel that UG has performed an immense service in saving people from gurus like that. What's the use of struggling endlessly following these street gurus? How he protects Guha too! If men could extricate themselves from the intoxication of these tricky gurus, their lives would become quite straight. If they could stop worrying about their future, their lives would become even happier.

You must be able to say, "I am not afraid of death." But you must know first what death is before you can fear it. Who knows what death is? How does he know? Who has seen anything about rebirth? How could they believe in them [other lives]? Who knows anything about one's own death except what one has seen by watching others die? The 'I' is what you imagine and think yourself to be; the 'I' is a bundle of information about yourself. It doesn't mean anything else. What does it matter if the 'I' lives or dies. I know I am writing all this – speculating about the 'I'; but this is a big addiction for me. That's how 'I' am continuing.

When I saw a purse under the car seat, how many crooked thoughts crowded my mind! They may be mean, but they are my true 'I'. I am a first-rate thief and liar. But can I announce this to everyone in public? How can others know what sort of vile serpents hiss within me when I am dazed with lust looking at Lisa's breasts? Is that the true 'I'? Can I tell that to UG? UG tells everything about himself to others; he doesn't hide anything. What's left of him to be protected? Where is it? If I look at myself, I only see my eagerness always to protect my image of myself hidden somewhere in me. Even when I am sitting in UG's presence, I am very watchful. There is always the effort to keep myself in control, to cover things in myself. Cover-ups and facades. There is this gargantuan effort to hide my true nature with a facade so that no one would notice it.

I detest my true nature. If I could denude myself in front of myself, I wouldn't be able to stand my true shape for one moment. When I stand in front of UG or talk to him, he denudes me like that; he removes all the safety covers and veils of thoughts. They are deceptive. Primarily they deceive *me*.

Francis said that he will come today at 7:30 am. He said he will write everything in a letter and bring it over. Why is he coming? What does he want from me? What can I give him? When I told UG about him yesterday, UG said, "I don't want to see him; I don't want to get involved in his problems." If UG doesn't want to be involved, how could I? It's different with Raju. UG has taken responsibility for him. UG may take responsibility for many people like that, but he remains unscathed. Responsibility for Lisa and Mario fell on UG. They completely submitted themselves to him. This time there was a big change in Henk too. "These three weeks with UG have been great; I'll never forget them in my life," he said, saying goodbye to me in Gstaad train station. UG, who usually teases and mocks him, has showered his grace on him this time. He forced Henk to stay when he wanted to go and then gave him enough money to stay. He also gave him food. How nicely he treated him this time! Henk has changed completely. I was so pleased.

* * *

Aruna and Venkat got off the plane Friday exactly at 5 pm. It took an hour for them to get out of the airport and get into the car. Then we were caught in the traffic. It took three hours to get back via Interlaken. Mario has been driving the car from 1 o'clock in the afternoon till 10 at night. We bought small watches in the Zurich airport. Suguna bought some dolls for Viswam's children. When we were coming back from Air France, I asked UG in terminal 'B' about body programming. "How do you do it? How does the body remember?" "When I give commands, then UG is there. That's all. He comes whenever there is a need. In between, he doesn't know anything about the body's experiences or pains," said UG. I didn't quite understand him. I must think about it some more. When the consciousness of 'I' is not there, is that programming which UG talks about possible?

The sky is somewhat overcast. It looks like it rained last night. Aruna and Venkat have not woken up yet. We spent a lot of time last night chatting. We presented a photo frame to Venkat. He said it was very nice. UG was saying at dinner that they have already seen half of Switzerland. Mario looked very tired. Today we must show them the whole town.

*　　　　　　　　*　　　　　　　　*

August 29, 1999 (Sunday)

This is the day we know has been coming, our last day here. We two will be in Zurich tomorrow by this time. This may be the last day we will be in this country for this lifetime. Or we might gather some more sunsets and then rise up here again. If

I think about it, how strange it is, the mind doesn't stay in the present; it only thinks about the past! I am writing as if my mind is different from me. Isn't this mind part of my nature? Do I have a nature? Because all these people pound it into me, I believe that I have one. If not, do I have a shape or existence?

Who is it that looks at the sunrises and sunsets and experiences them? Who is it that resides in this 'house'? It's vacant. Who is echoing my call? Who is asking me? I hear these words and am deluded into thinking that someone exists. He is joining his voice with mine and speaking with me each word I speak. O God, who is this chatterbox? I speak of 'God' again. Is there God apart from me? Doesn't He always exist in my heart? Why not? He is always there. When I open my eyes and look, I see my reflection in the form of UG. He too is God. But there is some fear, some hesitation. Although I know that the reflection is mine, there are some unknown vague screens, layers of snow. Something far away. The distance between me and UG must go. It must not be there.

When am I going to see UG again? Do I really see him now? Am I listening? What am I listening to? What do I see? Aren't all these my fabrications? I slip into this arid metaphysics. How do I know that this is all false either? Only because someone told me so, isn't it? If I don't accept any of them, then what is true? And what is false? Does the world exist or does it not? Do I or do I not exist?

My legs and thighs are aching. My fingers are hurting. As long as I have this ache, pain, suffering and anxiety, how can I tell myself that those things don't exist? Yesterday, when I woke up it was raining heavily. The sky was heavily overcast. I worried, "Oh, my God! What bad luck! Must we show this beautiful place to Aruna and Venkat in this rain?" We went in Mitra's car and showed them Saanen, UG's old house, the bench, Chalet Sunbeam, and such. Aruna picked some red roses from a rose bush in front of Sunbeam. She reminded me of what Lulu had written in her letter when Valentine died. I didn't know that she remembered it so well. Apparently she wrote: "I cannot forget those roses which bloomed day after day in front of Sunbeam Chalet and which Valentine liked the most." When she saw the red roses, Aruna remembered those words.

Everything is a memory – not just Valentine, I too am nothing but a memory. Someday, during the night or early in the morning, this memory will permanently disappear. Everything will end with that. That's it. Why all these entanglements just for that? I want to ask UG when I'll see him again. Will I see UG again in my life? What a strong bond it is! Can I brush it all off saying, "This is all nothing, it's a mere memory?" How real it all appears! Could UG's non-existence or my own non-existence not be real, by any chance? Do we really exist now or don't we? How do we know for sure that we don't exist? Isn't it just telling ourselves that we don't exist, as much as telling ourselves that we do exist? Which one of these is actually true? Which of these is real? UG, would you say that we two exist in this world or would you say that we don't?

This [*questioning*] has become an obsession. I am trying to separate myself from this question and stand apart. That's how I strive to continue. When will this gap, this distance go? What a noise inside! How many images! How many shadows!

Every moment lights and shadows on the screen – some near, some far.

*   *   *

Yesterday, Francis came at 7:15 am. He described his financial problems clearly in a letter and brought it. The trust he has developed recently in UG will certainly save him. He read the letter to me. While he was reading it, tears welled up in my eyes in spite of myself. He was able to present his sad state before UG. He pleaded, "Please help me, UG, and don't let my hand go."

The immediate threat of the government repossessing the house he is living in and turning him out into the street with nothing but the clothes on his back is pulling him down. His family and children are his responsibility. He has problems selling his house and he has problems buying another house. He is trying to mortgage his house to a different bank. But he needs 500,000 francs to redeem himself of his indebtedness, particularly to save his house from the government. He is an honest man. Society dealt him a blow.

UG listened to everything he said and reassured him. "Your wife's job, the property she is going to inherit and your retirement fund are your strong points. I believe that the bank will certainly take those into consideration and grant you a loan. But don't try for another job yet. The unemployment compensation of 6,000 francs which the government gives you is enough. Be brave," he told Francis. Yesterday, Francis sat in UG's presence till noon. When finally he was about to say goodbye to me, I too felt as if someone close to me was leaving. Without a prior thought, I said, "We'll meet again, somewhere, some time." I was so glad that UG took his matter into his hands. Francis is a lucky man. In this pitiable condition, his luck brought him to this great wish-fulfilling tree called UG.

*   *   *

UG got us to go out sightseeing in the car yesterday afternoon around 1:15 pm. Seven of us fitted ourselves in Mario's car. Venkat and I sat in the two seats in the back; in the middle three seats, Suguna, Aruna and Lisa; and UG in the front, by Mario's side. Where to go? UG said **Les Diablarettes**. I thought we would come back in an hour. But it turned out that by the time we returned it was 8:30 in the night. They showed us the peaks of Diablaret and the natural beauty on the way and directed the car toward Montreau.

We saw the castle there from a distance. The town is well known as the 'Swiss Riviera'. It's always sunny there. The rain-and-cloud climate in Gstaad suddenly disappeared and we were plunged in sunshine as soon as we got into Montreau. The city is on the shores of Lake Geneva shining in the sun. We walked around for an hour. Aruna and Suguna did some shopping. Apparently Francis's father worked as an administrator in the castle there for 25 years. Lord Byron made this his place of residence. The town inspired this great English poet to write the poem called "The Prisoner of Chillon". Lausanne and Vevey are the two neighboring towns. We then had coffee in the Palace Hotel in Montreau and continued on our way to Geneva.

Again we saw Valentine's old house and Lake Geneva and the fountain. We took the highway from the city again and returned to Gstaad via Bulle. Thus UG showed Aruna and Venkat almost the whole of Switzerland. Today we travel by train; and by cable car to Eggli. But the sky is still covered with thick clouds. Last night, Aruna and Venkat walked around in Gstaad for an hour and got back. If it is clear, they will go out to see the town some more. UG told us yesterday in Lausanne that Kamala Nehru died there. He also said that Indira Gandhi went to school in another town nearby. In those days, the lady warden of the hostel where she stayed had come to see Valentine once. Apparently, the warden had told Valentine that she used to see Indira coming out each morning after having spent the night with a different boy. UG recalled all that.

I liked Switzerland on the French side a lot. If there is such a thing as a future, I would like to go around those places again – those mountains, the shores of the lakes, the grape vineyards and Mont Blanc shining brilliantly in the distance. Looking at that mountain I think of Arunachala.

I don't know if I will have time to write more. Tomorrow we'll start our return trip. I will probably open this book again in Bangalore. This story stopped exactly on my birthday, March 26 [*in the diary*]. We will see how far more it will go.

*   *   *

"'You' have to go. You are the squatter there. As long as you are there, you want to change the world, change yourself. I am saying that no change is necessary. How can you be interested in what I am saying? You want to live for 60, 70 years and still continue. You are not interested in going. The body is trying to throw you out all the time. That is the constant battle that is going on there. You are the problem. There is no other problem."

      *   *   *

August 30-31, 1999 (Monday and Tuesday)

Camping in the Bombay airport. The four of us left Gstaad yesterday at 4 am in Mario's car. I am writing this sitting in the domestic air terminal in Bombay. Suguna has set her suitcase between two chairs and is dozing. The time now is 3:30 am. I must wait for two hours more in this Indian Airlines waiting room. Aruna and Venkat left Zurich at 12 noon and arrived in Bombay at 1 am. They must be waiting and napping in the waiting room of Jet Airways. It's better here than there.

The End

A view of Chalet Sunbeam, Gstaad, Switzerland

Chandrahaus with UG in Gstaad

Chalet Pfyffenegg Saanen, Switzerland

Chandrasekhar and Moorty in Gstaad, Switzerland

Chandrasekhar and Suguna on the 'Bench' in Saanen, Switzerland_1

Chandrasekhar, Suguna and Simon With UG in Gstaad

Moorty and Paul Sempe with UG in Switzerland

Suguna and Chandrasekhar with Julie in Gstaad

Suguna, Julie, Lisa and Mario

UG leading the friends down hill

Epilogue

I published my first book on UG Krishnamurti in 2001, introduced to me by Mahesh Bhatt. Not long after, I met K. Chandrasekhar – Babu, as his friends fondly call him – again through Mahesh. That meeting marked the beginning of a beautiful journey for me, one deeply intertwined with UG and his friends, including Mahesh and Babu.

Born in 1945 in Tirupati, the sacred temple town of Lord Venkateswara, Chandrasekhar Babu comes from a modest Brahmin family. Son of a staunch Gandhian, he navigated hardships and eventually acquired a Diploma in Mechanical Engineering, which led to a stable career at Hindustan Aeronautics Ltd. in Bangalore. After 18 years there, and another 10 at Hindustan Motors, he opted for voluntary retirement.

The real foundation of Babu's inner life, however, was laid much earlier. Raised by his maternal grandfather, a theosophist, he was exposed to spiritual thought from an early age. A chance encounter with Sai Baba at the age of 16 sparked a fire in Babu. That flame turned into a blaze, pushing him toward seekers and sages across the country. At 19, drawn by the pull of Arunachala, he went to meet Chalam and Souris, both disciples connected to the great sage Ramana Maharshi. The search for God-realization had truly begun.

But somehow, Babu's life reached a crossroads. The philosophical framework he had so carefully built had started crumbling. And then, in December 1969, he met UG.

UG didn't offer any solutions. In fact, he demolished the very need for one.

"When you are walking in a thick forest with dangers lurking all over amidst pitch darkness, what do you do?" UG asked.

Babu had no answer. He just stopped in his tracks.

And from that moment, his life became an inward journey… anchored to UG.

Babu began keeping a journal, an honest, unfiltered record of his encounters, insights, struggles, and revelations. Over time, these journals grew into volumes, eventually forming the basis of *Stopped In Our Tracks*, published in 2005. What began as a single book evolved into a trilogy. This volume marks its final chapter.

In these pages, you'll find more than just stories about UG. You'll see Chandrasekhar Babu's raw reflections – his admiration, confusion, resistance, surrender, sorrow, and unwavering devotion. His attempt to grasp UG's fierce, elusive presence mirrors the reader's own inner wrestling. His journey is not just about UG – it's about all of us who have ever stood in front of the unknowable and tried to make sense of it.

So, who was UG?

He was never bound to a place. He roamed the world without fear. Unconstrained by tradition, beyond morals and codes of conduct, he lived outside the rules. At times demonic, at others guileless, he never let go of his singularity. Even in the company of celebrities and madmen, drunkards and libertines, he remained untouched – like a lotus rising from the mud. Praise or blame left him unmoved.

He belonged to no order, no sect, no society. His message echoed across the globe, yet his ways were uniquely his own. Never caught in a groove, he mocked sages and saints alike, condemning what others revered. He rebuked those who came to him… yet they returned, drawn back to him again and again. He was enigmatic in how he aided true seekers, his impact slipping quietly into the hearts of those ready.

He was the embodiment of boundless spiritual force. He was a fire that burned through all illusions. He was UG.

And through the eyes of K. Chandrasekhar, we glimpse just a fragment of that fire... still alive in the pages of this book.

Sunita Pant Bansal
New Delhi, 2025